The Synonyms of *Fallen Woman* in the History of the English Language

STUDIES IN ENGLISH MEDIEVAL LANGUAGE AND LITERATURE
Edited by Jacek Fisiak

Advisory Board:
John Anderson (Methoni, Greece), Ulrich Busse (Halle),
Olga Fischer (Amsterdam), Marcin Krygier (Poznań),
Roger Lass (Cape Town), Peter Lucas (Cambridge),
Donka Minkova (Los Angeles), Akio Oizumi (Kyoto),
Katherine O'Brien O'Keeffe (UC Berkeley, USA),
Matti Rissanen (Helsinki), Hans Sauer (Munich),
Liliana Sikorska (Poznań), Jeremy Smith (Glasgow),
Jerzy Wełna (Warsaw)

Vol. 45

Bożena Duda

The Synonyms of *Fallen Woman* in the History of the English Language

Bibliographic Information published by the Deutsche Nationalbibliothek
The Deutsche Nationalbibliothek lists this publication in the Deutsche Nationalbibliografie; detailed bibliographic data is available in the internet at http://dnb.d-nb.de.

Library of Congress Cataloging-in-Publication Data
Duda, Bozena, 1979-
 The synonyms of fallen woman in the history of the English language / Bozena Duda. – Peter Lang Edition.
   pages cm. – (Studies in English Medieval language and literature; Vol. 45)
 Includes bibliographical references and index.
 ISBN 978-3-631-64450-8
 1. English language–Gender 2. English language–Synonyms and antonyms. 3. English language–Grammar, Historical. 4. Historical linguistics. I. Title.
 PE1211.D84 2014
 428.1–dc23
                                                                    2014020485

This publication was financially supported
by the University of Rzeszow.

ISSN 1436-7521
ISBN 978-3-631-64450-8 (Print)
E-ISBN 978-3-653-03140-9 (E-Book)
DOI 10.3726/978-3-653-03140-9

© Peter Lang GmbH
Internationaler Verlag der Wissenschaften
Frankfurt am Main 2014
All rights reserved.

Peter Lang Edition is an Imprint of Peter Lang GmbH.

Peter Lang – Frankfurt am Main · Bern · Bruxelles · New York · Oxford · Warszawa · Wien

All parts of this publication are protected by copyright. Any utilisation outside the strict limits of the copyright law, without the permission of the publisher, is forbidden and liable to prosecution. This applies in particular to reproductions, translations, microfilming, and storage and processing in electronic retrieval systems.

This publication has been peer reviewed.

www.peterlang.com

*To Professor Kleparski
with eternal gratitude*

Table of Contents

Introduction 11
List of Abbreviations 13
Typographic Conventions 15
CHAPTER ONE: On the Nature of Euphemism 17
   1.1 Euphemism: In search of definition 17
      1.1.1 Language restrictions 17
      1.1.2 Building euphemistic blocks over taboo 19
      1.1.3 The category of X-phemism: Pizza or the melting pot? 21
      1.1.4 Concluding remarks 26
   1.2 Mechanisms behind X-phemisms 27
      1.2.1 Structural tools 28
      1.2.2 Semantic tools 37
      1.2.3 Rhetorical tools 47
      1.2.4 Syntactic/Grammatical tools 62
      1.2.5 Concluding remarks 64
   1.3 Context as a disambiguating factor in the interpretation
       of X-phemism 65
      1.3.1 X-phemism and context 67
      1.3.2 Extralinguistic context in the act of X-phemism disambiguation 67
CHAPTER TWO: On the Specifics of Sexual Relations in the History of Mankind with Due Reference to Sex for Sale 69
   2.1 Conceptualisation of sex, gender and sexuality 69
   2.2 Historical variations in conceptualisation of sex relations 70
      2.2.1 From antique all-going permissiveness to Victorian restrictiveness 70
      2.2.2 The sexual revolution of the 20th century 81

2.3 Cultural variations in conceptualisation of sex relations 83
    2.3.1 Anglo-Saxon 83
    2.3.2 Romance 86
    2.3.3 Germanic 87
    2.3.4 Slavonic 89
    2.3.5 Non-Indo-European 93
2.4 Concluding remarks 94

CHAPTER THREE: Panchronic Developments of the Lexical Items Linked to the Conceptual Category **FALLEN WOMAN** 95

3.1 On the internal organisation of the conceptual category **FALLEN WOMAN** 95
    3.1.1 Historical foundations of the intricacies in the structure of the conceptual category **FALLEN WOMAN** 96

3.2 Historical growth of the lexical items linked to the conceptual category **FALLEN WOMAN** 100
    3.2.1 Formative historical mechanisms employed in the coinage of lexical items linked to the conceptual category **FALLEN WOMAN** 101

3.3 Methodology contour 109

3.4 Old English X-phemisms linked to the conceptual category **FALLEN WOMAN** 118

3.5 Middle English X-phemisms linked to the conceptual category **FALLEN WOMAN** 129
    3.5.1 Middle English synonyms and structural tools 130
    3.5.2 Middle English synonyms and semantic tools 136
    3.5.3 Middle English rhetorical tools at work 139

3.6 Early Modern English X-phemisms linked to the conceptual category **FALLEN WOMAN** 143
    3.6.1 Early Modern English metaphorically based X-phemisms 144
    3.6.2 Early Modern English metonymy conditioned synonyms 165
    3.6.3 Early Modern English and the mechanism of understatement at work 173

3.6.4 Early Modern English borrowing 181
   3.6.5 The role of eponymy in Early Modern English 191
   3.6.6 Early Modern English working of circumlocution 195
   3.6.7 Early Modern English employment of morphological deriva-
         tion 199
Conclusions 203
Index 213
References 215

Introduction

The issue of sex for sale is beyond any conceivable doubt culturally and socially topical, in terms of both human everyday verbal intercourse and the written literature on the subject published worldwide for a variety of reasons and with diverse intentions. Outside the world of language studies, suffice it to mention here Brundage (1987), Karras (1996), Trumbach (1998), Self (2003), Binnie (2004), Cook (2004), Outshoorn (2004) and McAnulty and Burnette (2006) as some of the most recent studies of the subject. From a linguistic point of view the roots of the analysis of pejoration of female-specific lexical items – which frequently accompanies the rise of negatively loaded women words – herald back to Bechstein (1863), and the study was continued in the first half of the 20th century by, among others, Jaberg (1901-1905) and Schreuder (1929) in his most extensive study *Pejorative Sense Development in English*. In the second part of the 20th century Schulz (1975), in the short, yet comprehensive study related to the morally negatively tinted nouns within the conceptual category **FEMALE HUMAN BEING**, opened a new phase in the linguistic enquiry into the semantic development of female-specific vocabulary. Other more recent contributions to the research in this field include Kramarae and Treichler (1985), Mills (1989) and Kövecses (2006), while in Polish tradition such works as Kleparski (1990, 1997), Kochman-Haładyj (2007a, 2007b), Kochman-Haładyj and Kleparski (2011) and Duda (2013) formulate many answers to the questions posed by the pejorative development of female-specific vocabulary at various stages of the history of English.

Likewise, this monographic study is meant to be a contribution to the body of analytic ventures aiming at analysing female-specific vocabulary in current linguistic research. By and large, this work continues the *RSDS* mainstream tradition, but it narrows down the perspective in targeting euphemisation forces operative in the rise of lexical items onomasiologically linked to the conceptual microcategory **FALLEN WOMAN**. In this sense the analysis proposed here continues the tradition of data-oriented studies, at the same time making a step forward in restricting its interest to euphemisms and dysphemisms with little regard for other types of change, such as narrowing, broadening or amelioration of meaning content.

The long-lasting pursuit of relevant semantic literature, data collection, attempts at partial data analysis and sharing their results with the like minded linguists both in Poland and abroad ultimately led to the completion of doctoral work at the *University of Rzeszów*, Poland, upon which this text has been based. Substantial sections of this monograph acquired their initial shape in several publications issued both locally, at the *University of Rzeszów, State School of Higher Vocational Education* in Jarosław, and also internationally at the Historical English Word-Formation and Semantics conference in Warsaw and the International Conference on Middle English 8 in Murcia, but also online in *Studia Anglica Resoviensia* and *Círculo de Lingüística Aplicada a la Comunicacíon (clac)*. The final shape of this monograph owes much to frequent exchange of views with a number of academics I had a chance to contact at various stages of writing this work, such as Professor Rafał Molencki of the *University of Silesia*, Professor Michał Bylinsky of the *University of Lviv* and Professor Ursula Lenker of the *University of Munich*. My special thanks go to the reviewers of my PhD thesis, Professor Pavol Štekauer of the *P.J. Safarik University in Kosice*, and Professor Ewa Komorowska of the *University of Szczecin*, who formulated a number of critical remarks, suggestions and improvements, which were taken into account during the preparation of the final version of this study.

Last but not least, let me take the opportunity to express my gratitude to the people without whom accomplishing the tasks set to this work would have been impossible. First and foremost, the greatest debt I owe to **Professor Grzegorz A. Kleparski** whose guidance, unprecedented support, encouragement and patience I felt at every single step of my work. I am especially grateful for the invaluable lexicographic, reference and analytical resources Professor Kleparski made available to me. He was also the one who made every attempt to bring the results of my work closer to a wider internatonal readership. In this context I also wish to acknowledge the strong academic backing of Professor Jacek Fisiak, who has supported this academic project from the very conception. Finally, I would like to express my gratitude to Mr. Donald Trinder and Mr. Ian Upchurch who contributed to whatever stylistic grace this work may offer. This work would not have been started at all if it had not been for the support and the fervent non-academic enthiusiasm of Jacek, Julia and Filip, my family members. Both my fellow academics and those dear to me helped me through the most critical periods by showing how to fight with subjective downs and not to bow to objective trials.

It remains for me to hope that this monograph – another fruit of the Rzeszów-based historical semanticists – will stimulate readers' interest and provoke further academic discussion, both in Poland and beyond. Obviously, I reserve for myself alone the blame for any remaining errors of facts or interpretation, editorial blunders and misfires.

List of Abbreviations

Alb.	Albanian
Am.E.	American English
Arab.	Arabic
ASD	*An Anglo-Saxon Dictionary*
Aus.E.	Australian English
BLACKWELL	*The Blackwell Encyclopaedia of Anglo-Saxon England*
Br.E.	British English
Bret.	Breton
BRITANNICA	*Encyclopaedia Britannica Online*
cf.	compare with
Cor.	Cornish
CSDD	*The Concise Scots Dialect Dictionary*
Cz.	Czech
Da.	Danish
Du.	Dutch
DRS	*The Dictionary of Rhyming Slang*
E.M.E	Early Middle English
E.Mod.E.	Early Modern English
Eng.	English
ENROM	*Encyclopaedia Romana*
EPSW	*The Encyclopedia of Prostitution and Sex Work*
Fr.	French
Gael.	Gaelic
G.	German
Gr.	Greek
HTE	*Historical Thesaurus of English*
Ir.	Irish
Ir.G.	Irish Gaelic
It.	Italian
Lat.	Latin
LDCE	*Longman Dictionary of Contemporary English*
L.G.	Low German
lit.	literally
L.Lat.	Late Latin
L.M.E	Late Middle English
L.Mod.E.	Late Modern English

List of Abbreviations

M.Du.	Middle Dutch
M.E.	Middle English
MED	*Macmillan English Dictionary*
M.L.G.	Middle Low German
M.Lat.	Middle Latin
Mod.Du.	Modern Dutch
Mod.E.	Modern English
Mod.Fr.	Modern French
Mod.G.	Modern German
Mod.It.	Modern Italian
Mod.Pol.	Modern Polish
Mod.Russ.	Modern Russian
Mod.Sp.	Modern Spanish
Mod.Sw.	Modern Swedish
Nor.	Norwegian
N.Z.E.	New Zealand English
O.Da.	Old Danish
ODO	*Oxford Dictionaries Online*
O.E.	Old English
OED	*The Oxford English Dictionary*
O.Fr.	Old French
O.H.G.	Old High German
O.Ir.	Old Irish
O.N.	Old Norse
O.Sp.	Old Spanish
O.Sw.	Old Swedish
Per.	Persian
Pol.	Polish
P.I.E.	Proto-Indo-European
Pr.	Portuguese
Pres.E.	Present-day English
Proto-Sl.	Proto-Slavonic
RSDS	*Rzeszów School of Diachronic Semantics*
Russ.	Russian
Sc.	Scottish
SJP	*Słownik języka polskiego*
Sp.	Spanish
SS	*The Slang of Sin*
Sw.	Swedish
Wel.	Welsh

Typographic Conventions

Bold capitals are employed for:
names of conceptual categories/domains (e.g. **FALLEN WOMAN**, **DOMAIN OF MORALITY** […]).

Angled bracketed capitals are employed for:
names of conceptual values/elements (e.g. <FEMALE$_{[NEU]}$>, <LOW$_{[NEG]}$>).

Capitals are employed for:
a) names of concepts/notions/conceptual spheres (e.g. PROSTITUTION, DEATH),
b) names of conceptual metaphorical extensions (e.g. SEX IS CONSUMPTION, A WOMAN IS AN ANIMAL).

Capitals in double backslashes are employed for:
names of conceptual metonymic contiguity patterns (e.g. \\LOCATION FOR PROFESSION\\, \\TIME OF ACTIVITY FOR PROFESSION\\).

On the Nature of Euphemism

1.1 Euphemism: In search of definition

In the beginning was the word (John 1:1). It may certainly seem somewhat unusual to commence any account of euphemism with a quotation from the Holy Writs. However, this clearly shows how significant what we say may turn out to be, and what power may actually be hidden behind verbal statements. Note that in the usual and natural course of events first we utter then we act, which simply means that words tend to precede our deeds, whether good, barely acceptable or bad. In other words, this is to say that words have the performative power of directing people's lives, or at least their actions. Power, as we know, should be subject to monitoring and control, and usually is, somehow – either overtly or covertly – regulated. Otherwise it may pose a certain threat to other members of a society.

1.1.1 Language restrictions

Somewhat obviously from the very beginning of human race, according to the Christian faith, words had to be kept under control. With the advent of Christianity Two of the Ten Commandments set early limitations on the use of language. As *Exodus*, 20[1] says, *You shall not take the name of the LORD, your God, in vain* and further *you shall not bear false witness against your neighbor*. Such restrictions as the ones formulated here, and many others besides, imposed on the users of language contribute greatly to the emergence or reinforcement of **taboo**. It is worth mentioning at this point that when Captain Cook introduced the word *taboo* (from Malayo-Polynesian, both Fijian *tabu* and Tongan *tapu*) into English in the late 18th century it referred, according to McArthur (1992:1019), to what may be qualified as *consecrated or limited to a special use, and therefore prohibited*. As McArthur (1992:1019) further clarifies, *in language terms, something taboo is not to be mentioned, because it is ineffably holy or unspeakably vulgar*. In turn, Polański (1995:545) stresses the importance of *the mystical identification of a word with a thing or a phenomenon the word refers to*.[2] Obviously, at that time nobody could possibly have predicted how overwhelming the career of the word *taboo* would be. It seems that we may

---

1 *The New* American Bible. St. Joseph Medium Size Edition.
2 Translation mine.

search for the origins of taboo subjects in various religious denominations, whether Christian, Hindu, Muslim or Judaic. Since normally religion lies at the core of the majority of societies, taboo – enrooted in the faith of the people – becomes an integral part of social life and social conduct. As some linguists, such as Widłak (1968) and Dąbrowska (1992), argue, taboo that evolved from religion is to be viewed as primary taboo. More to the point, Danesi (2000:224) points out that, by extension, taboo refers to *any social prohibition or restriction that results from convention or tradition*. Taking on a more recent perspective, Chamizo Dominguez and Sánchez Benedito (2005:12) justifiably add that, *[...] however, in our society, the last great remaining taboo seems to be sex. And although this taboo was originally related to religious beliefs or superstitions, nowadays religious taboo does not seem to have much relevance*. This point of view goes hand in hand with Polański's (1995:545) comment on the areas that are tabooed in contemporary western societies, namely sex, effluvia, underwear, dangerous diseases and death.

What needs to be stressed at this point is the natural variability in the attitude towards sexual and/or religious taboo across temporal and cultural dimensions. Thus, debauchery or innuendo were subject to sheer opprobrium in the Victorian age, whereas today a number of western societies seem to show a growingly relaxed point of view on all matters which were either unspeakable or at least were held to be unspeakable in 18th- and 19th-century England. A telling illustration of how transient people's ideas are of the appropriateness of language is the story of Sir Walter Scott's great-aunt.[3] Being presented, on her own request, with a book by Alphra Behn, the aunt asked Scott to burn it as she was unable to read something which had been the source of great amusement and entertainment in upper class circles sixty years previously. What is even more intriguing is her own surprise at the reaction she experienced. On the other hand, under no circumstances could you hear a member of the Victorian upper class say anything but *unmentionables* or *ineffables* for 'trousers', *bosom* for 'breasts' and *past* instead of 'disreputable sexual history'.[4] These two cases seem to point unambiguously to the fact that what seems to be the greatest taboo for one generation may be simply a standard word or phrasing for another. Note that this seems to be a part of a much broader regularity that may be discerned in the realm of language development. In grammar the irregularity of today (for example irregular verbs) need not be irregularity of the past. In inflectional morphology the irregular plural (for example *datum/data*) of the early 20th century may

---

3   Taken from Rawson (1989).
4   However, Ayto (2007:12) argues that this kind of "pathological reticence" might have existed only within the short margin of the society.

not be irregular in the next century when we find *data* used both for singular and plural. In sociolinguistics a colloquialism of today need not be a colloquialism of tomorrow. For example, in the middle of the 20th century *loo* was a colloquialism not to be used in polite circles, while it has since become a standard word in English without any hint of colloquialism or vulgarism.

It was the 19th century that witnessed the implementation of laws which – as O'Donnell (1992:12) remarks – were to serve a guardian function. Among other pieces of legislation can be included the Obscene Publications Act and the Comstock Postal Act introduced in Great Britain in 1857 and in the United States of America in 1873 respectively. Such legal restrictions were in full force, and even more than a century later instances of charges on the basis of these laws were not at all infrequent. O'Donnell (1992:15) illustrates the point with the case of a shop-assistant who was taken to court and charged with the use of *obscene, vulgar or profane language*. Although the charge was subsequently dropped, such instances provide a body of unquestionable evidence that, as O'Donnell (1992:28) puts it, *some sort of restriction on language in any society is inevitable.* Yet, the restriction of today need not be the restriction of tomorrow.

1.1.2 Building euphemistic blocks over taboo

Regardless of the formal restrictions that are imposed on some languages or – at least – on some aspects of communicative activity, people in certain situations have a tendency to avoid mentioning anything that could be considered offensive, vulgar, disgusting or too straightforward. The term **euphemism**, as defined by McArthur (1992:387), is commonly understood to mean a word or an expression which is delicate and inoffensive and is used to replace or cover a term that seems to be either taboo, too harsh or simply inappropriate for a given conversational exchange. In literary studies euphemism is described by Głowiński et al. (2002:132) as *a word or expression used to replace a certain word which for some reasons (of, for example, aesthetics, ritual or censorship) cannot be directly employed in an utterance.*[5] In language studies, Allan and Burridge (1991:11) provide a customary, yet comprehensive, definition, which goes along the following lines:

> A euphemism is used as an alternative to a dispreferred expression, in order to avoid possible loss of face: either one's own face or, through giving offense, that of the audience, or of some third party.

---

5   Translation mine.

As for the etymological roots of the term *euphemism*, the element *eu-* derives from Greek and means 'well, sounding good' and *-phēmē* means 'speaking'. Traditionally, both Pei and Gaynor (1954:68-69) and Danesi (2000:89) characterise euphemism as the substitution of a more pleasant or less direct word for unpleasant or distasteful one. Rawson (1981:1), in turn, remarks that euphemisms *[...] are so deeply embedded in our language that few of us, even those who pride themselves on being plainspoken, ever get through a day without using them*. The reason for this may be, as Polański (1995:138) and Gołąb at al. (1970:164) clarify, the neutral emotional load of euphemistic expressions which seems to attenuate the negative illocutionary force a taboo word or phrase has.

The omnipresence of euphemisms seems to be mirrored in the range of tabooed topics we face in our everyday communication. Thus, for instance, the death of a close person is euphemized to English *the loss* or *passing away* and to Polish *strata* 'loss' or *odejście* 'passing away' for the simple reason of sympathy, delicacy or fear. The second most deeply enrooted tabooed topic of today seems to be the sphere of sexual activity. Rather than talking bluntly about it with the use of four-letter words, though very common nowadays, most people prefer employing a whole range of words and expressions based on such conceptual metaphors as, for instance, SEX IS CONSUMPTION.[6] The main reason is the feeling of broadly-understood embarrassment as the ultimate outcome of a long-lasting and all-prevailing moral prudery which used to be, and, to a certain extent, continues to be, cultivated in some societies and in certain social circles. Yet another conspicuous area of euphemisation appears to be any topic related to racial or sexual otherness.[7] The already widespread and continually growing trend of political correctness makes people both more aware and more genteel towards various minorities from the white heterosexual perspective. Suffice to illustrate this with the preference for (in English) *dark-skinned*, (in Polish) *ciemnoskóry* 'dark-skinned' or, in Great Britain in the 1950s, simply *immigrant* for 'non-white person' or Polish *kochający inaczej* (lit. 'loving differently') and English *same gender oriented* instead of 'homosexual'.[8]

It seems that the omnipresence and figurative nature of euphemism constitute the core features of this linguistic mechanism which serves such a fundamental function in human communication. Undoubtedly, not many people fancy the idea of being labelled as either *rude* or *coarse*. Instead, in a typical $A \leftrightarrow B$ act of communication, they would rather resort to some auspicious term in order to

---

6   For more on sex-related metaphors see, Crespo Fernández (2008), Allan and Burridge (2006:190-202), Chamizo Dominguez and Sánchez Benedito (2005:22-25) and Allan and Burridge (1991:86-95) to name but a few.

7   On the issue of otherness, see Kudła (2010), among others.

8   For more examples, see Kleparski and Martynuska (2002).

be perceived as politically correct or so as not to hurt someone's feelings. Accordingly, as Chamizo Dominguez and Sánchez Benedito (2005:8) argue, the mechanism of euphemism – apart from its main function of concealing or veiling something unpleasant or apparently unpleasant – serves several other functions that may be itemised as follows:

1. the politeness or respect function,
2. the dignifying function,
3. the function of attenuating a painful evocation,
4. the function of naming the taboo object.

To venture a generalisation one may say that normally all the functions are jointly at work to a varied degree, depending on the social context of a speaker and the level of their delicacy and/or their involvement in a given situation. It is an undeniable fact that one may use the verb *depart* in English or Polish *odejść* on one occasion and – on other occasions – resort to the much idiomatic phrasing *kick the bucket* or *kopnąć w kalendarz* (in Polish lit. 'kick the calendar'), and in both cases reference is made to the same concept, namely DEATH. The questions that inevitably arise in this context are why people tend to choose one and not the other language tool and whether both can, and indeed do, convey the same functions.

1.1.3 The category of X-phemism: Pizza or the melting pot?

To put it bluntly, the answer to this seemingly simple question is neither obvious nor straightforward. Allan and Burridge (2006:29-34) draw a fine distinction between **euphemism**, which they refer to as 'sweet-talking'; the mechanism of **dysphemism**, or, in other words, 'speaking offensively', and **orthophemism**, which derives from the Greek root *ortho-* meaning 'proper, straight, normal'. McArthur (1992:328) defines dysphemism as *the use of a negative or disparaging expression to describe something or someone* with a note that its special subtype, which is cruel and offensive, is **cacophemism**,[9] which derives from Greek *kakós* 'bad'. Additionally, in the works of Allan and Burridge (1991, 2006), the term **X-phemism** is postulated to encompass any and every type of cover terms regardless of its illocutionary force.

---

9 For the sake of not offending the innocent ear the inside marking of the quoted cacophemisms in the form of an asterisk inserted after the first letter, for example *f*uck* shall be employed throughout this work.

It appears that the sole factor determining the choice of one against another is the intention of the speaker; a classic example being the polite *poo* used mainly by and to children, the offensive *s*hit*, especially employed as an interjection, and the bookish or neutral *faeces*. Yet another case in point is the group of words in which *toilet* is treated as standard,[10] *loo* is a genteel form and *s*hithouse* is reserved for those who do not mind being either impolite or downright vulgar.[11] Such trios that, generally speaking, refer to one and the same denotatum can be multiplied in any natural language.[12] However, as Chamizo Dominguez and Sánchez Benedito (2005:7) put it:

> [...] in many cases the dividing line between euphemism and dysphemism can be clearly drawn, in many other cases that line is so utterly blurred that it becomes difficult, if not impossible, to establish the boundaries between the two figures of speech.

One has grounds to say that it is the contextual environment in which the person speaks that plays a crucial role in distinguishing between the cases of euphemism and dysphemism. Taking *s*hithouse* as an example, the compound is incontestably vulgar and impolite when employed in a social, formal or semi-formal, verbal interaction among strangers. When we change the scenario, for example, in an army squad context never would this word be treated dysphemistically. Allan and Burridge (2006:32) go as far as to argue that among a group of soldiers *loo* may be perceived as a dysphemism because of its insulting load, as if someone was talking to them with baby talk.

It seems that the justification for the problem of determining the thin line of distinction between euphemism and dysphemism may be sought in **diachronic semantics**. As Kröll (1984:12) accurately points out *what today is a euphemism, may tomorrow be a dysphemism*, which doubtless works the other way round as well. Suffice it to mention the story of *gay*, which – according to the *OED* – started its drift in the 14th century in the positively loaded adjectival sense 'light-hearted, exuberantly cheerful, sportive, merry' (1310 Heo is... Graciouse, stout, ant *Gay*, Gentil jolyf so the jay. > 1880 I knew he was *gay* and careless.). The

---

10 It is worth noting at this point that *toilet*, which is linked to the concept WASHING, used to be employed as a euphemism for *lavatory* which was considered too impolite for the society. With the passage of time it lost its euphemistic power and needed other terms to replace it in a 'sweet-talking' way (Enright 2005:10-11).

11 Note, however, that from the diachronic point of view *loo* was, 30 years ago or so, still considered a vulgar slang term that has – with the passage of time – lost its offensive stylistic stigmata.

12 In Polish the counterparts of the trios mentioned would be *kupa* for 'poo', *g*ówno* for 'shit' and *odchody* for 'faeces' or *toaleta* for 'loo', *s*ralnia* for 'shithouse' and *WC* for 'toilet'.

early 17th century brought a euphemistic extension to 'of loose or immoral life' (1637 You'le not be angry, Madam. *Cel.* Nor rude, though *gay* men have a priviledge. > 1910 He felt rather a *gay* dog.). Subsequently, a euphemism developed into a sexual dysphemism when in the 19th century the lexical item *gay* acquired the negatively loaded sense 'leading an immoral life, living by prostitution' (1825 Two sisters – both *gay*. > 1885 She was leading a *gay* life.) with reference to woman kind. Rawson (1981:120) justifiably observes that the further development of *gay* must have been – at least to a considerable extent – inspired by the specifics of the Victorian, both homo- and heterosexual, underworld of the 19th century. At that time the greatest overtly tabooed topic of all was sex, along with anything connected directly or indirectly with the human body and body functions that – among other uses – served the purpose of having sex. Not surprisingly, the dysphemistic load remained with the lexical item *gay*, the semantics of which may be said to have undergone a shift from the conceptual category **FEMALE HUMAN BEING** to **MALE HUMAN BEING** in the early 20th century. As a vulgar and offensive item, *gay* continued well into the 1970s when it slowly began to neutralize its dysphemistic nature and finally entered the standard lexicon, washing off the 'dirt' that had clung for so long.

Grygiel and Kleparski (2007:88-90) observe that both *[...] taboo and euphemisms are linguistic mechanisms, which are influenced or – to put it more adequately – are created by the working of both overt and covert social and psychological factors*. True as it is, the generalisation seems to apply fully to all three mechanisms topical here, that is euphemism, dysphemism and orthophemism. The first two – as opposed to the last one – must be treated as figurative in nature, and should be viewed as kinds of conceptual metaphors in accordance with the theoretical framework proposed in the monumental work of Lakoff and Johnson (1980). A particularly intriguing instance of the working of metaphorical mappings in the formation of cover terms is, as observed by Kiełtyka (2008:137-139), the process of animal metaphorisation, also known as **zoosemy**.[13] This may be instanced with the zoosemic development of such lexical items as *alley cat* used in the sense 'prostitute' or *bitch* applied in the sense 'peevish, wrangling woman' in English or *ropucha* 'toad' meaning 'old fat and ugly woman' in Polish. It is worth pointing out that, for example, *filly*[14] developed its 17th-century metaphorical meaning 'young lively girl', and shortly afterwards came to be used euphemistically to refer to wanton woman.[15] Once the

---

13 On this issue see Kleparski (1990), Grygiel and Kleparski (2007).
14 For more examples, see Kleparski (1997) and Kiełtyka (2008).
15 Consider the following *OED* contexts: 1668 I believe nobody will be very fond of a Hide-Park *Filly* for a Wife.

euphemistic meaning of *filly* became lexicalized two centuries later (1849 Katherine's a young *filly* that will neither be led nor driven. > 1881 You are but a *filly* yet.), it lost its function of covering a dispreferred term, thus retaining merely a neutral sense 'young lively girl'.

Taking a lexicographic perspective on the way the three mechanisms in question are presented in dictionaries, it is befitting to quote Osuchowska (2010:30), who says that:

> The treatment of euphemisms and dysphemisms is yet another grey area. Whereas in the case of the latter, one may safely conclude that users' needs should be satisfied by having the meaning explained and a warning to avoid the word being defined, entries for euphemisms (such as social exclusion) should probably supply the level of detail needed for encoding, not just decoding.

Among other causes and conditionings, the problem lies – as observed by Burchfield (1986:15) – in the alphabetical organization of dictionaries. It seems to be a fact of life that there is a general lack of lexicographic works which would account for the synonymic strings from a given period of time with all the necessary information about their evaluative sociolinguistic load. Suffice it to consider the following O.E. synonyms of present-day *prostitute*:

bepǣcestre 'seducer',
cifes 'concubine',
cwene (survived as, now archaic, *quean*),
firenhicgend 'harlot, adulteress',
forlig(n)is (cf. *forlicgan* 'to fornicate'),
hōre (survived as *whore*),
portcwene 'town whore',
scand (also 'shame, scandal'),
scrætte (from Latin *scratta*),
synnecgei (used of Mary Magdalene).

To compile a list of synonyms like the one provided by Burchfield (1986:23), of any synonymic strings from a given period of time, one would hardly be able to make use of just one lexicographic source. This may be a consequence of the involved difficulty in unscrambling fully and explicitly the context of the writers of the past, as well as understanding and interpreting correctly the complex nature of the long-gone social arrangements and attitudes. Yet, what seems to be an attractive solution to all the aforementioned doubts is – propounded by Allan and Burridge (1991, 2006) – the compilation of all major features and functions of both euphemism and dysphemism in one and the same lexical item. Acting on their advice, let us now direct our attention to this issue.

On various communicative occasions people are bound emotionally by different circumstances and factors, and tend to choose either 'sweet-talking' terms, or offensive ones or – alternately, circumstances and emotional composition permitting – they try to remain neutral. There are, however, situations when feelings are mixed and the locution chosen for communicative purposes stands in direct opposition to the illocutionary force. Such is the case with acts of swearing using modified lexical items. To say that the lexical item *S*hit!* is a clear example of dysphemism is relatively obvious, but the exclamations *Sugar!* or *Shoot!* are in no way vulgar, and many would agree that only very choosy people would feel offended on hearing them. That is the reason why they are called **euphemistic dysphemisms**.

An analogous motivation, this time of the earlier mentioned biblical restriction which forbids us to call the name of God in vain, leads to phonological, thus euphemistic, modifications of such names as *God*, *Jesus*, *Christ* or *Jesus Christ* into *Gosh!*, *Geeze!*, *Chrissake!*, *cripes!*. The act of uttering them in the original form may bring about the opprobrium of those that treat such violations of the second of the Ten Commandments as a case of blasphemy. As Allan and Burridge (2006:39) observe *a euphemistic dysphemism exists to cause less face-loss or offence than an out-and-out dysphemism (although it will not always succeed in doing so)*. Similarly, as Kleparski and Grygiel (2003:19) argue, Puritans used legislation to censor the use of the name of God, which led to the employment of the so-called apostrophised forms in oaths or exclamations, such as *'zounds* for *God's wounds* or *'slid* for *God's lid*.

Quite the reverse is the case with impolite, vulgar or flippant forms that serve to refer to a neutral or, sometimes, serious situation. When the illocutionary force is neutral or calling for euphemistic treatment and the locution is either jocular or offensive, then we are justified to speak about **dysphemistic euphemisms**. One overwhelming tabooed issue that has always provoked fear or, at least, unease is death and its inevitability. As Enright (2005:29) observes, humans' long-lasting avoidance of the topic seems to function as a kind of a trigger for a wealth of X-phemisms used with reference to various aspects of death and dying. A puzzling story, for example, is hidden behind one of the classic expressions referring to dying, namely *kick the bucket*.[16] The origin of the idiomatic formation is disputable since the *OED* suggests two possible ways of development of the lexical item. Presumably, the word *bucket* was adopted from O.Fr. *buquet* 'balance, beam' or *buket* 'washing tub, milk-pail'. As for the former, its connection with the concept DEATH seems to be strictly bound with a slaughtered animal hanging from a beam and twitching. The latter supposedly comes from the idea of an execution or suicide by hanging. In either case a person

---

16 The Polish equivalent *kopnąć w kalendarz* (lit. 'kick the calendar') also seems to contain the element of degrading the concept DEATH with a dose of jocular note.

about to die has to kick something he or she stands on: either a bucket or a stool (Ayto 2007:241). Whatever the ultimate origin, the locution in this case fulfils the function of degrading the concept DEATH and making it seem less frightening. The illocutionary force, on the other hand, is euphemistic.

Yet another instance of a basically neutral concept expressed with a whole array of dysphemistic or semi-dysphemistic terms is menstruation; classic examples being *have the curse, off the roof* or *flying the red flag* in English, *mieć ciotkę* (lit. 'have an aunt') in Polish. For some, however, as argued by Allan and Burridge (2006:39), expressions such as *bleeding like a stuck pig* or *riding/surfing the red wave* are pure instances of dysphemisms because of their – sociolinguistically determined – strong vulgar load. Cockney Rhyming Slang undoubtedly deserves a mention at this point, as well. A whole wealth of rhyming expressions, such as *Bristols* (from *Bristol cities* 'titties') or *nellie dean* (for *queen* 'homosexual'),[17] offer substantial evidence that the jocular locution may, and in fact frequently does, cover a euphemistic illocutionary point.

1.1.4 Concluding remarks

Although the authority of Apostle Paul (Ephesians 4:29) warns against the foul use of language, the truth – as Oscar Wilde[18] puts it – *is rarely pure, and never simple*. The main aim set to this section was to make a case-marked search for a boundary line between the category of euphemisms and the category of dysphemisms, the functions of which are by no means identical. In short, euphemisms serve to dignify or express politeness and/or respect. The elements which are clearly absent from the scope of dysphemisms which serve to offend, insult or name a taboo object.

It was hinted long ago by such giants of European structuralism as Saussure (1916), Ullmann (1957) and, more recently, by Kardela and Kleparski (1990) and Kleparski (1997) that the explanation of many language phenomena must be aided by assuming a panchronic standpoint. It was not accidental that in the foregoing sections many cases of euphemisms and dysphemisms from various historical epochs were given and discussed. This was intended to show the universality of both mechanisms and, secondly, that the immediate conclusion emerging from our discussion is that the explanation of synchronic states must be sought in language history. More to the point, although the boundary line between the processes of euphemisation and dysphemisation is not always clear-

---

17 For more on sociolinguistic factors in word-formation and morphological processes, see, among others, Körtvélyessy (2010).
18 *The Importance of Being Earnest*, Act I.

cut synchronically, historical evidence may help one to find arguments that make it possible to classify individual cases of these mechanisms in one of the two relevant categories. Finally, despite the apparently clear, albeit subtle, distinction between the types of X-phemisms, it is vital to point out the indispensable role of the context and the intentions of the speakers in their choice of expressions.

1.2 Mechanisms behind X-phemisms

Having considered the theoretical background and the various dilemmas connected with defining the concept of euphemism and dysphemism let us now pass on to the subject of mechanisms that are employed in their formation. It needs to be stressed at the outset that the tools employed for the formation of X-phemisms are of varied nature, from structural to semantic and rhetorical devices. The question that may be formulated here is that of whether the processes to be discussed are equally operative in the formation of euphemisms and dysphemisms.

Not infrequently the mechanisms employed are mixed and mingled and the novel formation is hardly attributable only to a single category of formative tools. Such cases as the Polish compound *edzio-pedzio* 'homosexual' are the result of the mixture of several word-formation processes, namely eponymy *edzio* formed from the proper name *Edward*, which, together with the second constitutive element *pedzio* < *pedał* (a dysphemism for 'male homosexual'), are clipped, phonologically modified and compounded to form a nominal compound *edzio-pedzio*.

As for classifications of the mechanisms operative in the formation of X-phemisms, a number of linguists have offered partial discussions[19] without, however, attempting any transparent all-encompassing classification, if indeed such a typology is altogether possible. And so, Warren (1992) proposes a rather detailed taxonomic schema of the mechanisms in question, according to which the body of euphemistic processes fall into two main categories, namely semantic and formal innovations. The latter are further subclassified into word-formation devices, phonemic modification and loan words. In turn, word-formation devices include such processes as compounding, derivation, blends, acronyms and onomatopoeia whereas phonemic modification comprises back slang, rhyming slang, phoneme replacement and abbreviation. In what follows

---

19   See Crespo Fernández (2008), Chamizo Dominguez (2005), Allan and Burridge (1991) and Burchfield (1986), to name but a few.

an attempt will be made to include more sources of X-phemism formation of various types. The taxonomy may be diagrammed as follows:

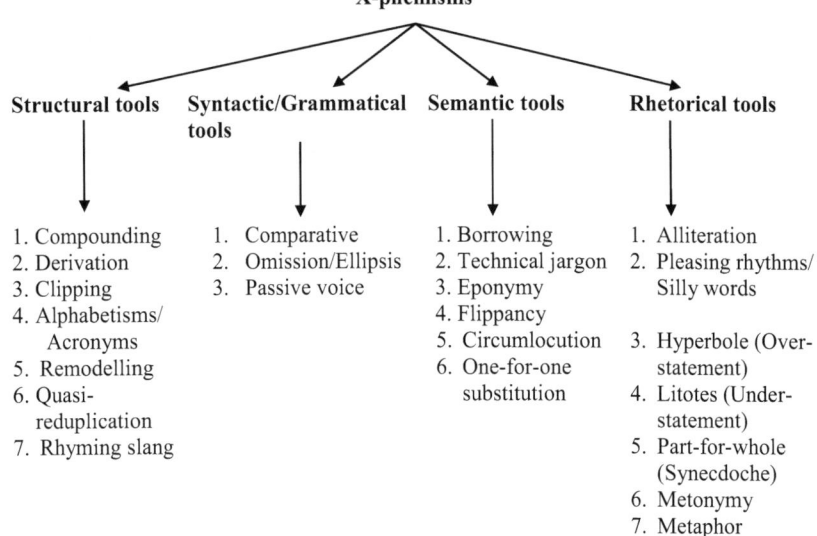

The above synchronic taxonomy, though seemingly minute in its taxonomic aim, largely depends on and evolves from the diachronic understanding of language. It seems that taking on a panchronic perspective is the only adequate standpoint to assume in the analysis of the tools involved in X-phemism formation. That is the reason why – apart from providing examples for each category of tools – some space will be devoted to the diachronic discussion of intriguing and historically-intricate cases. The vast majority of language data quoted and discussed in the sections that follow are taken from Rawson (1981), Burchfield (1986), Aman (1987), Ayto (2000, 2007), Green (2003), Dąbrowska (2005), Enright (2005) and Holder (2008).

1.2.1 Structural tools

In what follows the focus will be on the whole array of processes that may be referred to as structural; that is those mechanisms that interfere within and affect the internal phonological and/or morphological structure of a lexical item. Naturally, most frequently language users resort to their native language resources in order to perform a well-defined euphemistic or dysphemistic function. More often than not one and the same X-phemism may be analysed from either the structural or semantic perspective. Here, we shall start our account with the mechanism of compounding.

Being one of the traditional methods of manipulating the native word stock, the process of putting two free morphemes together to form a new lexical item – known as **compounding** – seems to be often at work in the process of the formation of the so-called concealing devices, which may be exemplified by such instances as *rodent operator* 'rat catcher', *sanitation engineer* (Am.E.) 'dustman' or, on some occasions, *freedom fighter* 'terrorist'. The mechanism may be illustrated with a multitude of cover terms for such a commonly visited place as a toilet, many of which being compounds. Some of them highlight the location without mentioning the function as in the currently used *smallest room* or *outhouse* as used in the earlier days. Similarly, in the set of Polish euphemistic compounds, such as *komórka potrzebna* (lit. 'necessary cubbyhole')[20] or *ustronne miejsce* (lit. 'secluded place'), one seems to operate with the sense of 'kind of place' rather than its function. In other cases we seem to be dealing with distorting the true reason of going to the toilet by adding some element specifying another function of the place, the case in point being, for example, the compounds *powder room*, *rest room*, *washroom* and *bathroom*. On the other hand, such compounds as *comfort station* or *modern convenience* appear to be linked to the concept of the relieving nature of the act itself; that is emptying one's full bowels/bladder. Another relevant formation is the neo-classical compound *sanctum sanctorum* (lit. 'holy of holies') used to refer to a place where one goes to be private and which, as Ayto (2007:186) argues, *has in the past been used for 'lavatory'*. The reference to the presupposed holiness of the place is also reflected in the semantics of the Polish compound *świątynia dumania* (lit. 'temple of contemplation'), which is clearly a jocular term. Let us highlight the fact that even during the Anglo-Saxon times, as Burchfield (1986:20) puts it, there existed several compounds which were used euphemistically in the sense 'toilet', such as O.E. *heolstor* 'place of concealment', or a number of formations which foregrounded the conceptual element <GOING[NEU]> seen in such compounds as *gang-pytt*, *gang-setl* or *forðgang*.

Note that most of the compounds mentioned above are instances of euphemistic devices, which seem to favour genteelism and politeness. There are, however, only a few composite determinants which may be said to have a negative illocutionary force, the relevant examples being *shithouse* or *bog house*, as well

---

20 This *toilet* euphemism, though in rare use nowadays, is semantically close to English *necessary house*, which, according to the *OED*, went out of general use in the 19th century to become a dialectal marker (1828 Written pleadings are of no more use in a court than they would be in a *necessary-house*).

as O.E. *earsgang* 'arse privy', and Burchfield (1986:20) comments on the latter as *scarcely euphemistic*.

The analysis of X-phemisms in terms of the working of **derivational** affixes seems to show that the most frequently employed – regardless of the tabooed sphere – are the negation encoding prefixes, such as *un-*, *in-*, *im-*, *il-*, *ir-*, *dis-*, *de-* and *ab-*. One is justified to say that in the history of Great Britain it was Victorian prudery that stigmatised and prevented the uttering of such words as *trousers* or *breeches*. Instead, the cover terms such as ***in**expressibles*, ***in**describables* or ***un**mentionables* were put to use to meet the need for socially unacceptable naming devices (see Burchfield 1986:16). In Present-day English lexical items which are clearly dysphemistic in nature include ***un**healthy*, ***un**married*, ***un**natural* and ***ab**normal* encoding the notion HOMOSEXUALITY, whereas ***un**balanced* and ***un**hinged* serve to convey the concept MENTAL ILLNESS while ***im**paired* and ***in**convenienced* are used as an alternative to *challenged* employed with reference to physical disability and – as such – are instances of genteelism and may be regarded as euphemisms, or when employed ironically, they may be treated as dysphemistic euphemisms (see Enright 2005:134-137). Another illustrative case of jocular effect of applying a negative prefix is seen in the formation ***un**installed* used in the sense 'dismissed'. There is also a *****dys**functional family* that stands for 'broken home', the verb ***de**contaminate* used in the sense 'destroy evidence', as well as ***un**classified* (used about information) frequently applied in the sense 'not secret, but accessible to the privileged few'. Curious as it may seem, the politically correct term that serves to convey the sense 'rude' is *politically **in**correct* and the act of lying was once referred to by Winston Churchill as *terminological **in**exactitude* (Enright 2005:155).

As for the Polish data, it is fairly evident that the negative prefix *nie-* 'not' is also relatively common, and it is especially frequently attached to euphemistic adjectives. To mention but a few, ***nie**cenzuralny* ('coarse, indecent'), ***nie**przyzwoity* ('coarse, indecent'), ***nie**ciekawy* ('sinister, suspicious', lit. 'uninteresting'), ***nie**świeży* ('stale', lit. 'not fresh'), ***nie**zdrowy* ('bad, weird', lit. 'unhealthy'), ***nie**trzeźwy* ('drunk', lit. 'not sober') or ***nie**parlamentarny* ('impolite, vulgar', lit. 'unparliamentary'[21]). For example, as shown by *SJP*, the bookish adjective and adverb ***nie**parlamentarny/**nie**parlamentarnie* are most frequently used with reference to public utterances which are in disagreement with the rules of conduct, as evidenced by the following *SJP* examples:

---

21 Note that the English literal equivalent was rather short-lived and its sense was always tied with the rules of Parliament, which is evidenced by the following *OED* contexts: 1626 I am come here to shew you your errors, and, as I may term them, *unparliamentary* proceedings in this Parliament. > 1876 A speech is *unparliamentary* when it does not agree with the rules of parliamentary debate.

1. *Obrzucili się **nieparlamentarnymi** epitetami.* – 'They threw vulgar insults at each other.'
2. *Na krytykę swojej pracy odpowiedział wręcz **nieparlamentarnie**.* – 'He answered in vulgar terms to the criticism of his work'.

However, it is not to be understood that Polish *nie*-qualified adjectives are universally negatively loaded. Take, for example, the adjective ***niekulawy*** which in spoken Polish is the antonym of English *lame*. As Chaciński (2005:165) elucidates, the adjective *niekulawy* is currently used with reference to girls in the evaluatively positive sense 'slim, attractive' and computers in the sense 'with a lot of memory'.

The search for suffixes employed to coin X-phemisms in English led to fairly inconspicuous results; the only instances that have been found are *ange**lina*** 'homosexual' or *leg**less*** 'drunk' and French-based *toil**ette*** the diminutive form of *toile* 'cloth', which – through borrowing into English – became the euphemism of *toilet*. On the other hand, the Italian language boasts a whole array of suffixes that are employed in the formation of X-phemisms to refer to the concept PROSTITUTE. As Radtke (1996:34-39) argues, the most frequently used suffixes are -***ona***, -***accia*** and -***ella***, which are exemplified by such formations as *caval**lona*** (*cavalla* 'mare' + *-ona*), *don**naccia*** (*donna* 'woman' + *-accia*) and *galli**nella*** (*gallina* 'hen' + *-ella*).[22] The author also provides a clear explanation of the semantics of these nominal suffixes, according to which Italian *-ella* is used to encode the conceptual element that may be formalised as <NICELY HARMLESS$_{[POS]}$> whereas the derivative suffixes *-ona* and *-accia* are inherently pejorative in nature and make the whole suffix-bound formation vulgar and dysphemistic.

Extensive investigation reveals that in the area of our interest it is virtually impossible to find instances of **fore** or **mixed clipping** and the cases of **back clipping** are still quite unimpressive in their number. Among the English examples for the employment of clipping in the formation of X-phemisms there is *bra* < *brassiere*, which was borrowed from French in the early 20th century where it now chiefly means, according to the *OED*, 'leading strings (of infant)'. As Allan and Burridge (1991:19) point out, *brassiere* itself should not be treated as a euphemism but its clipped form should. Although, as the authors claim, *the use of French is per se euphemistic* the lexical item *brassiere* may be perceived as a standard term (an orthophemism may be postulated here), especially when confronted with such native synonymous formations as *tit-covers* or *breastplates*,

---

22 It is worth noting that the lexical items *cavallona* and *gallinella* are, simultaneously, instances of zoosemic metaphorical mappings which will be discussed in the section on metaphor.

which are indeed dysphemistic in common esteem, at least for some language users.

As for such formations as English *sis, sissy, cissy, lesbie, lesb* or *les* and Polish *homo* or *homcio*, they all serve as evidence that clipping is fairly common as a mechanism employed for deriving cover terms encoding the conceptual element <HOMOSEXUAL_{[NEU]}>. Let us mention at this point that – as Holder (2008:65) explains – *cissy* used in the sense 'effeminate homosexual man' is *probably a corruption of sister via sissy or sis*. Evidently, out of the three forms the most typical instance of clipping is *sis*, as it is not modified either by the suffix *-y* or *-ie*.[23] Hence, the suffixed forms are the outcome of the mixture of two processes; namely the mechanism of clipping coupled with the process of suffixation. An analogous situation may be observed with the lexical items *lesb, les* and *lesbie* all used in the sense 'lesbian', in which case the last one is a mixed form, as well as Polish *homcio* a diminutive of *homo*, which in turn is clipped from *homoseksualista* 'homosexual'. Still in the same conceptual sphere HOMOSEXUALITY we find *Lizzie* 'lesbian' which may be viewed as an instance of clipping (from the proper name *Elizabeth*), but also – alternately – it may also be regarded as the eponym of *Liz* coupled with the suffixation of *-ie*.[24] Yet, it is not to be understood that back-clipping is the only tool operative in the formation of homosexual-specific terms. In Russian we find a case of – rare as it is – application of mid-clipping evidenced in the coinage жóпник/жóп(оч)ник used in the sense ' fag, homosexual', as evidenced by Kunitskaya-Peterson (1981:73).

As Enright (2005:122) puts it, *[...] it is an international sport to speak offensively of other nationalities, and these terms are usually used flippantly with no other intent than that*. A number of these obvious dysphemisms or dysphemistic euphemisms result from the process of clipping, frequently accompanied by suffixation and occasional slight graphic modification as well. The examples are not far to seek: *Yid* 'Jewish person' (from *Yiddish*), *Paki* (from *Pakistani*), *Paddy* 'Irishman' (a diminutive of *Patrick*), *Prod* (from *Protestant*) or *Gyppo* (from *Gypsy*).

Ayto (2007:187) analyses yet another example of clipping combined with the working of suffixation. English *lav* is said to have been derived from *lavatory* at the beginning of the 20th century (1913 Tell the army to line up behind the *lav*. At four o'clock.) and then provided the basis for the derivation of *lavvy*, which Ayto (2007:187) qualifies as *inappropriately winsome*. Some Polish ex-

---

23 Green (2003:1077) seems to accept the opinion that the ultimate origin of *sis* and *sissy* is *sister*, and also provides another spelling variation, namely *sissie* and *cissie*.

24 This is argued by Ayto (2007:106) that the formation *lizzie* in the sense of 'lesbian' was to some extent inspired by the proper name *Lizzie* whereas the *OED* treats this term as an abbreviation of the female Christian name *Elizabeth*.

amples include euphemistic dysphemisms such as *hera* from *heroina* 'heroine' or *kur!* from *k*urwa!* (an extremely harsh and derogatory vulgarism compared to English *f*uck!*). Note that, according to Stomma (2000:103-104), the etymological path of the lexical item *k*urwa*[25] goes back to Proto-Sl. *kurъva*, supposedly a feminine form of *kur* 'rooster' and not Latin *curva* 'crooked, curved'. Although the process of clipping is relatively frequently employed in the formation of X-phemisms it is often accompanied by the working of suffixation and/or graphic modification.

In several lexicographic sources (see, among others, Ayto 2007, the *OED*) the instances of clipping are referred to as abbreviations.[26] For the sake of clarity though, suffice it to mention that – for the purpose of this work – a hard and fast distinction shall be drawn between the mechanisms of clipping, acronymy and alphabetisms. **Clipping**, as exemplified above, is a process in which a lexical item is reduced, often to a monosyllable with the underlying assumption that a single lexical item is subject to alterations to create another lexical item of which the formation of *bra* < *brassiere* and *les* < *lesbian* are good cases in point. Following Crystal (1995:120), clipping is a type of abbreviation. In the case of **alphabetisms** and **acronyms** (other two types of abbreviation), at least two lexical items take part in the formation of a new one by taking the first letters or, sometimes, syllables of each lexeme in a cluster. The distinction between the two lies, as argued by Crystal (1995:120), in the fact that an alphabetism is pronounced as a sequence of individual letters of an alphabet, like *B.A.* '*b*ullshit *a*rtist' and *RTU* '*r*eturned *t*o *u*nit = failed, e.g. in a qualification force', and an acronym is uttered as a single word, as is the case with *snafu* used in the sense '*s*ituation *n*ormal, *a*ll *f*ouled/*f**ucked *u*p'.

In day-to-day communication there are extralinguistic contexts in which uttering the full form is either embarrassing, frightening or politically incorrect. An abbreviated form, whether an acronym or an alphabetism, seems to be of great help in levelling down any negative connotations. Examples that may readily be quoted are euphemistic expressions referring to illnesses, disorders or bodily functions, such as *the Big C* '*c*ancer',[27] *vd* '*v*eneral *d*isease', *bm* '*b*owel

---

25 Stomma (2000:103-104) observes that the Polish vulgarism *k*urwa*, except for its epithet function, is employed in at least five other senses, namely 'prostitute', 'promiscuous woman', 'unfaithful wife', 'ruthless person', 'person overusing their power, status'.

26 See Fromkin (2003:95-97) on the issue of the word coinage and the distinction between acronyms and abbreviation.

27 This example, in the view of Crystal's (1995:120) classification of abbreviations, would be treated as an awkward case since only one element *cancer* is abbreviated to *c*. An analogous case is *the Big D* for 'death'.

*m*ovement', *s/m* '*s*adomasochism' or *PTSD* '*p*ost-*t*raumatic *s*tress *d*isorder'. Linked to the conceptual spheres HOMOSEXUALITY and RACE there are such alphabetisms as *lgb* for '*l*esbian, *g*ay, *b*isexual', *sgo* for '*s*ame *g*ender *o*riented' or *FBI* for '*f*oreign-*b*orn *I*rish', a term employed in Am.E., as Enright (2005:125) explains, to refer to Irish immigrants who enter well-paid white-collar jobs. Another example of that type is an acronym *WASP* which stands for '*W*hite *A*nglo-*S*axon *P*rotestant' and – as Enright (2005:131) argues – it is not particularly offensive, and therefore, may be classified as a dysphemistic euphemism. Yet another instance of a euphemistic acronym is *RIF*, also spelled as *Riff*, which means '*r*eduction *in f*orce', and is used in Am.E. instead of 'summary dismissal from employment'.

Likewise, some dysphemisms tend to be abbreviated, presumably in order to attenuate their negative illocutionary force. Among such cases there are *P.E.E.P* which is used with reference to a woman in the sense '*p*erfectly *e*legant *e*ating *p*ussy' or *sob* employed instead of extremely arrogant and pejorative *son of a bitch*. As for the former, one can risk classifying it as a euphemistic dysphemism since its illocutionary force seems to be quite nicely and intricately concealed behind the innocent sounding acronym. However, undoubtedly women would object to such handling of the term. On the other hand, in the case of the latter, a person described with such an epithet is hardly likely to feel appreciated.

As for the mechanism of **remodelling**, Allan and Burridge (1991:15) define it as a process in which *either the onset or rhyme of the dispreferred term is matched with that of a semantically unrelated word*. It seems that this mechanism is most frequently employed in the formation of euphemistic dysphemism when uttering the dispreferred form would be considered either extremely vulgar or blasphemous. Interestingly, a single vulgarism usually has several remodellings. To illustrate the point one need only quote such lexical items as *Jeez!*, *Jeepers Creepers!*, *Chrissakes!*, *Cripes!* or *Jiminy Cricket!* which serve to replace *Jesus!* or *Jesus Christ!*. An analogous situation is found in Polish in which such morphophonological remodellings as *jeny!*, *jerum!* or *jeżu!* replace *Jezu!* (i.e. 'Jesus!'). Among the variety of crude cover terms which are levelled down through remodelling are the English *freak* instead of 'the f-word' and a whole array of the Polish substitutions of the most stigmatised vulgarism, namely *k*urwa*, in the form of *kurde, kurna, kurka* (also used in the sense 'small hen'), *kurcze* (also used in the sense 'chicken'), *chmurwa, kuchnia* (also used in the sense 'the kitchen'), *furwa, kutwa* (also used in the sense 'miser'), *kuźwa* and the metathetic *kuwra*.[28]

---

28   Note that Polish *kuwra* is an example of a different type of remodelling, namely **metathesis**, which involves change in position of two, usually neighbouring, sounds. As All-

Apart from a number of profanities and blasphemies, remodellings are found in cover terms referring to some parts of the body, bodily functions and in the sphere of SEXUAL OTHERNESS. And so, English *piddle* seems to be an auspicious remodelled version of *piss* although, as Ayto (2007:172) argues, it may be treated as a blend resulting from the combination of *piss* and *puddle*. In current Polish usage there are multiple examples of euphemistic terms denoting the bottom part of the body, that is *d*upa*[29] 'arse', formed with the use of remodelling. Those in current use are *dupcia, dupeczka, dupelinka, dupeńka, dupencja* and *dupka*, all being diminutive formations based on the base form *d*upa* 'arse'. Moreover, one can find other instances of the mechanism of remodelling based on the form *d*upa* 'arse' which are used in the sense 'unpleasant chap', namely *dupek* and *dupol*. The same process appears to be at work in the creation of such (euphemistic) dysphemisms as *pedryl, pedallo* or *pedzio* which serve the concealing function for *pedał* 'homosexual'. On the basis of the number of examples one may infer that the process of remodelling is quite readily exploited in the formation of different types of X-phemisms.

The two remaining mechanisms, namely **quasi-reduplication** and **rhyming slang**, appear to lie somewhere within the boundary area of structural and rhetorical tools as they involve the use of rhyme, which is inherently rhetorical in nature. More to the point, the use is frequently made of what Allan and Burridge (1991:15) refer to as **silly words**. As a result, the outcome is a mixture of two or three processes; specifically reduplication, rhyme and the working of jocular silliness.

Presumably, the conceptual spheres SEX and BODY PARTS constitute a very productive source of examples of quasi-reduplication. Examples here include such gems as *rantum-scantum* used in the verbal sense 'copulate', *hanky-panky* meaning 'flirtation, playing around' and *tuzzy-muzzy* for 'vagina'. Interestingly, out of a great number of X-phemisms expressing the sense 'penis' Morton (2003:91-96) enumerates 1300 such cover terms and – among them – a number of instances of the mechanism of quasi-reduplication. Here, we find

---

an and Burridge (1991:16) claim, metathesis is quite commonly used in 'secret languages' or 'play languages'. From the ongoing analysis it may be concluded that this process is not so popular in the formation of X-phemims.

29 The present-day Polish vulgarism *d*upa* 'arse', as Stomma (2000:44) argues, orginates in Proto-Sl. *d*upa*, which used to mean 'cavity, hole' and around the 15th century the word must have been employed euphemistically in the sense 'arse' to replace the older vulgar term *rzyć* 'arse'. With the passage of time the form *d*upa* acquired the negative evaluative colouring attached to the tabooed part of the body it was used to refer to. Moreover, as observed by Brückner (1985:104), the form *d*upa* is present in all Slavonic languages but only Polish, Bulgarian and Serbian have it employed in the sense 'arse'.

beaver cleaver, boy toy, bone phone, crumpet-trumpet, ding-dong, dingle-dangle, jig-jag, pax wax, pee-dee, placket-racket, tit-bit, tricky dicky and *wang-tang*. The jocular overtones linked to these dysphemistic euphemisms make them sound inauspicious in their locution whereas the illocutionary force is somewhat neutral since they are used to conceal the name of the body part.

Another group of cover terms that should be labelled as dysphemistic euphemisms are reduplicated names that serve to express the sense 'breasts'. In this case the process of reduplication seems to be employed with the aim of expressing, as Morton (2003:153) puts it, *the doubleness of breasts*. Such lexical items as *chi-chis, flip-flaps, lulus, knick-knacks, nay-nays, num-nums, boom-booms* and *bon-bons* provide rich illustration of the point. Beyond the conceptual spheres SEX and BODY PARTS examples are relatively scarce, *ping-pong* instead of 'pass a rich client from specialist to specialist' being the only instance that has been found. As for Polish, the mechanism of quasi-reduplication seems to be of low employment, with *boga-noga* (lit. 'god-leg') to euphemise blasphemous *Jak Boga kocham!* 'God gracious' and the already mentioned *edzio-pedzio* used in the sense 'homosexual'.

In turn, English **rhyming slang** has its roots in the Cockney dialect and it is a particularly intriguing sociolinguistic characteristic feature of the English language. As McArthur (1992:868) elucidates, this form of slang *may have originated in the 18th century, probably among the London Cockneys, as part of creative word-play and thieves' cant*. As far as its euphemistic function is concerned, it seems that concealing quite a number of naughty-sounding body part terms, as well as various sexual activities, makes rhyming slang an ample candidate as a tool for the formation of X-phemisms. Note that, as McArthur (1992:868) explains, there are two phases in the formation of rhyming slang. Firstly, two-element expressions are formed, such as *butcher's hook*, which rhyme with *look*. Then, the second element in a rhyming pair is dropped, and in this way *butcher's hook* becomes simply *butcher's*, as in *Take a butcher's at him* meaning 'Take a look at him'.

To illustrate the point, let us examine several relevant examples. Thus, for instance, cover terms for the sense 'homosexual' include *ginger beer* or *King Lear* 'queer', *iron (hoof)* 'poof', *nellie dean* 'queen' and *nellie duff* 'puff'. Among these, *ginger beer*, originating after the Second World War, is frequently reduced to *ginger*, and in Aus.E., as Franklyn (1975:69) observes, *The Ginger Beers* are a (Military) Corps of Engineers. In turn, the expression *groan and grunt* which rhymes with *c*unt* is also employed in the sense 'girlfriend'. There are a great number of terms referring to 'penis' out of which those rhyming with *p*rick*, namely *Hampton Wick, Pat and Mick* or *Giggle Stick* are but a few.[30] Such a formation as *Bristols* (= *Bristol Cities* 'titties') is fairly common, but there exists a whole array of rhyming slang items employed in the sense 'tits' or 'titties', namely *cat and kitties, brace and bits, Tale of Two Cities, thousand pities* or *fainting fits*.[31] More to the point, their jocular nature places the formations based on rhyming slang among dysphemistic euphemisms.

All in all, the data discussed in the foregoing seem to provide ample evidence that the mechanisms involved in the formation of X-phemisms are of complex and frequently intricate nature. A partial conclusion that may be drawn from the above outline is that – while such word-manufacturing processes as compounding and prefixation in most cases yield euphemistic formations – other mechanisms, including all types of abbreviation are at work in the formation of either euphemisms or dysphemisms. The process of remodelling is, to a large extent, exploited in the formation of euphemistic dysphemisms whilst the mechanisms of quasi-reduplication and rhyming slang prevail in the coinage of dysphemistic euphemisms.

1.2.2 Semantic tools

The general rule is that whenever language users try to avoid some taboo topic they tend to semantically 'beat about the bush', to put it in somewhat colloquial terms. Very frequently, instead of naming a taboo word or phrase they resort to other less laden lexical items that may be employed to conceal a dispreferred semantic equivalent. Whether the syntactic outcome of the semantic innovation is complex, as in the case of circumlocution, or simple, a good example being one-for-one substitution, all semantic tools have one thing in common, namely the conceptual nature of the exchange between a taboo word and its auspicious counterpart. One needs to bear in mind, however, that in the formation of X-phemisms the application of structural tools is not infrequently coupled with semantic devices, a good illustration being such cover terms as the compound *smallest room* and the alphabetism *sgo* < *same gender oriented* which also constitute examples of the semantic mechanism of circumlocution that serve to convey the senses 'toilet' and 'homosexual', respectively.

The process of **borrowing**, which has been one of the most common mechanisms of expanding the English lexicon, has been readily employed in the formation of X-phemisms. Abstracting from the nature of English, the intensity of

---

30 Note that *giggle stick* – according to Franklyn (1975:69) – is of Australian origin *where it is not rhyming slang, but is descriptive of a stick used for mixing drinks.*
31 For more relevant examples, see Franklyn (1975).

borrowing differs from language to language. However, as Rawson (1981:8) rightly observes, *foreign languages sound finer*, and classic languages in particular are perceived as superior and refined since, as Warren (1992:132) puts it, *they imply learnedness and matter-of-factness and so elevate "the tone" of the word*. Regardless of the language, whether it is English or Polish, Romance cover terms can be multiplied. It seems that the conceptual spheres BODILY FUNCTIONS and BODY PARTS are remarkably productive with such terms as *perspire, menstruate, copulate, defecate, urinate, expectorate, penis* and *vagina* in English and in Polish where such words as *perspiracja* 'perspiration', *menstruacja* 'menstruation', *kopulować* 'copulate', *penis* 'penis' and *wagina* 'vagina' are preferred against their native equivalents which most language users tend to perceive as either coarse, or – worse still – vulgar. Take, for example, English *masturbation* the sense of which may be defined as 'sexual gratification by self-stimulation'. Apart from the bookish Romance borrowing *masturbation* there are plenty synonymous native expressions, such as *whack off, choke the chicken, spank the monkey, kill a kitten* or *polish the dolphin* which – though for some vulgar – should be put among dysphemistic euphemisms because of their jocular overtones.

A synchronic perspective allows us to place the above-mentioned examples of borrowings among orthophemisms due to their neutral overtones, and the fact that each term also has euphemistic and dysphemistic counterparts. Suffice it to mention *urinate* that is technical and somewhat medical in nature, but may be euphemistically replaced with *spend a penny* or, simply, *go to the bathroom* and dysphemistically substituted for *piss* or, in a more jocular way, *siphon the python* for men and *squeeze the lemon* for women. The same is true for the Polish orthophemism *menstruować* which may be replaced with such euphemisms as *mieć te dni* 'have those days' or *być niedysponowaną* 'be unavailable' (for sexual purposes). The Polish dysphemism that is used in the place of the neutral *menstruacja* is *ciotka* 'aunt(ie)', as in the idiom *mieć ciotkę* 'have an auntie'. An intriguing case of a Latinate genteelism that entered both English and Polish is *in flagranti* which subtly points to being caught "red-handed" during a sexual intercourse or immediately before/after.

What is even more worthy of note is that, from a diachronic perspective, such Latin-based euphemisms as *coition, copulation* and *intercourse* were once, as Rawson (1981:4) observes, general terms for 'coming together, coupling and communication'. Only with the passage of time did their sexual connotations become dominant after they had been employed as euphemisms, irreversibly dropping earlier existing senses almost completely. Correspondingly, the English lexical item *prostitute* may boast a neutral beginning, when in the 17th century it came to life as a euphemism for *whore*.[32] Ample evidence exists, Rawson (1981:6) argues, that the lexical item *whore* itself may have entered the English lexicon as a cover term for some other expression that is beyond recognition today. According to the *OED*, O.E. *hóre* may have been based on O.N. *hór* 'adultery', but it is stressed in the literature that the corresponding Indo-European root *qār-* may serve as the basis for the assumption that Latin *cārus* 'dear' and O.E. *hóre* are cognates. There are grounds to believe that the sense of the O.E. equivalent of Latin *cārus* may have transferred its semantic range in Anglo-Saxon times for concealing purposes. Such a sequence of euphemism exchange, with one substituting another, is traditionally referred to as the Law of Succession. Rawson (1981:4-5) explains that

> [...] after a euphemism becomes tainted by association with its underlying "bad" word, people will shun it. [...] Once people begin to shun a term, it usually is necessary to replace the one that has failed. Then the second will become tainted and a third will appear. In this way, chains of euphemisms evolve.

The author exemplifies this law with the following chain of historical euphemisms: *mad > crazy > insane > lunatic > mentally deranged > mental*.

Another language that has acted as a source of English euphemisms and dysphemisms is French, which should be of no surprise due to a simple fact that its overall and fundamental influence upon the shape of English is predominantly visible in the wealth of synonyms that the English language gained from its southern neighbour. The body of euphemistic French synonyms is represented by *brassiere, derrière, lingerie, masseuse* and *enceinte* to replace dysphemistic *tit-covers, arse*, or neutral, *underwear, prostitute* and *pregnant* respectively. Other languages also have their representatives among the body of English X-phemisms, namely Portuguese, Yiddish and Sanskrit. For example, an expression of decidedly euphemistic force is a Portuguese borrowing *auto-da-fé* (lit. 'act of faith') which is employed to conceal the act of killing and its origins go back to the time of Inquisition, when "the act of faith" was performed by burning to death. As to the more exotic example, *yoni* 'vulva, source, nest' is a cover term incorporated from Sanskrit, which has been used, as Morton (2003:142) maintains, in the sense 'vagina' for about two hundred years. The word may have originated from the Proto-Indo-European cognate *yeug* 'unite' and is echoed in the word *yoke*, through the Germanic branch, and in the middle of *conjugal*, through the Italic branch. In American English the lexical items *tush* or *tushy* (remodelled versions of *tochus*) were borrowed from Yiddish *tokhes* 'beneath' to be used in the sense 'arse', and are – due to the presence of a jocular

---

32 Consider the following *OED* context: 1613 I haue seene houses as full of such *prostitutes*, as the schooles in France are full of children.

overtone – representatives of dysphemistic euphemisms. More to the point, Bluestein (1998:112) provides some contexts of its use, as in Rhinemaiden's observation about the Dwarf Alverrück: *Er kommt nicht der wasser zu trinken*, to which the Dwarf replies, *I came some tuschies zu pinchen*.

Needless to say, the Polish wealth of X-phemisms is, to some extent, made up of foreign elements as well. Apart from the Latinate element mentioned above, there are a number of lexical items borrowed from English, like *gej* (from *gay*), *sex*, *call-girl* or *sex-worker*, all linked directly to the conceptual sphere SEXUALITY. Still within the same conceptual sphere we find French borrowings in the forms of *pedał* and *pedryl*, both being dysphemisms for 'homosexual'.[33]

In turn, the process of employing **technical jargon** in the formation of X-phemisms encompasses the use of Latinate borrowings. Thus, such examples – most of which were mentioned above – as *perspire, menstruate, copulate, defecate, faeces, urinate, expectorate, penis, vagina* and many other such words provide evidence that the use of learned terms helps language users convey messages in the conceptual spheres BODILY FUNCTIONS and BODY PARTS, where calling a spade a spade would be construed either too embarrassing or socially inappropriate. Hardly anyone can imagine a sociolinguistic context of a doctor's surgery, for instance, in which a patient talks about *a pain in the tits* or *problems with the pussy*. Resorting to technical jargon that aptly fits medical terms is simply a marker of trying to save one's face and, hence, being perceived as polite, according to middle-class politeness criterion postulated by Allan and Burridge (2006:34-36).[34] Another plausible justification for the use of technical jargon and learned terms goes back to the 19th century when – as Allan and Burridge (1991:19) explain – the author assumed that *the Latin text would be uninterpretable to the uneducated – and therefore to the young and innocent*.

Unsurprisingly, what is true for the English language works perfectly well for Polish, too. Suffice it to illustrate the mechanism of using Polish technical jargon with such lexical items as *kał* 'faeces', *mocz* or *uryna* 'urine', *menstruacja* 'menstruation', *perspiracja* 'perspiration' and *współżycie* 'sexual intercourse' (lit. 'co-existence'), which are particularly favoured in formal and medical contexts. It is worth stressing that not all Polish cover terms, which in the case of technical jargon should be referred to as orthophemisms, are of Latin origin. The morphologically complex lexical item *współżycie* is obtained from

---

33   From Greek through French: *pais, paid* 'boy', *erastēs* 'lover'.
34   In order to be polite to a casual acquaintance of the opposite sex, in a formal situation, in a middle-class environment, one would normally be expected to use the euphemism or orthophemism rather than the dispreferred counterpart. The dispreferred counterpart would be a dysphemism (Allan and Burridge 2006:35).

the process of prefixation, in which both the prefix *współ-* 'co-' and the lexical base *życie* 'life, existence' are native elements of the Polish word stock. As for the orthophemism *mocz*, its Slavonic origin together with other Polish derivatives is argued for in Brückner (1985:343), and its cognates in other Slavonic languages, like *moč* in Czech, *mokraća* in Croat and *моча* in Russian, aptly speak in favour of the Slavonic roots of the Polish orthophemism *mocz*.

The fact that a proper name, like *Earl of Sandwich*, may enter the body of common nouns, in this case in the form of *sandwich*, has long been recognised. It may, however, be somewhat surprising to note that the same process – referred to as **eponymy** – is at work in the formation of X-phemisms. An example is the history of the word *pussy*, which functions as an auspicious cover term used in the sense 'vagina'. The evidence for its inclusion in the category of eponymy is to be sought for in language diachrony. As Morton (2003:62) clarifies, *puss* was used in the 16th century as a proper name given to cats, like present-day *Snowball* or *Whiskers* (a1530 I haue sene the day that *pus* my cat Hath had in a yere kytlyns eyghtene). A century later *puss* became a synonym of *cat* and – around the 18th century – was the word, according to the *OED*, gradually superseded by its diminutive form *pussy* (1726 My new *pussey* is… white,… with black spots). From the 17th to the 18th century, the word *puss* fell down the evaluative scale when it commenced to function in English as a derogatory zoosemy-based synonym of *woman*. Interestingly, its diminutive counterpart managed to remain on the neutral side when applied to women, though in the middle of the 19th century it started to be linked to the conceptual sphere BODY PARTS as it developed the sense 'female genitals'.[35]

Within the conceptual sphere HOMOSEXUALITY English boasts a number of cover terms which are the outcome of the process of eponymy. In vast majority, these are female-specific names that came to be used in the sense 'homosexual', examples being *lizzie, mary ann, annie, betty, molly, nellie, agnes, abigail* and *amy-john*. Apart from the fact that they exemplify the process of eponymy, as used in the formation of these apparent dysphemisms, at the same time they constitute lexical evidence for the existence of the conceptual metaphor HOMOSEXUALITY IS FEMINITY.[36] Needless to say, the rise of some of them,

---

[35] From the analysis conducted, it becomes clear that the lexical item *pussy* used in the sense 'pudendum', being a diminutive form of *puss* through the suffixation of *-y*, is an outcome of a mixture of processes, namely derivation coupled with eponymy. What is more, a zoosemic mapping between the conceptual categories **FELINE** and **HUMAN BEING**, as well as general-for-specific metonymy must have taken place in the historical development of the word *pussy*.

[36] For more on conceptual metaphors employed in the formation of X-phemisms, see section 1.2.3.

such as *lizzie, betty, annie* and *nellie*, results from the derivational process of suffixation, in which a diminutive suffix *-y/-ie* has been operative. Once again, let us stress that the data gathered so far suggests fairly unambiguously that hardly ever do we observe a single process at work in the formation of X-phemisms.

Yet another attention-grabbing case, though not so certain in its affinity to the category of eponyms is the conceptual sphere BODY PARTS with a relatively great number of dysphemistic euphemisms used either in the sense 'male genitals' or 'breasts'. The fact that these lexical items tend to be spelled with a capital letter makes us hesitate as to whether the process of eponymy can be claimed to have been fully completed. The list of examples includes *John Thomas, John Tom, John Willy, Julius Caesar, little Elvis, (little) Peter, (little) willy, Oscar (Meyer), Pat and Mick* used in the sense 'penis' and *Mickey and Minnie, Thelma and Louise, Wilma and Betty, Lucy and Ethel* meaning 'breasts'.

The inherent feature of another semantic mechanism, namely **flippancy**, is its total lack of seriousness or – in extreme form – uncritical disregard for a taboo topic a given expression helps to encode and convey. The conceptual sphere that seems to be particularly prolific in flippant cover terms is DEATH. Very frequently, language users resort to flippancy in the context of death as a type of self-defence mechanism. As Enright (2005:30) puts it, *[...] the flippancy is more accurately a kind of defiance, the apparent insensitivity a form of whistling past the graveyard, a refusal to recognize or accept the fact of death, or that it worries you in any way*. What is more significant, however, is that the mechanism of flippancy seems to be tightly linked to and interwoven with another formation process discussed below, namely circumlocution. One gets the impression that there exists a certain relation between the two mechanisms based on the semantic relation of hyponymy. Seen in this light, it may be assumed that each flippant expression simultaneously exemplifies the process of circumlocution, but the rule does not work in reverse; not all instances of circumlocution have flippant overtones. It stands to reason that, at least for some, the two mechanisms should be discussed under the same heading. However, conditioned by the specific nature of flippancy, which puts such cover terms among dysphemistic euphemisms, here it seems reasonable to discuss the two mechanisms separately.

A good number of dysphemistic euphemisms that are used to denote the notion DEATH provide a good illustration of the mechanism of flippancy. The body of English examples includes such idiomatic expressions as *turn up one's toes, kick the bucket, pop one's clogs, hang up one's hat/the spoon, go to the happy hunting grounds, push up (the) daisies* and *bite the dust/ground*. Similarly, in Polish many instances of flippant cover terms that serve to encode the sense 'dying' are there to be found, such as *strzelić kopytami* (lit. 'shoot one's hooves'), *kopnąć w kalendarz* (lit. 'kick the calendar'), *odwalić kitę* (a hunting term; lit. 'lay one's tail up'), *wąchać kwiatki od spodu* (lit. 'smell flowers from underneath') and *przekręcić się* (lit. 'turn oneself').

From a synchronic perspective all the examples enumerated here are variously jocular and seem to be somehow degrading and trivialising the concept DEATH. Diachronic analysis of some of the idiomatic expressions reveals their literal, and – in most cases – axiologically neutral character. The most intriguing example, apparently, is the expression *kick the bucket*, the origin of which – as Ayto (2005:241) puts it – remains notoriously in dispute.[37] Some euphemisms – interestingly not only those that are found in English – centre on the position of a dead person with respect to plants' roots that grow above, and thus we obtain such phraseological formations as English *turn up one's toes to the daisies* or *push up (the) daisies*, Polish *wąchać kwiatki od spodu* 'smell flowers from underneath', German *das Radieschen unten betrachten* 'watch radishes from underneath' and French *manger les pissenlits par la racine* 'eat dandelions by the roots'. Along more technical lines, Enright (2005:39) explains that the apparently misplaced notion PUSHING is the consequence of a dead body becoming part of the nitrogen cycle, thus helping the daisies to grow. English *bite the dust/ground*, Polish *gryźć ziemię* and German *ins Gras beißen* 'bite the grass' provide yet another illustration of a special treatment of the concept DEATH, in which it is the sense 'falling down face first' that seems to be hidden behind the discussed euphemisms.

On finding that sociolinguistic status is almost indefinable some language users find it hard to go through a day without saying, for example *at this point in time* instead of *now* or, something like, *little girl's room* instead of *toilet*. This type of pragmatic 'beating about the bush' – according to Allan and Burridge (1991:16) – *is a kind of componential analysis; the senses of taboo terms are unpacked and each of the meaning components are listed*. As shown in the previous section, a considerable number of cover terms coined on the basis of **circumlocution** are flippant or jocular in character. Here, the focus will be on purely euphemistic expressions which, through a complex form, are aimed at levelling down the negative illocutionary force that their straightforward counterpart has.

An incredibly useful arithmetic device proposed by Rawson (1989:10-11), that bears the name FOP Index (Fog or Pomposity Index), equips language users with a tool for measuring the level of euphemistic complexity or – to put it more bluntly – the element of 'beating about the bush'. Rawson (1989:10) maintains

---

[37] The analysis of the plausible origins of the dysphemistic euphemism *kick the bucket* is provided in the section on dysphemistic euphemisms.

that *the longer the euphemism the better*, however, in scientific terms it seems to imply that the higher the FOP Index for a given euphemism, the longer it is with respect to the corresponding inauspicious cover term. To illustrate the way it works, let us compare the monosyllabic and normally neutral *now* with its long euphemistic, often legal, equivalent *at this point in time*. What the FOP Index takes into consideration is how many letters are used in a euphemistic term and how many more syllables and words are employed in order to express the same referential meaning. In the case of *at this point in time*, 17 letters are used with 4 syllables more and 4 words more than in the case of *now*. To calculate the FOP Index it is necessary to work out the total of 17+4+4 and then divide it by the number of letters used in the neutral term, here 3. The result of the calculation should be 8.3 (25:3), which makes a relatively high FOP Index for the euphemism *at this point in time*. On the other hand, it is comparatively low for a different euphemism, namely *break wind*, which, with the score of 11 (9+1+1) calculated against 4 of the vulgar *fart* yields a FOP Index of 2.75.

The mechanism of circumlocution seems to be an inherent feature of the process of euphemisation since, as Rawson (1981:10) points out:

> As a rule, to which there are very few exceptions (*hit* for 'murder', for instance), euphemisms are longer than the words they replace. [...] This is partly because the tabooed Anglo-Saxon words tend to be short and partly because it almost always takes more words to evade an idea than to state it directly and honestly.

One may say that whichever conceptual sphere stigmatised by taboo we consider, be it DEATH, SEX, BODY PARTS, BODY FUNCTIONS or any other, a multitude of circumlocutory expressions concealing the direct terms substantiate Rawson's (1989:10) claim that – in order to be genteel or indirect – language users show a tendency to opt for a longer word or multiple-word expression. With the FOP Index provided in brackets below, let us now analyse a number of other examples to illustrate the point further and better.

The notion LYING is frequently disguised, especially in the world of politics, in such vague and seemingly innocent expressions as *economical with the truth* (10.6) or *terminological inexactitude* (11.6). Interestingly, in the Polish language the euphemism that veils *kłamać* 'lie' is *mijać się z prawdą* (3.6) which has a comparatively low FOP Index. As for concealing another shameful conceptual element <DRUNK$_{[NEG]}$> lexically, both Polish and English use similar expressions, that is *pod wpływem alkoholu* (4) instead of *pijany* 'drunk', which in fact semantically corresponds to English *under the influence* (4.8).

The conceptual sphere DEATH has attracted a considerable number of circumlocutory expressions, some of which were discussed earlier in the section on flippancy.[38] Those expressions conspicuously euphemistic in nature are such English cover terms as *pass away* (3.6), *no longer with us* (7) and *give up the ghost* (6.6) and the Polish euphemisms for *umierać* 'die', such as *zejść z tego świata* (3), which literary means 'leave this world' and *wyzionąć ducha* (2.3) corresponding semantically to the English expression *give up the ghost*. Moving on to the conceptual sphere SEX, one encounters a whole array of idiomatic coinages formed by the mechanism of circumlocution. Finally, let us mention the concept of PREGNANCY which is mirrored in the semantics of such cover terms as *in an interesting condition* (4.1) or – somewhat outdated – *in the family way* (2.6). Similarly, the sense 'being pregnant' is lexically represented by means of such Polish euphemistic expressions as *w odmiennym stanie* (3.3) lit. 'in a different condition' or *spodziewać się dziecka* (4) 'be expecting a baby'.

Yet another circumlocutory-prone notion within the conceptual sphere SEX is PROSTITUTION. And thus, for instance instead of a short and overtly vulgar *whore* in English and *k*urwa* in Polish, language users frequently resort to such longer auspicious terms as English *nymph of the pavement* (4), *lady of the night* (4.2), which is now, as Ayto (2007:98) puts it, *decidedly superannuated*. Such cover terms as *commercial sex worker* (5.4) and *sex care provider* (4.2) were coined, as Ayto (2007:100) elucidates, by a politically correct lobby with a view to rehabilitating the connotations that the lexical terms expressing the notion PROSTITUTION have had over the centuries. In fact, the two terms in question make language users think of a job connected with a social service sector rather than *the oldest profession* (5.2). As for the Polish euphemisms that serve to conceal the sense 'prostitution', the expression *najstarszy zawód świata* (5.6) is conceptually equivalent to *the oldest profession* and *kobieta lekkich obyczajów* (6.4), literally meaning 'woman of loose morals', where the constitutive element *lekki* that means both 'light' and 'loose' seems to convey the notion of total lack of morality, if not hardcore immorality. It is worth noting at this point that, as Ayto (2007:100) also observes, in western cultures the notion PROSTITUTION is gradually creeping out of the tabooed spheres. Among other explanations, the more or less successful attempts in several countries to legalise paid love and harbouring places where paid love is offered seem to constitute ample evidence for this out-of-taboo trend.

---

38 The calculation of the FOP Index shows that in many cases flippancy seems to boost up the level of circumlocution. This may be observed in the following examples (the FOP Index provided in the brackets): *turn up one's toes* (6.6), *kick the bucket* (6), *pop one's clog* (5), *hang up one's hat* (6.3), *push up the daisies* (7.6), *bite the dust* (5) and *go to the happy hunting grounds* (12.6), the unquestionable winner in the competition for the longest circumlocutory euphemism in the conceptual sphere DEATH.

In our discussion countless examples have already been provided of yet another semantic mechanism, namely **one-for-one substitution**, which takes place whenever a single form – disfavoured by language users to be used on certain occasions – comes to be replaced with another single form, which is considered (more) appropriate in a given communicative event. Out of a variety of mechanisms already discussed the most illustrative examples of one-for-one substitution are to be found among the representatives of eponyms (*annie, bettie, willy*), technical jargon (*perspire, copulate, faeces*) and borrowings (*brassiere, enceinte, tushy*). It needs to be stressed, however, that the remaining instances to be given in this section are simultaneously the so-called by-products of other mechanisms that are at work.

The conceptual sphere BODY PARTS abounds with cases of one-for-one substitutions, such as *tits, boobs, bosom* for 'breasts', *pudendum, keyhole, beaver* for 'vagina', *manhood, organ, key* for 'penis' and *behind, bottom, rear* for 'arse'. Whichever tabooed part of the body is taken into consideration there are at least a few, if not many, euphemistic or dysphemistic single-form equivalents. Significantly, one-for-one substitutions trigger all types of X-phemisms, which makes this mechanism particularly attractive. Other conceptual spheres boasting a considerable number of single-form cover terms are APPEARANCE, DRUNKENNESS and RACE with such illustrative examples as *wrinkly* 'old', *homely* 'plain, ugly', *chubby* 'fat', *caned, hammered, plastered* for 'drunk' and *taffy* 'Welshman', *skip* 'Aborigine term for a white Australian of British birth', *kiwi* 'New Zealander'. Beyond the scope of these three conceptual spheres, the euphemisms that encode the sense 'lover' seem to be particularly intriguing as – in several individual cases – they are coupled with the mechanism of understatement. This mechanism is observable in such expressions as *roommate, partner* and *companion*, which – taken literally – have nothing to do with a sexual relationship. Only an appropriate context reveals the true meaning intended by a speaker.[39]

Once again what seems to be a natural conclusion emerging from our discussion on semantic tools is the perspicuously complex nature of X-phemisms in that they – in the majority of cases – appear to arise from the simultaneous application of two or more mechanisms. Suffice it to mention here the most illustrative cases, namely the cover terms *bettie* and *willy*, which result from derivation by means of the diminutive suffix *-y/-ie*, the working of eponymy and one-for-one substitution. Some euphemistic coinages, such as the lexical item *bra*, are the result of applying both structural and semantic tools; here the processes of borrowing, clipping and one-for-one substitution seem to have been jointly at work.

---

39 For more on the relation between euphemisms and context, see Chamizo Dominguez (2005) and Allan and Burridge (1991).

1.2.3 Rhetorical Tools

Superficially, there is no substantial difference between semantic and rhetorical tools, and all rhetorical tools are either structural, like alliteration, or semantic, like hyperbole. Such an argument is easily justifiable and relevant, at least from the synchronic perspective. However, the purpose of a more detailed taxonomy of all the mechanisms is to stress the literary roots, since several of them originated as devices for making oral and written communication effective or persuasive. The adjective *rhetorical* was first used in Late Middle English in the sense 'eloquently expressed' and for centuries the term has served the task of naming literary devices prevailing in poetry and other literary genres. Hence, it is worthwhile examining the issue of how sophisticated means of expression are employed in the formation of, more often than not, colloquial cover terms.

Let us commence our discussion of rhetorical devices with the mechanism of **alliteration**, which – apparently – is merely restricted to poetic verse. However, a closer inspection of its scope of application reveals that among jocular cover terms, that is dysphemistic euphemisms, instances of alliteration are not too far below the surface. As Cuddon and Preston (1998:23) and Danesi (2000:12) explain, the term *alliteration* – originating in Latin – refers to the practice of repeating and playing upon the same letter. What is even more intriguing is the fact that in English verse alliteration is an older device than rhyme, yet – according to Cuddon and Preston (1998:23) – it *becomes increasingly rare after the end of the 15th century*. Beyond the scope of literature, as observed by McArthur (1992:29), instances of alliteration are found in speech-making, collocations, idiomatic phrases and proverbs, such as *look before you leap* or *bed and breakfast*; similes, for example, *dead as a doornail*; reduplicative words, such as *tittle-tattle*; tongue twisters, for instance *She sells sea-shells on the seashore*; and advertising, for example, *Guinness is good for you*.

From the perspective of the analysis attempted here, it seems that dysphemistic euphemisms exploit the rudimentary form of alliteration. This is clearly observable in the phonetic shape of such jocular cover terms as *mad mick*, *big bird*, *cunny catcher*, *dangle-dong*, *inch instrument*, *lance of love* or *doodle, diddle, dink, dong*, all being euphemistic replacements for an orthophemism *penis*. Generally, the conceptual sphere BODY PARTS has attracted a considerable number of euphemistic formations formed by means of alliteration. Needless to say, the process of euphemisation most actively revolves around those body parts that are euphemistically termed *naughty bits/parts*. Hence, for example, the sense 'breasts' is expressed by means of such dysphemistic euphemisms as *beef bags, butter-bags, baby bar, silicon sacks, skin sacks* or *hee-haws*, to mention but a few. Yet another constituent of the human body for which jocular cover terms are formed through alliteration is a vagina, which becomes veiled by such alliteration-powered coinages as *gristle-gripper* and *groan and grunt*.[40] As for the Polish instances of X-phemisms coined by means of alliteration in the conceptual sphere BODY PARTS, these are relatively scarce in number; the phrases that may be quoted here are *cięższa część ciała* (lit. 'heavier part of the body') and *twarz tylna* (lit. 'rear face'), functioning as jocular cover terms for 'arse'.

Beyond the conceptual sphere BODY PARTS, it becomes increasingly difficult to find instances of alliteration operative in the formation of X-phemisms. Such playful idiomatic expressions as *go to the happy hunting grounds* used in the sense 'die' or *gruesome Gertie* employed in the sense 'electric chair' that are linked to the conceptual sphere DEATH are rarities in the scope of alliteration. What is characteristic about all the cases of alliterative cover terms is that they are characterised by the presence of the conceptual element <JOCULAR$_{[NEG]}$> and – consequently – they all may be classed to the category of dysphemistic euphemisms.

The mechanism of applying **pleasing rhythms** and **silly words** in the coinage of cover terms may be said to be conspicuously analogous to the processes of alliteration, rhyming slang and quasi-reduplication in that they all trigger the formation of dysphemistic euphemisms. Of apparent prominence is the fact that Allan and Burridge (1991:14-16) refer to all the four mechanisms as verbal play, and – in this way – they stress their playful and jocular nature. It is worth noting, however, that despite their relatively high productivity in the formation of dysphemistic euphemisms, they differ substantially in their nature. For this reason rhyming slang and quasi-reduplication are categorised as structural tools whereas alliteration, pleasing rhythms and silly words must be taxonomised as rhetorical devices. In turn, it seems virtually impossible to define, in scientific terms, either the mechanism of pleasing rhythms or silly words. The only appropriate starting point is **rhythm**, which, as *BRITANNICA* defines the notion, is:

> [...] patterned recurrence, within certain range of regularity, of specific language features, usually features of sound. Although difficult to define, rhythm is readily discriminated by the ear and the mind, having as it does a physiological basis. It is universally agreed to involve qualities of movement, repetition and pattern.

One is tempted to ask the question of how this account should be extended to include the conceptual element <PLEASING$_{[POS]}$>. Let us assume, for the purpose of the present analysis, that any rhythm that is discriminated by the ear and the mind as regular or harmonious should be treated as an instance of a pleasing rhythm. Yet, this does not solve the problem of the highly idiosyncratic nature

---

40 This is also an example of Cockney rhyming slang in which it rhymes with *c*unt*.

of an individual approach to the conceptual element <PLEASING[POS]>.[41] As for the terminological obscurity intrinsically involved in any attempt at explaining the mechanism of employing silly words,[42] let us resort to Morton (2003:153), who provides a sound account of the formation of silly words to euphemise the concept BREASTS. In order to explain the extralinguistic conditionings behind the rise of such cover terms as *bamboochas, cadabies, chalubbies, chumbawumbas, smosabs* or *meguffies*, Morton (2003:153) argues that all such terms:

> [...] seem to be merely nonsense formations, almost as if the very notion of breasts can transport men back to [...] a pre-linguistic age when they delighted in experimenting with all the sounds and syllables that their pudgy little cheeks and lips could make.

Other intriguing instances, this time, of a pleasing rhythm coupled with either alliteration or rhyme are the lexical items *big brown eyes*[43] employed to refer to breasts and *over-shoulder boulder-holders* used in the sense 'bra'.

Still within the conceptual sphere BODY PARTS, or – more specifically – its subsector **NAUGHTY BITS**, there are a considerable number of cover terms used in the sense 'penis' which are formed with the aid of at least one of the mechanisms discussed here. For example, such dysphemistic euphemisms as *ding-a-ling*, *jing-jang* and *teenie-weenie* are typical instances of a combination of the three mechanisms, namely pleasing rhythm, reduplication and silly words. Another cover term, that is *inch instrument*, appears to result from both alliteration and pleasing rhythm while such cover terms as *libido bandido* and *main vein* are formed by means of the operation of pleasing rhythm coupled with effects of rhyme and reduplication.[44]

The inference that may be drawn from the data gathered so far is that a substantial number of dysphemistic euphemisms are hardly ever the outcomes of applying a single process, but rather such euphemistic devices are formed by means of an amalgamation of several mechanisms, such as rhyme, quasi-

---

41   Thus, it is the author that takes full responsibility for the adequacy of examples cited in this section.

42   The question may arise at this point whether the mechanism of employing silly words should be discussed together with rhetorical tools. After all, they are new formations with a completely new structure given. On the other hand, however, the ultimate outcome of this mechanism is words that are based on rhyme, quasi-reduplication, alliteration or rhythm. It is, presumably, the strong correlation between rhythm and silly words that puts the two mechanisms in the same section.

43   Cf. the Polish use of *(duże) niebieskie oczy* '(big) blue eyes' used in the sense 'breasts'.

44   For more examples of cover terms employed in the sense 'penis', which are based on a whole range of mechanisms, see Morton (2003:91-96).

reduplication, alliteration, pleasing rhythms and silly words. Therefore, one may speak of certain **non-exclusiveness** of the application of X-phemism-forming mechanisms, which means that the application of one frequently conditions/ precedes/requires the application of another one for the successful rise of the X-phemising variant that will meet the contextual needs, goals and ends of the speaker involved in the communicative event. Obviously, the combinatory nature of X-phemising processes is in no way an exception but rather goes hand in hand with the complex nature of many other semantic processes in the evolution of language (see Kleparski 1997).

As for the mechanism of **hyperbole**, it is defined by Pei and Gaynor (1954:94) as *a figure of speech representing an obvious exaggeration* while McArthur (1992:491) and *BRITANNICA* see **overstatement** as a deliberate exaggeration employed for emphasis or comic effect that is not meant to be taken literally. It is frequently exploited in political rhetoric and advertising slogans. In fact, as May (1986:122) observes, *exaggeration in advertising is common place: it is, one might say, the soil in which the fine flower of euphemism grows*. Curious as it may seem, it also has its share in the formation of X-phemisms beyond the scope of politics and advertising. The application of an intentional exaggeration seems to be particularly useful when, for example, language users wish to upgrade someone's status. This is the case with euphemisms that serve to express the concept of low professional status, such as *maintenance person* 'caretaker', *extermination engineer* 'pest controller' (especially in Am.E.), *executive assistant* 'secretary', *close protection officer* 'bodyguard', *door supervisor* 'bouncer', *sanitation engineer* (in Am.E.) and *refuse collector* 'dustman'.[45] In effect, the overall result of applying hyperbole is a grander and, seemingly, more respectful name, or a name with an air of respect, at least in the case of some professions.

As for the scope of advertising, the mechanism of hyperbole is frequently employed in order to attenuate negative connotations a given product might evoke in the minds of (potential) customers. This is the reason why *terraced house* becomes *town house* in advertisements of estate agents and Harpic lavatory cleaner makes use of a *Star Wars* line that goes *May the bleachmatic force be with you* (May 1986:124-126).

Within the conceptual sphere BODY PARTS the main role the mechanism of hyperbole performs is to build up the importance in the function of a given organ. This intentional exaggeration, however, may contribute to the fact that such cover terms as *atom bombs, flesh bombs, torpedoes, cannons, howitzers,*

---

45 It is worth noting at this point that all these names of professional terms simultaneously exemplify the mechanism of compounding discussed in section 1.2.1.

scuds, *warheads* and *bazookas* referring to 'breasts' are undoubtedly dysphemistic in their illocutionary force. Note that the perception of a sexual body organ as in terms of a weapon (of mass destruction) is also observable in the formation of some dysphemistic euphemisms used in the sense 'penis', namely *guided missile* or *love gun*. Surprising as it may seem, even in the Anglo-Saxon times the sense 'penis' was expressed in a very much similar way, and O.E. *geweald* 'power control' and *wǣpen* 'weapon' are representative examples. Another instance of intentional exaggeration seems to be at work when the male sexual organ is referred to as *matrimonial peacemaker* or *means of generation*. As for the conceptual sphere BODILY FUNCTIONS, the mechanism of hyperbole is employed in the formation of such dysphemistic euphemisms as *the curse* or *being a woman for a week*, which are formations that serve to express the sense 'menstruation'. A particularly puzzling case is the latter expression, the semantics of which may imply – through intentional exaggeration – that only one conceptual element, that is <MENSTRUATION$_{[NEU]}$>, stands for a person's womanhood. Alternately, a much more degrading interpretation is that a woman deserves the proud name of *woman* only during the period of menstruation.

On the contrary, *understatement reduces risks* claims Rawson (1981:10), but justifiably adds that, at times, using this *mild roundabout* may lead to the distortion of the true meaning. After all, is *freedom fighter*[46] always 'terrorist' or are all *friends* 'lovers'? In the majority of cases it is usually the context of the utterance that disarms the ambiguity of such expressions as *help* or *patients* in the sense 'servant' and 'corpses' respectively. To put it in strictly rhetorical terms **litotes (understatement)** may also be referred to as **meiosis**, which *BRITANNICA* defines as *understatement generally*, and Głowiński et al. (2002:261) treats meiosis as an interchangeable term with litotes. In turn, Cuddon and Preston (1998:501) elucidate that meiosis *contains an understatement for emphasis [...] and also for dramatic effect*. Here, no distinction shall be drawn between meiosis and understatement, the primary reason being that the former originates from the Greek word *meiōsis*, which literally means 'lessening', hence semantically corresponds with the term *understatement*.

Let us point to the fact that such one-for-one substitutions as *bottom* 'arse', *the monosyllable* 'pudendum' or *sleep/depart* 'die' are also illustrative examples of the mechanism of understatement. When we assume a diachronic perspective we see that the last two instances enumerated above, namely *sleep* and *depart* have remained euphemistic since the Anglo-Saxon times when their O.E. respective equivalents *swefan* and *ellorsīð* were employed to conceal the notion

---

46 This lexical item is also an example of structural tools, namely compounding and as such is mentioned in section 1.2.1 as well.

DEATH.[47] Another example of understatement that triggered semantic change is the French verb *baiser* which used to mean 'kiss' but began to be employed as a euphemism of *f*uck* in the 17th century. As a euphemism for a much tabooed activity the word acquired the air of "dirt" attached to its novel meaning. Consequently, another French word *embrasser* (lit. 'embrace') became the substitute for *baiser*, which has remained a cover term.

Among other instances of euphemisms formed through the mechanism of understatement are those lexical items that refer to feared or hunted animals, such as *the striped one* for 'tiger'. Interestingly enough, the traditional names that express the sense 'bear' in Germanic and Slavonic languages were presumably the ultimate outcome of avoiding the direct reference. While Germanic languages tended to apply the Proto-Indo European root **bher-* meaning 'bright, brown', Slavonic languages, as observed by Brückner (1985:360), concealed an apparent fear in referring to either the animal's diet by calling it *medved* in Russian or *niedźwiedź* in Polish (both meaning lit. 'honey eater') or in Lithuanian *lokys* lit. 'licker'.

Last but not least, there are a considerable number of synchronic euphemisms based on understatement which are notoriously employed by politicians, officials and employers. For fear of losing public support they resort to calling 'war' *a state of armed conflict*, 'riots' *disturbances* or *troubles* and 'civil war' *civil disorder*.[48] Employers, on the other hand, frequently turn to euphemistic expressions when they need to dismiss their employees. Instead of using the direct verb *dismiss*, more often than not they choose a genteelism, such as *let you go* and when there is a need to dispense with a large number of superfluous employees we hear of *planned reductions*.

The analysis of the mechanism of understatement would be somewhat incomplete without making a mention of its subtype, that is **litotes**, which – according to McArthur (1992:622) – derives from Greek (through Latin) *litotēs* 'meagreness', though *BRITANNICA* defines the term as *conscious understatement in which emphasis is achieved by negation*. Here, instances employing a negative prefix or adverb can be multiplied. Classic examples are *a little intoxicated* for 'drunk', *unmentionables* or *inexpressibles* for 'trousers', *disadvantaged* for 'poor', *not a great reader* for 'illiterate' and *not bright* for 'stupid'. At the same time, there are cases when negation takes the form of the opposite notion, as in English *liberate*, *pacify* or Polish *pacyfikować* used in the sense 'invade' or in Gealic *Am fear mór* (lit. 'the great fellow') to convey the sense 'the Devil'. The common feature of all those instances of understatement is that they

---

47 On this issue, see Łozowski (2000), among others.
48 For more examples on political and official euphemisms, see Hoggart (1986:181).

are auspicious terms aimed at attenuating and degrading negative illocutionary force evoked by taboo topics they conceal.

The remaining three mechanisms, namely synecdoche, metonymy and metaphor are cognitive processes which deserve special attention and treatment in the discussion on the nature of cover terms. To begin with, one may say that analysing the mechanism of **synecdoche** separately from metonymy amounts to taking on a traditional rhetoric approach.[49] First and foremost, the reason for such a distinction adopted in the present analysis can be found in the roots of both devices. Traditionally, especially in the rhetoric of antiquity, the two mechanisms, namely synecdoche and metonymy, were treated as distinct figures of speech. Here, a distinction is made, as well, in order to account for dissimilar illocutionary forces evoked by each of the two mechanisms. Synecdoche is frequently seen as a subtype of metonymy which is concerned with parts and wholes, whereby either the part represents the whole or the whole represents the part (see, among others, Danesi 2000, McArthur 1992:1014, Rayewska 1979:168).

In the case of the synecdochic relationship \\PART FOR WHOLE\\, and \\BODY PART FOR PERSON\\ in particular, the majority of examples that have been registered point to the existence of a conceptual mapping between the categories **MALE SEX ORGANS** and **MALE HUMAN BEING**, as well as **FEMALE SEX ORGANS** and **FEMALE HUMAN BEING**. Moreover, as for the illocutionary force, a preponderance of cases belong to the category of dysphemisms. To begin with, three lexical items, that is *cod*, *dildo* and *p*rick* represent the synecdochic relationship \\MALE SEX ORGANS FOR MALE HUMAN BEING\\. The lexical item *cod* started to be used in a novel sense 'scrotum, testicles'[50] towards the end of the 14th century and – at the turn of the 17th and 18th centuries – through synecdochic extension, the word developed the senses 'fool' and 'friend, pal'.[51] In turn, the form *dildo*, as evidenced by the *OED*, entered the English language in the 16th century as a euphemistic cover

---

49 It needs to be mentioned at this point that there is no unanimous agreement among linguists on the issue of the relation between synecdoche and metonymy. Some, like Bredin (1984) and Seto (1999), consider synecdoche a distinct process, but bearing similarity to metonymy, while others, such as Lakoff and Johnson (1980), Lakoff and Turner (1989), Kleparski (1997), Gibbs (1999), Koch (1999) and Kopecka (2009), treat synecdoche as a specific subtype of metonymy.

50 Consider the following *OED* examples: 1398 The *codde* of the genetours. → 1783 [Ruptures] are called inguinal, scrotal, femoral… as they happen to make their appearance in the groin, *cod*, thigh.

51 These senses emerge from the following *OED* contexts: c1690 *Cod*, also a Fool. An honest *Cod*, a trusty Friend. → 1878 Ye vile drunken *cod*.

term used in the sense 'penis'.[52] The 20th-century Am.E. slang brought a *pars pro toto* extension when *dildo* developed a human-specific sense-thread 'clumsy or stupid fellow'. Undoubtedly, the most inauspicious cover term in this relation is *p*rick*, which from the end of the 16th century has functioned in English as a vulgar locution employed in the sense 'penis',[53] and since the 20th century the word has also been employed through a synecdochic extension as a term of abuse in the sense 'man/male human being'.[54] Last but not least, the lexical item *mug* seems to represent a more general *pars pro toto* relationship, namely \\BODY PART FOR PERSON\\, since its 18th-century sense 'face'[55] shifted to the epicene sense 'stupid, incompetent person/simpleton' in the mid-19th century.

Analogous synecdochic mappings can be ascertained between the conceptual categories **FEMALE SEX ORGANS** and **FEMALE HUMAN BEING**, where the ultimate outcome in the form of – not infrequently – terms of objectification are negatively loaded dysphemisms. Suffice it to sketch the historical meanderings of such lexical items as *quim*, *brush*, *buttock* and *c*unt* to illustrate the point. As the *OED* informs us, in the 20th century the word *quim* – originally used in the sense 'vagina' from the 18th century – developed a new sense based on *pars pro toto* relationship when it began to stand for 'woman' or 'women collectively' in Am.E. slang.[56] Similarly, the sense of the lexical item *brush* developed from 'female pubic hair', according to Spears (1991:58), to a derogatory reference term for 'girl/young woman' in Aus.E. and N.Z.E. slang in the 20th century. In turn, the body part term *buttock* temporarily acquired a novel sense, namely 'common strumpet', in the 17th and 18th centuries. Interestingly, the synecdochic extension failed to survive in the

---

52 The *OED* examples: c1593 Curse Eunuke *dilldoe*, senceless contrafet. → 1965 Why does it matter so much to them whether lesbians use a *dildo* or not?

53 See the following *OED* quotations: 1592 The pissing Boye lift up his *pricke*. → 1976 Jocko had... a very small pecker... Blood on the bulging pectorals, tiny contradictory *prick*.

54 The following *OED* examples testify to this sense: 1929 *Prick*, one in authority who is abusive or unjust. → 1978 They have good jobs, big futures. And the *pricks* won't even do their service.

55 This sense is seen in the following *OED* contexts: 1708 My Lawyer has a Desk, nine Law-books without Covers, two with Covers, a Temple-*Mug*, and the hopes of being a Judge. → 1897 Look at old Rufus Abrane. I see the state of the fight on the old fellow's *mug*. He hasn't a bet left in him.

56 Consider the following *OED* examples: 1935 *Quim*, a female. → 1974 The key to success in this contest is a flashy car; and if the car is both expensive and impressive 'you have to beat the *quim* off with a hockey stick'.

language and the last *OED* quote for this sense dates from the middle of the 18th century.[57]

Originating in the 20th century, the most vulgar term of abuse one can use of a person, especially a woman, is *c*unt* and this sense also derives from the synecdochic extension in question. The origins of Mod.E *c*unt* are obscure and the so far unresolved dispute, as shown by Mills (1989:59), is the question of whether it derives form the Latin *cunnus* 'vulva' or from the Germanic *kunton* through M.L.G. *kunte* meaning 'female pudendum'. Note that the *OED* restricts its discussion to Germanic origin without mentioning the possible Latin roots. More to the point, before the 15th century the form *c*unt* was Standard English used in the sense 'female pudendum'[58] and it was, as Partridge (1984:278) puts it:

> [...] owing to its powerful sexuality [that] the term has since C15th been avoided in written and polite English [...] and since 1700 it has, except in the reprinting of old classics, been held obscene, i.e. a legal offence to print it in full.

It is worth stressing that – as a term of abuse – the form *c*unt* is considered the most vulgar of all, much nastier than *p*rick*, which, according to Mills (1989:60), may reflect the attitude of fear and hatred associated with female sexuality that seems to be deeply enrooted in our culture.

Last but not least, there are lexemes, such as *tail*, *skin* and *ankle*, whose primary senses all belong to the conceptual category **BODY PARTS** and, in each case, diachronic analysis reveals the presence of the synecdochic relationship \\BODY PART FOR PERSON\\. The history of the word *tail* clearly represents this path of development when its sense 'vulva' (originating from the 14th century) developed into 'prostitute' or 'female sexual partner'[59] in the 19th century.[60] In turn, in Am.E. slang in the 20th century the word *skin* acquired the sense 'at-

---

57 1743 The... capacity which qualifies a mill-ben, a bridle-call, or a *buttock* and file to arrive at any degree of eminence in his profession.

58 Consider the following *OED* contexts: a1325 Yeue þi *cunte* to cunnig and craue affetir wedding. → 1956 His young wife had abandoned all hope of bringing him to heel, by means of her *cunt*, that trump card of young wives.

59 The following *OED* examples testify to this sense of *tail*: 1846 I takes my pitch last night on Fleet pave, then... a swell was sweet on me for a *tail*. → 1977 He would yell, 'How y'all doin, chief? Gettin much *tail*?'

60 In Polish *ogon* 'tail' has developed human-specific sense 'someone who stands in the way' or 'someone who lags behind' while the diminutive form *ogonek* is occasionally used humorously in the sense 'penis'. Note that incidentally, in Latin *pēnis* used to mean 'tail' before it started to be employed in the sense 'male sex organ', thus being employed as a euphemism itself.

tractive woman/woman considered sexually'[61] and the lexeme *ankle* developed the sense 'attractive young woman or girl'.[62]

All in all, one may propose a rule that the presence of the synecdochic relationship \\BODY PART FOR PERSON\\ almost inevitably yields a dysphemistic illocutionary force.[63] The ultimate reason may be that many of the body part terms are under a stigmatising taboo, thus contaminated by the semantic element <FILTHY_{[NEG]}>. Curiously enough, the synecdochic relationship in question seems to be somewhat universal as in Polish, for example, the lexical items referring to male/female sex organs (as such under a strong taboo), namely *ch*uj*, *k*utas* both used in the sense 'p*rick' and *c*ipa* 'c*unt' also developed a secondary sense of a vulgar term of abuse used towards males and females, respectively.

In accordance with Lakoff and Johnson (1980) and Lakoff and Turner (1989), to name but a few relevant publications, the synecdochic relationship \\BODY PART FOR PERSON\\ is one of numerous contiguity relations found in the mechanism of metonymy that triggers the formation of X-phemisms. Here, according to Panther and Radden (1999), **metonymy** is understood as a conceptual operation, which – despite its rhetorical origin – has become deeply rooted in the human perception of the world. Firstly, a concealing device seems to be represented by the metonymic contiguity pattern \\ACTIVITY FOR CONSECUTIVE ACTIVITY\\. This is reflected in the use of such phrases as English *go to bed* or *lie with* (arch.) to convey the sense 'have sex', *go to the toilet*, *spend a penny* used in the sense 'urinate' or 'defecate' and *fall (in a fight)* for 'die'. Corresponding euphemistic expressions are found in Polish, namely *iść do łóżka, pójść z kimś (do łóżka)*[64] 'go to bed', *iść do toalety/ubikacji* 'go to the toilet' and *polec/paść (w walce)* 'fall (in a fight)'. Other cover terms used in the sense 'have sex' include English *to bed* and Polish *łóżko ich pogodzi* lit. 'the bed will reconcile them' and *rozwiedli się przez łóżko* lit. 'they got divorced because of bed' representing the effects of the metonymic contiguity pattern \\PLACE FOR EVENT\\ and *sleep with* that represents the \\SUCCESSIVE SUBEVENT FOR (COMPLEX) EVENT\\ contiguity pattern.

---

61 Note that the history of Polish has witnessed a very similar kind of semantic transfer. In the last decades of the 20th century Polish *skóra/skórka* 'skin' developed a secondary sense 'attractive woman', particularly used in such exclamations as *Ale skóra!* 'What a skin!' or *Ale (młoda) skórka!* 'What a (young) skin!'
62 For more detailed analysis of these and other metonymic relationships within the category **HUMAN BEING**, see Kopecka (2009, 2011).
63 See Allan and Burridge (2006:79-89) on different types of dysphemistic terms of insult based, among others, on metonymy and zoosemic metaphor.
64 The part *do łóżka* lit. 'to bed' is frequently elliptically skipped.

In turn, the metonymic extension based on \\FEATURE FOR PERSON ADORNED WITH THIS FEATURE\\ contiguity pattern seems to be mirrored in the semantics of such lexical items as English *glassy-eyed, tired* for 'drunk', *street walker, hooker* for 'prostitute' and *bender, bent* for 'male homosexual' or Polish *ślepiata* (from *ślepy* 'blind') used in the sense '(woman) with big eyes' (northern Polish), *zmęczony* lit. 'tired', *wczorajszy* (from *wczoraj* 'yesterday') employed in the sense 'drunk' and *cichodajka* (from *cicho* 'quietly' and *daj* imperative form of *dawać* 'give') used to express the sense 'woman who generously and somewhat indiscriminately offers her body to men'. Needless to say, it appears that the features represented by the names clearly point to types of people characterised by them. After all, drunk people do have glassy eyes and look tired. Homosexuals may stereotypically assume a bent position during sexual acts, and a female walking up and down a street hooking or attracting men is quite likely to work in the oldest profession.[65] More importantly, however, scrutinising the features per se leads to an obvious conclusion that, theoretically, they fail to be sufficient conditions for determining the type of a person. At this point one is tempted to address a series of questions: *Are all people in a bent position homosexuals? Are all girls walking in the streets prostitutes? Are people who look tired always drunk?* Nevertheless, being employed as referential terms, most of the features mentioned become conspicuous regardless of the context. The only exception seems to be the form *tired*, which is highly dependent on the context of an utterance.[66]

Curiously enough, as recently observed by Kudła (2010:149), there seems to exist a metonymic relationship that triggers a dysphemistic illocutionary force, namely \\FOOD FOR NATIONALITY\\. The author observes that in order to employ the name of a particular type of food to refer to a representative of a specific nationality this food has to be stereotypically associated with a given nationality. To illustrate the point, let us mention such dysphemistic terms as *frog-eater* 'Frenchman', *macaroni* 'Italian', *potato-eater* 'Irishman' and *beef-eater* 'Englishman, British' (in Am.E.).

---

65 Note that in Polish the movement is frequently seen as taking place in the air since the word *latawica* implies aerial movement (from the verb *latać* 'fly'). In German the euphemistic cover term *Horizontale* seems to centre on the horizontal movement of prostitutes.

66 The issue of context-dependent ambiguity is strictly linked to the level of lexicalization of an X-phemism. Here, lexical items, such as *streetwalker, hooker, bender, bent* and *glassy-eyed* are lexicalized X-phemisms whereas *tired* is semi-lexicalized and as such needs a context for the appropriate interpretation. The issue of X-phemism lexicalization is thoroughly discussed in, among others, Chamizo Domínguez and Sánchez Benedito (2005:13-26).

Yet another metonymic relationship worth directing attention to is \\GENERAL FOR SPECIFIC\\, which is relatively widely exploited at a lexical level, especially when it comes to naming sexual body organs. Hence, instead of calling a spade a spade and saying *penis* or *male genitals* one has a whole array of more general terms at their disposal, such as English *person* (legal), *equipment*, *bits*, *business*, *the thing*, *machine*, *instrument*, *organ*, *gadget* or, in Polish, *sprzęt* 'equipment', *organ*, *instrument*, *interes* 'business'. Similarly, the term *arse* is skilfully avoided with such vague cover terms as *bottom*, *backside*, *behind*, *rear*, *posterior*, *latter end*, *derriere* in English and *tyłek* lit. 'backside', *siedzenie* lit. 'seat' in Polish. In turn, the sense 'breasts' is veiled with such auspicious cover terms as *bosom*, *bust*, *chest*, *front* and *lungs*. The Polish equivalent of the last English form, namely *płuca*, works the same way. Last but not least, the word *genitals* itself is not general enough to suit all contexts, or may be perceived as too technical, and is frequently replaced with one of numerous euphemistic expressions based on the metonymic contiguity pattern \\GENERAL FOR SPECIFIC\\. Those in most common use today include English *down there*, *down below*, *downstairs*, *nether regions* or Polish *tam* corresponding to English *down there*, which stress the location of the embarrassing organs, or *private parts*, *privates*, *naughty bits/parts* and *bits*.

It has long been established that the mechanisms of metonymy and metaphor are not merely literary figures of speech. They are far more omnipresent conceptual operations than traditional linguistics considered them to be. In the light of cognitive linguistics **conceptual metaphor** is strongly embedded in human perception and experience of the world.[67] Conceptual mappings between different domains of experience are also observable, at a lexical level, in the case of X-phemism formation.

To begin with, within the structural metaphor LIFE IS A JOURNEY the notion DEATH is conceptualised either in terms of a stage of a journey or its specific type (e.g. to an unspecified place). At a lexical level such a mapping is reflected in a number of euphemistic cover terms, namely *depart this life*, *reach the end of the road*, *last journey/voyage*, *go to meet one's Maker*, *check out* (Am.E.), *go to a better place*, *go to the other side*, *go upstairs* (jocular) and *pass away*. It needs to be stressed that the last example is already fully lexicalized in the English language, and the metaphorical mapping can only be traced in an etymological account. The sole verb *pass*, as Ayto (2007:234) puts it, is *of considerable antiquity* as it developed the sense 'die' already in the 14th century and

---

[67] For an in-depth analysis of conceptual metaphor, see, among others, Lakoff and Johnson (1980) and Kleparski (1997), and for most recent account in Polish cognitive literature, see Strugielska (2012).

the phrase *pass away* entered English in the 19th century. The distinction needs to be drawn between *go* and *pass (away)* in that the latter, as Ayto (2007:234) argues, *encapsulates perfectly the element of sentimental pretence that cannot even come straight out with go*.

Furthermore, the conceptual sphere SEX seems to abound in metaphorical mappings from such source domains as **FOOD, WAR, GAME, TRADE** and **ANIMALS**.[68] Linguistic material proves the existence of a whole range of conceptual metaphors. First and foremost, let us consider how the conceptualisations SEX IS CONSUMPTION and THE OBJECT OF SEX IS FOOD[69] are portrayed in English. Suffice it to mention, after Chamizo Dominguez and Sánchez Benedito (2005:49), such expressions and such utterances as *I'll eat you up, have/get a bit of meat/mutton/jam, cook, cut the mustard, make a sandwich, make jam* and *roll the dough*, which are linguistic representations of the conceptual metaphor SEX IS CONSUMPTION. In turn, the conceptualisation THE OBJECT OF SEX IS FOOD is reflected in a great number of, more often than not, colloquial or slang terms referring either to a person, be it a man or a woman, or to a sex organ. Thus, language users can choose out of a whole menu of words, such as *dish, dishy* for 'good-looking person', *cookie, cheesecake, cream puff, honey-bunny, sugar, sweet meat* for 'attractive female', *hot dog, sausage, salami, beef, mutton, pork, banana, cucumber, gherkin, candy stick, lollipop* for 'penis', *apricot, cabbage, cauliflower, bun, jam, jelly, lunch-box, muffin, cookie* for 'vagina', *apples, coconuts, grapefruits, lemons, mangoes, pumpkins, melons, watermelons* for 'breasts'. Note that all the aforementioned examples represent what has come to be known as **foodsemic** metaphorical extensions.[70]

Secondly, the conceptualisation of sex in terms of fighting and war in the form of the metaphor SEX IS FIGHT/WAR finds its linguistic outlet, as exemplified by Chamizo Dominguez and Sánchez Benedito (2005:41), in the rise of such cover terms as *stab, pierce, nail, bang, poke, knock* to express the verbal sense 'copulate', *knife, cleaver, prick, sword, weapon, stick, whip, club, pole* for the sense 'penis' and *wound, cut, scar, cleft, mortar, push* as synonyms of *vagi-*

---

68 Chamizo Dominguez and Sánchez Benedito (2005) provide an exhaustive collection of euphemisms and dysphemisms based on conceptual mappings between the domain **SEX** and various domains of experience.

69 The conceptual metaphors SEX IS CONSUMPTION and THE OBJECT OF SEX IS FOOD, together with SEXUAL DESIRE IS HUNGER, were first postulated by Lakoff (1987) and elaborated on by Kövecses (2006).

70 The term foodsemy was coined by Kleparski (2008) and refers to a semantic change based on conceptual mappings between the category **FOODSTUFFS** and the category **HUMAN BEING**. On this issue, see also Cymbalista (2009b), Kudła (2010) and Kleparski (2013).

na. An intriguing picture drawn from this metaphorical mapping is that, in this fight, a male is the attacker and a female the victim or the casualty.

Thirdly, the conceptual metaphor SEX IS GAME/PLAYING with its various lexical realizations, such as *have a roll in the hay, hanky-panky, jazz, rock and roll, sport, pocket the red* (from billiards or snooker), *score between the posts* (Aus.E.). Chamizo Dominguez and Sánchez Benedito (2005:47) place this metaphorical mapping, together with the metaphor SEX IS CONSUMPTION, in pleasurable spheres, that is *those conceptual spheres or networks of euphemisms which [...] highlight hedonistic aspects in all their multifarious ways.*

Yet another conceptual mapping discussed by Chamizo Dominguez and Sánchez Benedito (2005:54-56) has its source domain in the conceptual category **TRADE** and it gives rise to the conceptual metaphor SEX IS TRADE. This mapping is reflected at a lexical level with the employment of such phrases as, for example, *trade, trader, be on the job, business, buy love, sell one's body* to refer to the oldest profession. Interestingly enough, as Chamizo Dominguez and Sánchez Benedito (2005:55) observe, the sense-thread of the word *business* has developed in such a way that it can refer to anything related to sex. Thus, such cover terms as *get down to business* or *give her the business* (Am.E. slang) serve to convey the sense 'copulate' and *his/her business* means 'male/female genitals'.[71]

Last but not least, metaphorical extensions based on **zoosemy** have shaped another substantial group of X-phemisms. The working of the general metaphor A HUMAN BEING IS AN ANIMAL may be exemplified by means of several more specific individual conceptualisations, namely A PROSTITUTE IS AN ANIMAL, A BELOVED PERSON IS AN ANIMAL and A WOMAN IS AN ANIMAL. The first category is represented by zoosemic senses of such English lexical items as *chicken*, which secondarily means 'individual young male homosexual prostitute', *curtal* 'short-tailed horse' > 'prostitute' or *nag* 'old poor horse' > 'prostitute' and, following Radtke (1996:34-37), by a group of Italian lexical items meaning 'prostitute', such as *cagnaccia* < *cagna* 'bitch', *cavallona* < *cavalla* 'mare', *gallinella* < *gallina* 'hen', *vaccaccia* < *vacca* 'cow', *pocella* < *porca* 'sow', *scrofaccia* < *scrofa* 'sow' and *troiaccia* < *troia* 'sow'. The universality of the discussed conceptual mapping to the target domain **PROSTITUTION** seems to be evidenced, as exemplified by Kiełtyka (2008), by metaphorical zoosemic extensions in other European languages, that is Mod.Sp. *zorra* 'vixen', Mod.Fr. *poulette* 'small hen', *pouliche* 'young mare', Mod.Pol. *mewka* '(little) sea-gull', Mod.Russ. *бабочка* 'butterfly' and Mod.G. *Mähre* 'old mare'.

---

71   Cf. Polish *interes* lit. 'business' used in the sense 'male genitals'.

As for the zoosemic metaphor A BELOVED PERSON IS AN ANIMAL, it is represented by a group of terms of endearment, for example *lambkin, turtle, mouse, ladybird, sparrow, coney* and *marmoset*, most of them – as Morton (2003:52) points out – having been far more popular from the 15th to the 18th century rather than in the English of today. Polish present-day terms of endearment exploiting zoosemic extensions include, among others, *żabcia* diminutive of *żaba* 'frog', *kotek* 'kitten' and *myszka* 'small mouse', *misiek* '(small) bear', *ptaszek* '(little) bird). It needs to be stressed at this point that the metaphor A WOMAN IS AN ANIMAL is deeply enrooted in a number of natural languages.[72] Suffice it to mention Mod.E. *chick, filly, bird* and Mod.Fr. *pouliche* 'young mare' used in the sense 'attractive girl', Mod.Sp. *foca* (lit. 'seal') used figuratively in the sense 'fat person, particularly a woman', Mod.Fr. *haridelle* (lit. 'old horse'), employed metaphorically in the sense 'thin and ugly woman' and Mod.Pol. *kobyła* (lit. 'mare') used contemptuously in the sense 'stupid large woman'.

Moreover, metaphorical zoosemic extensions also take place between the conceptual spheres SEX and HUNTING, thus forming the metaphor SEX IS HUNTING, which may be illustrated with such English cover terms as *go bird's nesting, go cunny-catching, run a course* to refer to a man as 'hunter',[73] *crack-hunter, cranny-hunter, bush beater/whacker, horn* to mean 'penis' and *bird's nest, nest in the bush, happy hunting grounds, cunny-burrow, bunny, shooter's hill* for 'vagina'. Within the scope of the metaphor SEX IS HUNTING yet another conceptualisation at work can be found, namely SEX ORGAN IS AN ANIMAL. This schema seems to underlie the formation of such zoosemic extensions as *beaver, mink, cat, coney/cony/cunny, dormouse, kitty, kitty-cat, monkey, moosey, mouse, puss/pussy/pussycat, squirrel, poodle* to replace the word *vagina* and *big boa, cum cobra, snake, serpent, lizard, one-eyed trouser snake, one-eyed mamba, tiger, bull, chicken, cock, cockerel, rooster, donkey, dog, pup, frog, cuckoo, worm, dinosaur, dragon, unicorn* used in the dysphemistic sense 'penis'.

An interconnected conceptual sphere that deserves particular attention is SEXUALITY, and HOMOSEXUALITY, as its specialised variant, in particular. Conceptual mappings that are observable have their starting points in the conceptual spheres PLANT, FEMINITY and OTHERNESS, thus giving rise to the conceptual metaphors A HOMOSEXUAL IS A FLOWER, HOMOSEXUALI-

---

72 On this issue, see Kleparski (1997) and Kiełtyka (2008).
73 Note that in Polish such expressions as *zapolować na coś* lit. 'hunt something' and *ustrzelić coś* lit. 'shoot something down' frequently employed in boys-will-be-boys situations also represent the conceptual metaphor SEX IS HUNTING.

TY IS FEMINITY and HOMOSEXUALITY IS OTHERNESS. To illustrate the point discussed here, let us consider such linguistic material as *buttercup, daffodil, daisy, lily, pansy* (arch.), *petal, lavender, flower* (arch.) or *abigail, amy-john* ('lesbian'), *annie, agnes, auntie, belle, betty, ethel, fairy, jessie, margery, marge* ('lesbian'), *mary, mary ann, maud, molly, nancy* (arch.), *nellie* ('lesbian', 'gay'), *nola, quean, queen, sissy* or *abnormal, curious, funny, left-handed, odd, peculiar, unnatural*.

The analysis of the rhetorical tools involved seems to show their multifarious nature in terms of X-phemism formation. Note that, for example, the mechanisms of alliteration and pleasing rhythms and/or silly words are frequently forms that are at work in the formation of dysphemistic euphemisms, the mechanisms of general-for-specific metonymy, hyperbole and understatement, in the majority of cases, trigger the formation of euphemisms while the process of synecdoche is used in the coinage of dysphemisms. The mechanism that seems to be somewhat omnipresent – or at least frequently present – in the formation of all types of X-phemism is that of metaphor, which undoubtedly provides yet another piece of evidence for the long-established assumption about metaphors being deeply enrooted both in human perception and understanding of the world.

1.2.4 Syntactic/Grammatical tools

On the whole, syntactic and grammatical tools constitute a relatively small fraction in the whole array of X-phemism forming mechanisms. Nevertheless, they also deserve analytical attention with regard to their share in the formation of X-phemisms. The basic distinction between syntactic/grammatical tools and structural, semantic or rhetorical devices that is drawn here lies in the fact that syntactic or grammatical tools tend to work on a higher level of linguistic analysis, that is phrases and sentences whereas structural, semantic or rhetorical mechanisms are found operative mostly at a lexical level of analysis.

Apart from having a whole range of cover terms at their individual disposal, language users may also resort to what is – apparently – the simplest and the least costly way; namely not uttering a taboo word at all. In this case, as Allan and Burridge (1991:17) maintain, language users either decide to delete the taboo part in the form of **full omission** or replace it with some kind of non-verbal expression, which is known as **quasi-omission**. As for the latter, they may take the protect-the-sensitive form of asterisks or dashes in writing and *mhm* or *er-mm* in speech. Burchfield (1986:17) discusses a relevant quotation from *Tristram Shandy* to illustrate such a substitution along the following lines *My sister, I dare say, added he, does not care to let a man come so near her *****. Obviously, in this case the use of a sequence of asterisks replaces a tabooed body part term frequently referred to as *the monosyllable*. To visualise the spoken counterparts of asterisks and dashes, let us make use of Allan and Burridge (1991:17) who quote Pinero's *The Gay Lord Quex* (1929:116f), in which a lady comments on French novels in the following manner *This is a little – h'm – isn't it?* Curiously enough, the answer to this is *I read those things for their exquisitely polished style; the subjects escape me.* Some would call it a diplomatic reply, others, like Allan and Burridge (1991:17), *a likely story*!

It needs to be stressed, however, that some authors, such as Cuddon and Preston (1998:256) encompass both full and quasi-omissions within the working of **ellipsis**, which they characterize as *a rhetorical figure in which one or more words are omitted*. As the authors argue, in the late 16th century various ellipsis marks occurred in printed texts, such as a continuous rule (–), a series of hyphens (- - -), a series of points (…) or asterisks (***), to indicate an intended omission, a pause or an interruption. From a contextual viewpoint, it is worth noting that ellipsis is seen as a cohesive factor of textual structure. Crystal (1987:119), for example, defines it as *a piece of structure [that] is omitted, and can be recovered only from a preceding discourse*. In this sense, which clearly goes hand in hand with Polański's (1995:132) elucidation as well, ellipsis is what Allan and Burridge (1991:17) refer to as an act of full omission. Within the scope of X-phemism formation, the cases of full omission may be further exemplified by such expressions as *I need to go*, where the element *(to the toilet)* does not follow at all, or in Polish *muszę zrobić* (lit. 'I have to do') where the element *kupę/siku* (lit. 'poo'/'pee') remains purposefully dormant. Another instance is observable in a common proverb, namely *There's the pot calling the kettle black*, which leaves out the element *arse* from the end, and – in this way – language users may feel free to use the proverb whenever they need without appearing rude or vulgar.

In turn, the employment of **comparative** seems to be strictly linked with the use of circumlocution. Needless to say, when language users wish to refer, for example, to poor countries in what is commonly perceived as a politically correct way they will usually opt for a longer circumlocutory structure, such as *less developed*, or even, *lesser developed countries*. Note that the FOP Index for both cover terms, that is 4.25 and 5 respectively, is relatively high. An unquestionably elaborate structure is the veiled bureaucratic term *those on the lower end of the ability scale* or, in other words, *less able students* instead of the blunt, for some presumably offensive, *stupid students*. As for the FOP Index, here the value 7.83 – though relatively high – seems not to reflect the complexity and ridiculousness of the cover term itself. One can hardly escape the impression that such formations as those mentioned above are also instances of understatement, or, to be more precise, litotes as the auspicious illocutionary effect is achieved by grading the opposite term downwards the axiological scale. What may be observed is an evident, one may assume, conscious substitution of negatively loaded *stupid* for its opposite, and positive, *able* or *ability* that is graded with the use of the negative adverb *less* or adjective *lower*. The ultimate result is a term that is inoffensive, safe and perfectly appropriate in the present-day world driven and guided by ubiquitous political correctness.

The employment of comparative forms in the process of X-phemism formation may also be exemplified – to a certain extent – by the variety of cover terms representing the conceptual sphere BODY PARTS. Here, such an English dysphemistic euphemism as *nether regions* used in the sense 'genitals' is an example of a cover term as the comparative sense 'lower' is concealed by the Germanic form *nether*.[74] In turn, a Polish cover term used in the sense 'arse' which evidently employs a comparative form is *cięższa część ciała* (lit. 'heavier body part') or *tam gdzie słońce rzadziej dochodzi* (lit. 'the place where the sun gets less frequently'). What seems to be noteworthy at this point is that whereas the English cover term grades the position (*nether*) of the body part, the Polish one focuses on its weight (*ciężar*).

It should be stressed that the mechanism of the employment of the **passive voice** seems to lie on a boundary line among the types of X-phemism forming tools, the primary reason for this being the subtlety of the passive syntactic structure which only indirectly and contextually attenuates a painful evocation or expresses the same sense in a more polite way. Suffice it to mention two superficially distinct structures for the same intended sense, such as *They didn't inform me about the meeting.* and *I wasn't informed about the meeting.* Even though the deep structure seems to be basically the same, it may be true that the passive structure is less accusatory as it avoids pointing to the person responsible for not passing the message further, which stems from the nature of the passive voice.

1.2.5 Concluding remarks

One of the partial conclusions which may be drawn at this point is that the body of examples that we have gathered so far is by no means comprehensive. However, all the cases taken *en bloc* serve as ample evidence that today's communication is ruled by X-phemism whether language users wish to avoid a taboo topic in a polite, jocular or vulgar way they have a whole array of concealing tools

---

74 As evidenced by the *OED*, the origin of the word *nether* is common to many Teutonic languages and goes back to O.E. *neoþera, niþera*, M.L.G. *ned(d)er*, O.H.G. *nidari* and O.N. *neðri* with the sense 'lower, under'.

at their disposal. As shown in the foregoing sections, from the synchronic point of view, X-phemisms are formed at all levels of linguistic analysis, starting with phonology through syntax. The formation of X-phemisms by means of such a wide range of linguistic tools undoubtedly proves the assumption that we live by X-phemism, and one may expect that another groundbreaking monograph with the tentative yet very much telling title *X-phemisms we live by* will be produced before long. It is the deeply entrenched human instinct not to call a spade a spade that seems to be responsible for yielding innumerable cover terms and thus making X-phemism an omnipresent cognitive mechanism.

1.3 Context as a disambiguating factor in the interpretation of X-phemism

To start with, the significance of context in language interpretation has been acknowledged since at least the 19th century and the widespread study of the nature of context has led to the formulation of a number of relevant definitions and analytical approaches. To enumerate but a few, Pei and Gaynor (1954:47) and Pisarek (2006:104) both define **context** as the surrounding of a linguistic element, such as a word or a complete utterance, and – in this way – they lay stress on the importance of the linguistic aspect of context. More recently, Danesi (2000:67) elaborates on his definition to include the *whole situation, background, or environment (physical, social, psychological) that determines the meaning*, thus making his definition all-inclusive with regard to both linguistic and extralinguistic elements. For the purpose of the ongoing discussion, let us approach the issue of context following the instructions formulated by Chamizo Dominguez and Sánchez Benedito (1994:82-83). According to the authors, in order to interpret the semantic purport of utterances correctly the following criteria must necessarily be met:

1. the criterion of knowledge normally shared by the speaker and the hearer in a natural way,
2. the criterion of a certain immediate contextual knowledge,
3. the element of interpretative instructions that speakers themselves provide in their own utterances.

In Polish literature, Płóciennik and Podlawska (2005:167-168) maintain that the notion of context also encompasses the entirety of elements of life experience of both the speaker and the hearer. In his seminal work, Cruse (1986:52-54) names two effects of a context upon the lexical item included, namely **modulation** and **contextual selection**. In short, the former is meant to refer to certain semantic traits of an individual sense that come to be emphasized while others are backgrounded or suppressed altogether. The latter involves the activation of different senses associated with semantically polysemous words. Most importantly, however – as Cruse (1986:52) stresses – *the two types of variability are normally operative together; that is, a selected sense is also subject to modulation by the context which forced its selection.*

It is believed that phrasal ambiguity exists only in the scope of a sentence because, in the scope of an utterance, ambiguities regarding the interpretation are disambiguated by the context of use, and this includes the extralinguistic context, too. Nerlich and Clarke (2001:4) explain this mechanism along the following lines:

> Another widespread assumption in polysemy research is that words **in isolation** can have more than one meaning, but that words **in context** always have only one specific meaning. It is thought that as comprehenders, "we aim at **specifying meaning**, at selecting, out of the many possible interpretations, one interpretation that coheres with our background default assumptions and other contextual considerations" (Kittay, 1987: 80). According to this view, the speaker intends words to have one meaning and the hearer 'disambiguates' polysemous words automatically in context. [...] We are not so much interested in 'disambiguation in context' but instead in what one might call 'ambiguation' in context.

Obviously, these remarks are particularly justifiable for all types of figurative language which are detectable in the context of an utterance. As Palmer (1981:49) argues, *[...] to recognise the anomaly and the ambiguity we need to have the relevant information about [the context]* and to prove his point, the author provides two sample sentences (adapted from Bierwisch 1970), namely *My typewriter has bad intentions* and *John was looking for the glasses*. The underlying reason for the anomaly of the former, as well as the causes of the ambiguity of the latter must ultimately be sought both in linguistic and physical context whereby information may be conveyed about the typewriters and kinds of glasses. Moreover, already in the first half of the 20th century Malinowski (1948:300-301) stated that words we utter are in a way *active forces* and they help us or, even, enable us to manipulate the world around us. The famous Polish anthropologist, therefore, maintains that *there is much in common between words and magic, for both give power*. Naturally, the spheres of taboo and X-phemism inevitably link words with the world of magic, at least in their roots. Originally, it was the primary taboo of religion that abounded with rituals, myths and magic, thus giving power to those responsible for religious conducts. However, the interpretation of the illocutionary power of both taboo words or phrases and X-phemisms is strictly dependent on broadly-understood context.

1.3.1 X-phemism and context

All in all, the role of context in the process of disambiguating X-phemisms seems to vary according to the nature of a given type of X-phemism. For example, the so-called lexicalized X-phemisms[75] do not normally require (extensive) context for their disambiguation and interpretation. Thus, for instance, the context *Uncle Tom passed away last night* or *The psychopath kicked the bucket at the age of forty* do not require further context to be interpreted unambiguously. According to Bloomfield's (1933:153) behaviourist theory, there are particular predisposing factors[76] the function of which is to trigger different lexicalized responses for the same communicative situation. Interestingly, regardless of the level of lexicalization of a given X-phemism several, if not more, varied linguistic responses may be found and incorporated either in one and the same situation or to name one and the same concept or object. What changes, however, with the not-yet-conventionalised X-phemisms is that they require both extensive and clear context for the process of disambiguation. This is because, as Nerlich and Clarke (2001:4) claim:

> [...] people love juggling with ambiguities. They are less concerned with communicative efficiency and much more with the pragmatic 'effects' they want to achieve. In fact, we seem to have evolved an amazing ability to slide effortlessly up and down a scale of semantic options from being precise and monosemous in some circumstances to being vague and polysemous in others, depending on the conversational style and the situation of discourse.

Perhaps the best way to illustrate the point made in the quotation given above is the use of different cover terms to refer to the activity of having sex. Obviously, when one uses a lexicalized phrase *go to bed* or *bang* one leaves little room for misunderstanding. When, however, one resorts to such a novel metaphor-based euphemism as *collaborate together* or *do it*, then it is not always altogether clear whether the wording should be understood literally or figuratively as a cover term for what is not named/what is not to be named directly.

1.3.2 Extralinguistic context in the act of X-phemism disambiguation

Let us stress here that the disambiguating function of language segments that depend mainly on the extralinguistic situation and conditionings, such as vary-

---

75 The notion of lexicalised X-phemisms is understood here after Chamizo Dominguez and Sánchez Benedito (2005).

76 By predisposing factors Bloomfield (1933) understands the entire life history of the speaker and hearer.

ing cultural context, different value systems or different social contexts including their euphemistic potential may be both disambiguated and modulated. Interestingly enough, when we consider the joint appearance of both verbal and non-verbal signals between the semantics of which there appears a gap, speakers tend to rely on the extralinguistic message rather than on the semantic contents of a verbally-communicated message. Take, for example, the following statement (uttered in conjunction with an extralinguistic act of winking of an eye): *Isn't she a paragon of chastity?* It appears fairly obvious that the addressee to whom such a verbatim evaluatively positive statement is directed will inevitably treat the expression *paragon of chastity* to be a euphemism which, in fact, closely approaches here the sense of being considerably far from the chaste side.

Likewise, various gestures and body movements often serve the purpose of modulating, that is either increasing or decreasing the euphemising power of linguistic elements. Take, for example, the Mod.It. exclamation *Qe barba!* (lit. 'What a beard!') which is used euphemistically in the sense 'What a bore!' or 'What a boring thing!'. This exclamation – in case of need – comes to be intensified with a repeated sweeping movement of one's open hand under the chin. More to the point, varying cultural contexts may disambiguate a euphemistic message in a given language community. This may be illustrated with the following Polish statement: *Tata poszedł na śledzika i była awantura w domu.* (lit. 'Daddy went to have a bite of herring and there was a row at home.'). To understand the message conveyed by the statement one needs to be aware of the Polish pre-Christmas tradition, still present in the 20th century, when groups of men would organise a drinking randevous consisting of a quick series of alcoholic shots usually consumed both in boys-will-be-boys conditions and scouting tempo before they joined their family-based Christmas celebrations. Hardly surprisingly, wives were far from pleased on seeing their hammered husbands who turned out completely useless at the busiest time of Christmas preparations and festivities. Thus, the Polish expression *pójść na śledzika* (lit. 'go to have a bite of herring'), where the name of the fish represents the disgraceful pre-Christmas tradition and exemplifies a metonymic euphemism can only be successfully disambiguated in the appropriate sociological context by the language users familiar with the Polish Christmas customs and habits, however intolerable they might be.

On the Specifics of Sexual Relations in the History of Mankind with Due Reference to Sex for Sale

2.1 Conceptualisation of sex, gender and sexuality

It seems that an ample starting point for any discussion on sex relations seems to be a theorising passage on how the concepts of **sex**, **gender** and **sexuality** may be understood. Since it seems extremely difficult – if at all possible – to come up with definitions of the concepts that would be acceptable for all discriminating scholars dealing with widely-understood sexuality, let us resort to the understanding of sex, gender and sexuality along the lines proposed by Ember and Ember (2003:3). Following the two authors, the concept of **sex** will be understood here as referring to the chiefly biological function and characteristics. Human beings can be of one of the two sexes, with marginal cases of supernumerary sexes which refer to, as Ember and Ember (2003:3) explain, *cultural categories that did not fit the Western European and North American bipolar paradigm*. One needs to bear in mind, however, that sexual physiology is tightly linked with the cultural norms of a society which dictate appropriateness in the choice of sexual partners, sexual activities and, even, clothing in terms of being sexually provocative or not.

In turn, the concept of **gender** is meant to refer to *a culturally based complex of norms, values, and behaviours that a particular culture assigns to one biological sex or another* (Ember and Ember 2003:3). Whereas sex and gender are rooted in the culture, the concept of **sexuality** is taken to refer to the ways in which *individuals structure their sexual and gender performances, and the partners toward whom they direct their behavior and emotional attachment* (Ember and Ember 2003:3). It is worth stressing that the three concepts are mutually interdependent and interconnected, and it seems that the most appropriate approach is to treat them as a **sex-gender-sexuality system**. Furthermore, the cultures of North America and Western Europe organise their conceptualisation of sex-gender-sexuality along such sets of dichotomies as feminine – masculine and homosexual (forbidden) – heterosexual (permitted). Obviously, the conceptualisation of sex-gender-sexuality systems varies across time and space. To account for this variety, in what follows, an attempt will be made to provide a brief account of both temporal and cultural variations in the conceptualisation of sex-gender-sexuality systems.

2.2 Historical variations in conceptualisation of sex relations

Variation in the attitudes to sex, gender and sexuality is portrayed in numerous publications both older and recently issued, such as, for example, Licht (1932), Dover (1978) or Garton (2004). What strikes one almost immediately is a relatively uniform classification of historical epochs which are characterised by different views on questions of sex and sex relations. Thus, in the following sections an attempt will be made to provide an account of the variety of attitudes across time. In accordance with the spirit of this work, a particular focus will be placed on the treatment of sex irregularities, especially paid love (both female and male).

2.2.1 From antique all-going permissiveness to Victorian restrictiveness

All in all, one may venture a generalising statement that humankind seems to have gone through a far-reaching transformation in their attitudes to sex and sexuality. Recently, Garton (2004) describes extensively *how seemingly timeless and natural behaviours shape and are in turn shaped by history*. As the author observes *sexual practices may persist through time but history [...] illuminates how sex and sexuality are surprisingly mutable*. Suffice it to juxtapose the two attitudes. The permissiveness of antiquity – on the one hand – when, as Licht (1932) claims, masturbation, perversion, tribadism, prostitution and sexual licence were supposedly widespread and compatible with civilisation. And, on the other hand, the officially restrictive approach of Victorianism when upper classes of the society formally disapproved of sexual licence and perceived sexuality as contained and controllable, a feature of either men or fallen women. What seems particularly intriguing is the question of how and under what circumstances the phenomenon of, for example, homosexuality developed from widely practiced and acceptable in antiquity to stigmatised as openly unnatural, illegal and, thus, generally prohibited in Victorian times. Hence, such potentially influential developments as the emergence of Christianity and the Reformation movement need to be discussed with their reference to the standpoint on the widely-understood sexuality of humankind. Let us now turn to the characteristics of each period in terms of their treatment of sex-gender-sexuality systems in order to arrive at a relatively complete picture of human sexuality across space and time.

It seems that a sex-gender-sexuality system constituted a significant aspect of the social life of ancient Greece and Rome, and was largely based on and centred around male dominance. At least that is the impression one may have when one familiarises themselves with the literature of antiquity, which was authored exclusively by males. In other words, one could say that sex in antiquity was a kind of arena for showing mastery and superiority over other citizens, regardless of their sex or gender. As Garton (2004:32) has put it, *the central trope of Greco-Roman sexual culture was activity/passivity not homosexuality/heterosexuality*. In day-to-day practices, male citizens tended to impose sexual submission and humiliation upon their wives, partners, lovers, concubines or prostitutes, and – in this way – they asserted their masculine dominance. Typically, men married and had children with their wives to whom they demonstrated love and affection, but this in no way interfered with getting involved with other (frequently manifold) extramarital sexual relations with slaves, prostitutes and concubines.

An interesting aspect of antique sexual life is a seemingly open approach to – what we call today – homosexuality, at least from the present-day perspective. As Garton (2004:31) states, *the Greco-Roman world provided an abundant source of evidence to demonstrate that homosexuality was natural, not 'deviant'*. Some authors go to extremes saying that same-sex relationships were the cornerstone of Greek culture (see, for example, Dover 1978). It is believed that love relationships between older men and youths of male sex were especially common and even perceived as the supreme form of human love. The author goes as far as to postulate new terms to describe ancient Greek sexuality, namely **sexual** and **quasi-sexual** to reflect the inclination of ancient Greeks to *recognise the alternation of homosexual and heterosexual preferences* (see Dover 1978:1-3). It would, however, be somewhat erroneous to think that the existing relationships between two men were beyond any society-imposed constraints. Since the idea of dominance was by all means both well-rooted and prevailing in the structure of ancient societies, relationships between male citizens of the same social status were forbidden as they posed a threat to the codes of masculine dominance.

As for the status of women in the time of antiquity, they were fully subject to all-prevailing male dominance, regardless of their social role. What needs to be mentioned, however, is that, as Garton (2004:36) remarks, *the lives of wives, daughters, slaves, freed slaves, concubines and prostitutes are particularly elusive* as we learn about their social status from texts produced by male citizens. In general, it seems that women were perceived as mere commodities and sexual objects, and in sexual relations they were expected to assume the passive role in contrast to the man's all too evident all-pervading dominance. However, there exists a body of linguistic evidence which suggests that – in Latin myth and literature – women were seen as threatening, licentious and powerful. This point is illustrated, according to Garton (2004:37), by the presence of the word *virago* (lit. 'man-woman') which was used in Latin in the sense 'threatening voracious female sexuality', but – oddly enough – no equivalent of this word exists in Greek. The conclusion that Garton (2004:37) draws is that *images of threatening female sexuality were more common in Latin culture*. Another piece of evidence is the differentiation in meaning of the common words *moecha/moicha* which in Greek was used in the sense 'adulteress', though in Latin meant 'sexually dominating woman'.

Turning now to the issue of sex for sale, it needs to be said that in the ancient world prostitution was as common as it was normal, the reason for that being arranged marriages and the role of wives restricted to the biological function of child bearing. Some sources go as far as to say that in ancient Greece, for example, the services of prostitutes were subject to taxation, and in this way sex traffic was included both in the financial and legislative system of the country. Simultaneously, as *Encyclopaedia Romana* (henceforth: *ENROM*) informs us, prostitution was not practised by Athenian women, which means that the profession involved either slaves or those women who were born outside Athens.

Interestingly, *ENROM* names two types of prostitutes in the ancient world. The first one is labelled **pornê** (lit. 'buyable woman'), and was a term to refer to a common prostitute and the second one, **hetaera**, was an accomplished courtesan or a companion, frequently more educated than the wives of respectable citizens.[77] Generally speaking, the most suitable extralinguistic scenario for "employing" companions was a drinking party, known as a symposium, during which a privileged male elite was accompanied by either female or male companions (or both). It is worth noting at this point that Romans called male prostitutes *publici cinaedi*, where the noun *cinaedi* was used in the sense 'effeminate man who is passive in an erotic relationship'. In short, broadly-understood **prostitution**, whether female or male, was yet another area of demonstrating male dominance and showing that only truly masculine citizens deserved to be surrounded by wives, slaves, concubines, female and male prostitutes.

Evidently, with the advent of Christianity we observe a dramatic shift in the relationship between sexual relations and religion. In fact, as Garton (2004:49) remarks, *there is little agreement over the importance of Christianity in these shifts*. In turn, Foucault (1985:33) observes that – what the author calls – *'moral problematisation of pleasures' had moved away from an interest in the regula-*

---

77 As will become evident later, the line of differentiation between **pornê** and **hetaera** seems fundamentally crucial for the systematics of paid love vocabulary.

tion of pederasty and the 'proper' uses of slaves and concubines towards a concern with women, marriage and the self. The most striking attitude of Christianity seems to be summarised in the semantics of one single term, that is **chastity**. In a nutshell, it was expressly believed that women were the source of men's spiritual fall and thus women, especially those sexually active, were condemned by early Christianity, although the outlook is not altogether uniform in certain geographical regions of the world of today. Bullough and Brundage (1982:3) draw our attention to the fact that St Paul decided to systemise male-female sexual relations, and the only condition when a man could touch a woman was within the limits of wedlock. St Paul preached along the following lines: *[...] if men and women could not contain themselves, let them marry* (quoted after Bullough and Brundage 1982:3). With such authorities involved, the ultimate result of such preaching and teaching was the confinement of sex and desire within marital bonds. What is more, any form of sexual activity was seen as a means of procreation rather than a source of shameful pleasure.

Thus, sex – and with it – the human body, especially the female body, became the scope of fervent hostility in early Christianity. Interestingly enough, Garton (2004:57) argues that already before the era of Christianity there was *a growing apprehension about the bodily effects of sexual desire*. Consequently, Garton (2004:57) sees the immediate link between this fear of the destructive power of sexual drive and the growing importance of marriage in Christianity when he claims:

> [...] sex was associated not just with the problem of mastering desire or justly asserting one's status over others, but with pervasive problems of evil and disease. [...] The heightened fears and concerns about the potential evil effects of sex went hand in hand with a greater valorisation of marriage as an institution that fostered moderation.

The next seemingly natural step, if not leap – on the part of the Church – was to take control of the functioning of marital relationships. Among others, this was done in the act of imposing a new form of self-scrutiny; confession.

What needs to be stressed at this point is that the institution of the Church lacked a completely uniform approach to the value of asceticism, virginity or the extent of pollution due to menstruation. As Brown (1990:481) argues, there were chiefly three pressures that shaped the value system at the time of early Christianity, that is:

1. to treat sexuality as a privileged ideogram of all that was most reducible in the human will,
2. to herald sexual renunciation as a privileged emblem of human freedom,

3 to regard the body itself, by reason of its sexual components, as a highly charged locus of choice, of admiration in its virgin state and of avoidance in its sexually active state.

One may say that the new Christian perception of sexuality and the human body as something to overcome and renunciation as a means of liberation put a human being at war with their body and – in particular – sexuality. Nevertheless, one should bear in mind that – most frequently – ideas and practices are two separate things which – much as one tries – do not always go hand in hand with each other. Some scholars, such as Boswell (1994), go as far as to claim that the typically extramarital activities, like concubinage or prostitution, remained common in Christian Europe throughout the Middle Ages. Generally speaking, one may say that licentiousness continued uninterrupted especially among aristocratic and court circles despite the Church's teachings. Worse still, it seems that the Church itself failed to control its representatives, and – as historians suggest – there is evidence that in the words of Garton (2004:67), *despite the strictures on celibacy, by the sixteenth century as many as 45 percent of rural clergy in parts of Germany had, or were suspected of having concubines.* More to the point, the fact that prostitution and concubinage were widespread, especially among the patrician classes may simply point to a high level of one-sided tolerance of male extramarital relationships and activities. This tendency of the society and authorities of the Renaissance is reflected in such acts and facts as legalisation of brothels in certain towns and apparent indifference to them in others; a practice not entirely unknown in modern times.

Interestingly, one may speak of two approaches to the definition of a **prostitute** from before the 19th century. Karras (1999) argues that before the 19th century the terms *a prostitute* or *a meretrix* covered 'any woman who has multiple sexual partners' or 'engages in sex outside marriage'. In this understanding a prostitute is a permanent social identity of a sinful and disreputable character. However, Freccero (1999) – along entirely different lines – argues that the concept PROSTITUTE, at that time, should rather be connected with a psychosexual orientation, and it is not the number of sexual partners that is important, but rather the public nature of the transgression of a prostitute. Freccero (1999) also explains that the way Karras (1999) understands the sense of the term *prostitute* is closer to the definition of *a whore*, which is based on social transgression. As for the treatment of same-sex relationships by the Christian Church, Garton (2004:76) observes that *medieval and Renaissance anxieties about 'unnatural' acts created a context in which same-sex unions were widely condemned.* On the one hand, the general lack of tolerance imposed restrictions upon the society, but

– on the other hand – different forms of regulation clearly indicate that such 'unnatural' practices were common.

When we narrow down the perspective to the impact of Christian teachings upon the Anglo-Saxon society, it needs to be said that – as Lees (1997:19) notes – Pope Gregory the Great suggested *restraint, tolerance and flexibility about the implementation of Christianity, paving the way for the distinctively syncretic model of English Christianity that is the hallmark of Anglo-Saxon culture.* Likewise, Lees (1997:29) points out that the institution of marriage was understood in a different way than the moral duties of the Christian Church would unconditionally suggest. For example, concubinage and serial polygamy are evidenced throughout the Anglo-Saxon period. Still, at the close of the Anglo-Saxon times, serial polygamy and concubinage are prevalent among ruling families. Furthermore, as *The Blackwell Encyclopaedia of Anglo-Saxon England* (henceforth: *BLACKWELL*) informs us, in the Anglo-Saxon times *prostitute* was understood as 'any promiscuous woman', thus the present-day aspect of **payment of money** fails to correspond with the core of the Anglo-Saxon notion of prostitution. It was the later medieval period marked by the coming of urbanisation – and with it the rise and growth of capitalism – that provided a suitable ground for individual mobility and anonymity. As a result, young women found it easier to turn to the oldest profession without being immediately condemned by the nearest community, and many probably started to believe there was nothing wrong in engaging in the commercial sex trade.

One has an overriding impression that once Martin Luther nailed his 95 theses against the Catholic Church to the door of the church in Wittenberg in 1517, the European approach to sex relations underwent a sudden and all-pervading change.[78] Theoretically, as Garton (2004:81) argues, sex matters were one of the most crucial aspects of the Reformation movement. This was due to the fact that Luther believed that *sexual desire was natural and part of God's plan* and *refusal to have sexual relations within marriage constituted grounds for divorce* (Garton 2004:81). Simultaneously, Protestant ideals condemned fiercely any form of sexual and sex-related irregularities, such as sodomy, prostitution, adultery, contraception and abortion. To illustrate the point, suffice it to mention the attempts of the Anglo-American and northern European branches of Christendom to bring sexual behaviour under the control of the Church. For example, the Scottish Presbyterian Church formed special Church courts which imposed pun-

---

78 Interestingly, it needs to be mentioned that the Morning Star of the Reformation was John Wycliffe, an Oxford Professor, who inspired the idea of translating the Bible into the language of the people so that even the lowest orders could understand the word of the Gospel.

ishments of excommunication or imprisonment for any detected cases of birth out of wedlock.

Another aspect of the Reformation that was typically English was the emergence of Puritanism as a form of Counter-Reformation against what Elizabeth I had failed to alter within the newly-formed Anglican Church. Porterfield (2007:69) informs us that – in order to eliminate the evils of prostitution – for example, all the theatres in London were closed between 1642 and 1660 because Puritans associated them with licentiousness and sexual excesses.[79] In fact one may repeat after Porterfield (2007:64), that *all Christian cultures of the sixteenth and seventeenth centuries were becoming more intrusive about regulating marriage and punishing irregular sex*. Interestingly, it is the American frontier of the New World that is frequently perceived and portrayed as the venue of sexual freedom. However, Puritans tried as much as they could to control sexual life, especially of the young. For example, as Godbeer (2002:246-255) informs us, in New England Puritan families preferred to keep an eye on the sexual life of their growing children and allowed the so-called "bundling", which was a euphemistic term for inviting young men to spend the night in the company of their daughters. Even though sexual contact – and not infrequently pregnancy – was almost an inevitable outcome of such family-engineered meetings parents believed that the practice of "bundling" was less of a threat than uncontrollable and unrestrained sexual behaviour out of their sight. Porterfield (2007:70-71) argues, however, that the downside of the Puritan Revolution – both in England and in America – was the loss of legal power and status by women. The English common law, for instance, gave married women no property right, failed to recognise cases of rape if pregnancy occurred or treated ten-year-old girls as grown-up enough to legally consent to sexual intercourse. Significantly, in the American colonies, on the other hand, cross-racial marriages were strictly forbidden, that is – at least officially – any intercourse between white slave-owners and African slave women was disallowed, which obviously put the latter in an extremely inferior position in terms of their rights. Yet, sexual contacts, exploitation and child-bearing across racial lines were both widespread and common. As Porterfield (2007:68) points out, *denial of marriage to slaves made race into a more and more absolute category in the Protestant areas of North America and the Caribbean, despite the sex that continued to produce children across racial lines*.

---

79 To the modern eye this may seem somewhat unthinkable to see a direct link between licentiousness and the world of theatrical performances, though the same may be said about Polish history of culture.

As to the treatment of homoeroticism, it seems that even though any form of homosexuality was officially persecuted much in the same manner as bestiality or witchcraft, Puritans seemed to have frequently turned a blind eye to this issue. For example, there was merely one execution for homosexual practices in New England in the 17th century, but the same number of trials as those for bestiality. Furthermore, as Porterfield (2007:70) claims, *definition and control of homosexuality would not become a major issue until the late nineteenth century*. The author provides an example of the great Anglican poets of the 17th century who addressed God and their friends in homoerotic terms with hardly any objection or open criticism from the authorities. Another issue of apparent negligence is turning a blind eye to the officially banned prostitution. The growth of city life allowed more personal freedom, and sexual *outlets*, as Garton (2004:87) calls them, were seen as places for either letting off male sexual passion and desires or experimenting ground for young inexperienced males.[80]

One of the turning points in sexual matters may have been the emergence of libertine culture in 17th-century Court society, which was characterised by a frivolous, licentious and promiscuous attitude to sexual relations. Stone (1992:511-525), for example, describes this period as *a release of libido from the old-age constraints of Christianity* when *sexual promiscuity became the hallmark of fashion*. The changing conditions and attitudes are observable in changing female fashion patterns, which – among others – promoted accentuated buttocks and exposed or lightly covered breasts, as well as in growing expectation for countless mistresses and illegitimate children, especially among men from the upper strata of society. Moreover, special clubs for men opened in London and in Paris, where men could experiment sexually to their hearts' content. More significantly, however – as Stone (1992) argues – there was the tendency of libertine attitudes to spread down the social scale in the 18th century among gentry and middle classes. It is noteworthy that the growth of libertine culture went hand in hand with the growth of urban centres, which offered mobility and a life free from the constraints of country life. Consequently, an increasing number of men frequented pubs and brothels – not necessarily in that order – and more and more women undertook prostitution as a means of obtaining additional or basic income. Needless to say, the ultimate result of this general trend was bitter for women themselves as they were reduced, as Garton (2004:93) puts it, *to the image of the whore, ever available and compliant in the*

---

[80] Note that in the 16th and 17th centuries the average marriage age for young men was in their late twenties or early thirties, which meant that adolescence was a time of sexual (inter)play and avoidance of wedlock.

satisfaction of man's needs [...] to being sexual objects, limiting their capacity for sexual autonomy.

Yet another peculiarity of the sexual reality of the 18th century was an increased interest in physiology and anatomy, which resulted in a fundamental change in the way the human body was now treated and perceived. The previously-held concept of the one-sex body, whereby the female body was an inferior variant of the male body, gave way to the new concept of the two-sex body, whereby male and female bodies were seen as fundamentally distinct. This new approach to human corporal qualities led to an altered viewpoint on sexual relations that rested in the intercourse of the two types of bodies. In the 18th century the distinction was no longer between active and passive, regardless of the sex of the partners, but it was heterosexual as opposed to homosexual. Both taxonomies, however, retained the traditional conceptual element <ACTIVE$_{[POS]}$> and <PASSIVE$_{[NEG]}$> with men being basically promiscuous and active and women being chaste and passive in any heterosexual relation. As for the notion of HOMOSEXUALITY, Trumbach (1998:3-22) argues that towards the end of the 17th century a third gender emerged within European sexual cultures, namely that of the **adult effeminate sodomite**. The third gender was esentially characterised by conspicuous effeminacy; that is behaving, speaking and dressing like women. In the course of the 18th century, however, general public condemnation of this distorted form of manhood started to take shape, and an increasing number of men were arrested for sodomy and punished with a fine, imprisonment, a pillory or hanging. The conclusion that appears to be obvious is, as Garton (2004:99) argues, that:

> [...] the emergence of this third gender meant that increasingly men, out of fear, began to constitute themselves around the identity of being sexually interested only in women. Thus the specification of the third gender was integral to the emergence of the idea of a heterosexual identity. In this context sex ceased to be seen as something between an active and a passive partner, regardless of gender, but ideally as an act between men and women. Those who flouted this ideal risked legal and social retribution.

Interestingly, as Trumbach (1998:8) claims, an equivalent lesbian subculture occurred only towards the end of the 18th century although already in the 16th century there was a visible female homoerotic culture in European countries.

Assuming a first-things-first attitude, in order to discuss the characteristics of Victorianism, establishing the demarcation lines for the period seems to be an indispensable starting point. Most historians seem to agree that the term **Victorianism** applies to a longer period than the actual reign of Queen Victoria, that is between 1837 and 1901. According to Garton (2004:103), more conventionally the Victorian era is seen as a synonymous term either for the 19th century or for the period between the end of Napoleonic Wars (1815) and the beginning of the First World War (1914). The author, however, argues at the same time that chronology is relative here and it should be viewed differently for different parts of the world. For example, the starting point of Victorianism for France is believed to be the 1780s, for New England we should speak of the 1800s and for Germany or the Southern States of America one should talk about the mid-19th century. Regardless of the lack of complete consensus among historians, which puts the concept of Victorianism as a specific period in the history of sexuality into doubt, one should take into account the mainly English perspective set to this work. That is the reason why theories on the development of sexuality regarding the era of Victorianism deserve at least a brief mention, and the Victorian era will here be seen as approximately the 19th century up to the end of the First World War.

In fact, there have been two major theories on the sexuality of the Victorian era. The first of them is a product of early historians of sexuality[81] who portrayed the era as the period of Puritan moralism, excessive sexual austerity, repression and all-pervading prudery. This early assessment – combined with a later attitude of taking Victorian repression of sex matters for granted – resulted in the common public easily, and even eagerly, accepting Victorianism as a time of hypocrisy; morally strict on the surface, but sexually rotten inside. Another widespread belief is that it was the repression of sex and sexuality that actually triggered, produced or at least conditioned the elaborate flourishing of a Victorian **sexual underground** abundant with prostitution both female and male, pornography and all-prevailing sinful lust. In turn, since the late 1970s an increasing number of historians, referred to as revisionist historians,[82] have argued that treating Victorianism as a period of heightened sexual repression is far from the truthful image of the period in question. On the contrary, revisionist historians believe that such a simplistic historical cliché falls flat when confronted with the abundance of evidence in the form of diaries, popular literature, magazines and advertisements for the proliferation of sexual discourses and varied, or even contradictory, sexual customs and practices. For example, Foucault (1978:15-50) goes as far as to say that Victorians were far from repressing sex, and they were actually the ones who invented sexuality in the present-day sense of the word.

As for the status of women in the 19th century, a clear distinction may be drawn between a chaste passionless middle-class woman and an insatiable and morally corrupt **fallen woman**. Garton (2004:116) informs us that prostitution flourished in 19th century Britain, Europe and America. For example, rough es-

---

81 See, among others, Marcus (1966) and Pearsall (1969).
82 See, among others, Foucault (1978), Gay (1984) and Mason (1994).

timates say that there were at least fifty thousand prostitutes in Victorian London alone. The extent to which prostitution developed in 19th-century Great Britain may serve as ample evidence that male sexuality was treated differently than that of women in that men could both feel and find a vent for sexual desire while women could neither. Furthermore, it was believed that when left unsatisfied male desire could pose a threat to other people and turn into brutality or violence. As to Victorian wives – unlike their husbands – they were supposed to restrain and control their sexual passions and – as a matter of fact – they were believed to have none. Consequently, there was a visible clash between male expectations and female response within marital boundaries. Here, prostitution turned out to be the most welcome, and a necessary evil to fill in the existing gap. Through this extramarital vice male desire could be satisfied leaving wives chaste and still passionless.

More importantly, there seems to have existed a certain contradiction in the approach to the issue of prostitution among the 19th-century authorities. As Garton (2004:117-119) observes, while some medical doctors, social and moral reformers saw prostitutes as lowly, morally corrupt back-street females with rotten, foul-smelling and disease-afflicted bodies, others argued that such women were mainly victims of aristocratic libertines, frequently forced into the state they were in by poverty or human trafficking. A growing tendency among Victorians was to link unconditionally prostitution – and thus eroticism and sexual desire – with working-class women. Truly, there were innumerable cases of married or single working-class women who turned to prostitution as a means of supporting their families or themselves. In this context, prostitution was frequently approached as **women's work**, not sexual pathology.

However, it needs to be stressed that the hostile attitude towards prostitutes, and the growing fear of diseased degeneration ultimately led to abolitionist campaigns in order to eradicate Victorian vice altogether. The *Encyclopedia of Prostitution and Sex Work* (henceforth: the *EPSW*) informs us that a series of official documents were issued which regulated or banned prostitution. In the United Kingdom the first Contagious Diseases Act was passed in 1864 and two consecutive ones followed tout suit in 1866 and 1869. Their primary aim was to avoid an epidemic of venereal diseases in the British Army by an obligatory examination of every woman suspected of prostitution. Interestingly, prostitutes' male clients were not subject to the medical procedure despite many of them being infected and posing a threat to other female members of the society. This legislation, however, triggered a movement against the acts, the leader of which, Josephine Butler, founded the Ladies' National Association in order to fight against unjust treatment of women or – in other words – double standard of morality. Consequently, with social purity movements spreading to the United

States of America the beginning of the 20th century one observes a gradual shift in the attitude to sex and sexual relations which is becoming increasingly relaxed and liberal among different social classes, first in the New World and then in the Old Country.

Turning now to the issue of male prostitution, it needs to be mentioned that – as the *EPSW* informs us – at the turn of the 19th century the most widespread pattern of male prostitution was a biological man dressed like a female prostitute working in 'all-fairy' brothels or saloons.[83] Still in the middle of the 19th century, men dressed as female prostitutes were difficult to categorise, and even police officers were baffled on meeting fairies who had letters mentioning cash exchanges with clients. The police arrested male prostitutes, but lacked official regulations about how they should treat them in the face of the law. However, the Cleveland Street Affair of 1889[84] and the trial of Oscar Wilde together with the writings of sexologists on the issue of a newly created term *homosexuality* provided sufficient knowledge as for the way the police should react to such cases of male disorderly conduct. It was now obvious that male prostitution would be prosecuted by authorities and it began to take different forms from – what we call today – family cross-dressing over the weekends.

2.2.2 The sexual revolution of the 20th century

It is virtually impossible to determine with absolute certainty the beginning point of the 20th-century sexual revolution. Several events may be treated as fundamentally significant in the transformation of the social attitudes to sexual matters during the course of the 20th century. First of all, it may all have started with the so-called social purity movements of the late 19th and early 20th centuries. At that time a number of middle-class women, such as Josephine Butler and her campaign followers, began to fight publicly against discrimination towards women and white slavery. Although their primary aim and concern was the eradication of prostitution through the successful attempt at repealing the Contagious Diseases Acts and closing down of brothels – at the same time – women like Josephine Butler seem to have been the first advocates for women's rights. Secondly, the upsurge of sexual liberalism may have been triggered by abundant scientific literature which – in the second half of the 19th century – introduced

---

[83] Note that in the United States of America biological men dressed as women were called *fairies* in the 19th and the beginning of the 20th centuries.

[84] As the *EPSW* explains, the Cleveland Street Affair refers to the situation in which messenger boys of 15 or 16 years old were caught moonlighting as occasional prostitutes for aristocratic gentlemen at a West End male brothel. Supposedly, one of the upper-class gentlemen who also patronised the venue was Prince Albert Victor.

new definitions and new terms for the concepts, such as *contrary sexual feeling, inversion, uranism, intermediate sex* and *homosexuality*, and made attempts at explaining distinct types and manifestations of sexuality. In this way a separate science was born, namely **sexology**. Seemingly, one of the most crucial factors that shaped the emergence of this new science was the greater visibility of various sexual subcultures. The newly emergent sexual research constructed ideals of normality and perversion, by which, for example, homosexuality was no longer a crime, but rather sexual abnormality requiring special treatment. This, on the other hand, went hand in hand with the growth of large cities in both Europe and America in the 19th century. For example, Garton (2004:173) tells us that, at the time of the Enlightenment, London had a rich underground of brothels, gin palaces, music halls and "molly" clubs, which came to light mainly through the social surveys that Victorians had a particular liking for. Ultimately, however, the true, or second, sexual revolution, marked by sexual freedom, feminism, gay liberation and permissiveness was still a few decades ahead.

As Garton (2004:210) observes, *one of the most popular cultural narratives of the late twentieth century has been the 1960s and the 1970s as an age of 'sexual revolution'*. Although some historians are ready to claim that moral codes relaxed already in the 1920s and hence prefer to see this decade as the first phase of sexual revolution, there are countless reasons why it is the time of "flower-power" that is commonly associated with sexual liberalism. Firstly, the 1960s witnessed the proclamation of the end of Puritanism in American magazines. Young women, for example, were openly encouraged towards sexual promiscuity,[85] especially when guilt-free sex was made possible with the advent of the pill. Secondly, the concept of unrestrained sexual freedom was employed in a larger context of anti-racist movements and mass protests against the Vietnam War, colonialism, class oppression and conservatism in education. The best-known slogan of the time was *make love not war*. Thirdly, a new form of feminism began to take shape, which meant that – instead of fighting for political emancipation – women of the 1970s concentrated on gaining personal liberation from the oppression of the male-dominated world. Last but not least, the gay liberation movement breaking with the Stonewall riots of 1969 in Greenwich Village gave the issue of homosexuality a new phase and face.

Hardly surprisingly, the ideas of sexual permissiveness combined with the emerging capitalist modernity may be said to have formed the core of the sexual revolution of the 1960s. Allyn (2000) describes the time along the following

---

85 In 1962 Helen Gurley Brown advised nice single girls to engage in sex a lot, to say yes to sex. She was one of the first to publicly express the view that having dozens of sexual partners was more fun.

lines: *[...] deeply American revolution... spiritual yet secular, idealistic yet commercial, driven by science yet coloured by a romantic view of nature.* It seems that the power of the sexual revolution of the 1960s and 1970s lies in its mythical nature and stories around the revolution have been told and retold, and thus survive in society as a living memo of the past; still living past that is continually acquiring a new face.

2.3 An outline of cultural variation in conceptualisation of sex relations

It goes without saying that within the canvas of this work one can hardly attempt any fully-fledged panorama of world sexuality. Rather, one can hope to draw a representative picture of sex relations by selecting highlights from a number of various cultures. The survey offered in what follows will centre on a number of parameters, such as the attitude to sexuality, the status of homosexuality and the legality of prostitution, yet the pivot of our discussion will be formed by the axis of sexuality and – in particular – the issue of sex for sale. Somewhat arbitrarily the choice has been made here to sample the following cultural zones:

1. Anglo-Saxon: English, American,
2. Romance: French, Italian,
3. Germanic: German, Dutch,
4. Slavonic: Czech, Ukrainian, Polish,
5. Non-Indo-European: Hungarian, Israeli.

The primary reason for portraying approaches to sex matters in the cultures that have been selected here is an attempt to find at least a partial answer to the question of why sexuality is treated differently in different corners of the European continent, with one example from Asia.

2.3.1 Anglo-Saxon

Being of primary interest to the goals of the present work, the Anglo-Saxon cultural zone deserves to be discussed first of all, and its historical outline was sketched in the preceding sections. There we drew a picture of the path of development in the treatment of sex matters mostly in Great Britain, but also in the United States of America. Additionally, with regards to the issue of sex for sale in England – as contrasted with other European countries – one observes an intriguing shift of trends. As pointed out by Karras (1996:7), on the one hand, in medieval England *municipal brothels were not as common [...] as they were elsewhere in Europe*.[86] On the other hand, at the end of the 18th century, according to the *EPSW*, London was a harbouring place of thirty thousand prostitutes,[87] which was twice as many as in Paris at the same historical time. Generally speaking, the overall attitude towards prostitution in medieval England was, as Karras (1996:6) puts it, *combined toleration with marginalization*. The author adds that *prostitutes had their place in society, though not a respected one*, which went hand in hand with the St Augustine-triggered approach of treating prostitution as a kind of "necessary evil". As to present-day statistics, according to the *EPSW*, the number of prostitutes declined to eight thousand at the outset of the 21st century. Typically, frequent places of their employment are the escort industry, private houses, massage parlours and saunas. They advertise their services mainly through press, the Internet and printed cards (those placed in phone boxes are called *tart cards*). With regards to the legality of prostitution,[88] in 1957 – according to the *EPSW* – the Wolfenden Report, officially called the Report of the Committee on Homosexual Offences and Prostitution, triggered the implementation of the Street Offences Act of 1959. This ultimately led to the criminalization of prostitutes soliciting on the streets, but – curiously enough – not their clients. It was only in 2009 and after the amendments made by the Policing and Crime Act that the shift was observed from criminalizing only prostitutes to criminalizing clients, as well as prostitutes soliciting, but only those acting in a persistent manner.

Interestingly, when analyzing the occupational stratification in the American West of the 19th century one may conclude that the four categories singled out in the *EPSW* correspond roughly to the classification of prostitutes in ancient Greece.[89] Here, they are itemised in order from the highest position on the economic ladder to the lowest:

1. brothel dweller,

---

86 Although municipal brothels are said to have been relatively scarce in medieval England there was one brothel that left a permanent trace in the history of the country and its language; that is the 12th-century brothel in Southwark established on the premises of the Bishop of Winchester.

87 Note that Garton (2004:116) provides estimates of more than fifty thousand prostitutes working in Victorian London.

88 Note that the first legally regulated red light district in London was established by the order of King Henry II in the 12th century. As the *EPSW* informs us, the regulations imposed protected both the prostitutes working in the district and their clients. The prostitutes living there became known as *Winchester geese*, a term which entered general English as a synonym of *prostitute*.

89 For more on different classifications in the conceptual category **FALLEN HUMAN BENG** see section 3.1.1.

2. saloon/dance hall girl,
3. crib woman,
4. street walker.

To start with, the category of brothel dwellers included those who were usually younger and more attractive, and thus could successfully demand higher prices for their services. As they got older they either became saloon or dance hall girls or they rented cribs, which was much cheaper than renting a room at a brothel. Note that street walkers occupied the lowest position on the economic ladder because they could neither afford to rent a crib nor demand a decent rate for their occupational skills. Consequently, they were fully dependent on their clients as to the rate and place of stay.

Turning now to the question of the legality of prostitution in the United States of America, general regulations that would work simultaneously for the whole country are difficult, if not downright impossible, to formulate as each state has had its own legal approach to dealing with the issue. To draw a short outline, let us take four major American cities into consideration to serve as examples, namely Chicago, New York City, New Orleans and Los Angeles. What seems to be a common feature in the legal treatment of prostitution in the four places is – first of all – a lack of official legal regulations throughout the 19th century that would control commercial sex, and – secondly – the introduction of certain restrictive measures at the beginning of the 20th century. At that time, the councils of Chicago and New York City passed laws which banned prostitution altogether while the authorities of New Orleans and Los Angeles limited prostitution to restricted areas, where it flourished. Little is mentioned of male prostitution, especially when contrasted with the abundance of information about female vice. Yet, the overall picture we obtain is, as the *EPSW* observes, that male prostitution was a fact of life as well, and it centred either in separate brothels, such as Paresis Hall in New York City in the 1890s or West Hollywood bar Numbers in Los Angeles in the 1990s, or was realized in soliciting in the mixed zones, where female prostitutes were at work as well. To show the mixed-bag character of the problem in America, let us add that today – curiously enough – according to the *EPSW*, in Los Angeles clients of female prostitutes tend to be arrested together with street walkers though in the case of male prostitutes, clients are set free and a male hustler is subjected to legal prosecution.

2.3.2 Romance

Romance culture, which derives linguistically from the Latin language and historically and culturally from ancient Rome, should – at least theoretically – bear a strong resemblance to the ancient Roman way of life and conduct. Indeed, it was an Italian city of Pompeii where, according to the *EPSW*, the most relics of prostitution were found. Obviously, it was first Italy and, later, France that were under a great influence of the Roman Empire and its approach to earthly matters. The Vatican and – in the Middle Ages – Avignon were the capitals of the Catholic church, and thus centres of religious lives, but ironically prostitution flourished in both places. To illustrate the point, suffice it to mention the popular local proverb which said that *one could not cross the bridge of Avignon without encountering two monks, two donkeys and two whores*. To resort to statistics, at the Council of Church in Constance from 1414 to 1418 there were approximately one thousand four hundred prostitutes who offered their services to citizens, including clergy. Another characteristic feature of the medieval Avignon – labelled in the *EPSW* as the 14th-century capital of French prostitution – was its famous brothel called *the Abbey*.[90] Similarly, during the Second Empire (1852-1870) under the reign of Napoleon III prostitution was a fact of Parisian life, especially among members of the upper strata of the society. Significantly, the indication of man's wealth and status was a kept woman, a *grande horizontale*,[91] who was catered for in the highest style possible. Interestingly, those high-class prostitutes were beyond official municipal restrictions which were imposed on common women (of the town), for example registration with the police or medical checks.

In turn, the ancient Roman tolerance and acceptance of homoeroticism seem to have continued well into the 15th century in Florence; a feature of which was a common practice of young boys between 12 and 20 engaging in financially beneficial sexual relations with older men – usually in their 20s, or older. What is even more intriguing is the attitude of the parents who were not merely aware of their sons' involvement in sex-and-money relationships, but not infrequently the parents supported their sons as they also participated in the financial side of the arrangements. The *EPSW* reports that these intergenerational same-sex relationships had transformed significantly by the end of the 19th century, and – in

---

90 Note that the popularity of the place must have influenced the application of the term *abbey* in a more general sense 'brothel'. Furthermore, prostitutes began to be called *nuns* or *abbesses*, first in French, and then – through the process of borrowing – in English.

91 According to the *EPSW*, the term *grande horizontale*, which was employed to refer to the highest rank of prostitution in 19th-century France, was linked to the way the women worked, that is horizontally or lying down, and to the level of accomplishment, that is *grande* 'great'. Other names used at that time were *grandes cocottes, grandes abandonees, la haute galanterie, la Haute Bicherie* and, last but not least *la garde* reserved to refer to the greatest of the great.

the course of the 20th century – they were completely ruled out from social life. The transformation in question involved the change of the age and class pattern of men engaged in sex trade. Basically, towards the end of the 19th century the age of rent boys was on the increase while their social status was much in decline. In other words, in the 15th century young boys or young men who got involved in business-like sexual relationships came from all social backgrounds while by the end of the 19th century they were mainly working-class boys in their late teens.

As for the present-day state of the legality of prostitution in France and Italy, the *EPSW* informs us that until around 2000 the only legal place for sex work was the street as France, for example, decided to close brothels in 1946. Eventually, in France it was the Sarkozy law that criminalised soliciting in 2002. It seems that – despite the general tendency to close down brothels after the United Nations Convention for the Suppression of the Traffic in Persons and of the Exploitation of the Prostitution of Others in 1949 – escort agencies continued to develop and offer their services. In Italy, in turn, formerly tolerated brothels were closed down starting in 1958, and – although today prostitution is not illegal – such forms of sex work as brothels and pimping remain banned.

2.3.3 Germanic

It seems to be common knowledge that Germanic cultural zones, represented here by Germany, Holland, Denmark or Sweden, are the most liberal in their approaches to sexual matters in general, and prostitution and sexual minorities[92] in particular. As Ember and Ember (2003:405) observe *actual knowledge about sexuality is very high, while social taboos connected with sexuality hardly exist at all*. What is certainly somewhat surprising, however, is the fact that it had not always been so. According to the *EPSW*, before 1927 prostitution in Germany had been legally banned and – except for strictly state-regulated brothels in restricted areas – not tolerated either. Subsequently, under the legislative system of the Weimar Republic the approach was altered completely to decriminalization of prostitution and proclamation of the illegality of state-regulated brothels. This was enforced together with the introduction of a new Law for Combating Venereal Diseases in 1927. Consequently, the legal and civil status of prostitutes

---

92 Note that in Germany, according to Ember and Ember (2003:406), homosexual couples can formally register their relationship since 2001. Furthermore, already in 1994 the law forbidding homosexual activities was removed. Not surprisingly, however, there has never been any formal prosecution of female homosexuality, like in other European legal systems.

improved to such an extent that they were even able to sue police officers who overused the existing regulations in order to arrest them or persecute them.

The fate of sex workers changed dramatically together with the commencement of Hitler's Nazi Germany in 1933. As the *EPSW* comments, *Nazi moral agenda throughout the 1930s was characterized by heightened homophobia, a brutal "racialization" of sex, as well as attempts to reorganize and politicize sexual life*. At that time legal acts were passed which criminalized any form of street soliciting and which enabled the police to conduct numerous raids and mass arrests of streetwalkers throughout Germany. Furthermore, severe punishments were imposed on those found guilty of street soliciting or contracting sexually transmitted infections. Curiously enough, the new head of the police, Heinrich Himmler, who was a keen proponent of state-regulated prostitution, promoted the spread of brothels, which were supposed to serve as a form of *"safe" sexual opportunities for (male) extramarital sex* (the *EPSW*). In this way the German army tried to prevent male homosexuality from spreading among its troops. As a result, Nazi Germany – though abolitionist in its policies towards prostitution – never managed to eradicate the vice. On the contrary, the practice of accepting state-regulated brothels that began in 1930s has survived, and today takes the form of large "Eros Centers", which are state-supervised venues.

At present it is, however, Dutch Amsterdam that seems to be the unquestioned queen of prostitution with its globally acknowledged reputation of the city of prostitution or – for some – a modern Sodom. Although prostitution has been legal and granted all the rights of a normal occupation only since 1999, in historical perspective it is reported that women performing the oldest profession in Amsterdam have been in operation for approximately seven hundred years. As the *EPSW* informs us the first record of any traces of sex trade in Amsterdam dates from the 13th century when the present-day city was still a small fishing port. In the latter part of the Middle Ages, like in most other parts of Europe, prostitution was restricted to specified areas where neither priests nor married women were allowed. From the time of Protestant Reformation until the beginning of the 19th century prostitution was widely prosecuted with twenty percent of all judicial cases directed towards working girls in Amsterdam. Nevertheless, prostitution was never eradicated as sailors constantly coming to the port of Amsterdam had their needs which they expected to satisfy in harbouring places, and – whether legally or illegally – girls of the town were always – overtly or covertly – at their disposal.

The first official step in the general acceptance of commercial sex in Holland was the introduction of the Code Pénal in 1811 which decriminalized prostitution. Brothels and other places of sexual entertainment flourished in the long-established red light district, and even though – theoretically – all brothels were closed down in 1897 prostitutes still operated, but in the form of other professions, such as waitresses, hostesses, singers, masseuses and shop assistants in tobacco shops. Amsterdam's sex workers began to provide their services openly again in the 1930s, when the worldwide-famous form of window prostitution started, and later developed further during the sexual revolution of the 1960s and 1970s. The origin of this specifically Germanic way of illicit soliciting[93] began when prostitutes were banned from the streets of Amsterdam in the early 20th century and they moved to rented houses or rooms whereby – if downstairs – they sat behind windows and, as the *EPSW* describes, *from behind closed curtains they lured their customers with a tap on the window.* The spread of this form of illicit soliciting to the rest of the red light district was further encouraged by the permissive attitude of the police patrolling the area.

Not surprisingly, it was in Amsterdam that the prostitutes' union named Rode Draad (lit. 'red thread') was established in 1984, and the first World Whores' Congress was organized in 1985 (the following year it was held in Brussels). Obviously, the complete legalization of prostitution has had its downsides as well. Drug addiction and women trafficking have been serious problems for the authorities, especially since 2003, and they undoubtedly continue to show the dark side of the sex business, in all its forms.

2.3.4 Slavonic

Within the Slavonic cultural zone the Polish, the Czechs and the Ukrainians are worth comparing and contrasting primarily because of the considerable length of time the respective countries and their people belonged to and were under the great impact of the Habsburg Monarchy.[94] Hence, the legal status of prostitutes and their trade was relatively the same throughout the monarchy and corresponded roughly to the overall existing European trends of the Middle Ages or Reformation. For example, as the *EPSW* reports, after the time of medieval tolerance and business-like approach to prostitution, the advent of the 16th century witnessed the closure of brothels, which was greatly helped by the spread of syphilis and was personally encouraged by Habsburg Emperor Ferdinand I, a keen proponent of abolitionism.

---

93 According to the *EPSW*, window prostitution is typically found in Dutch, Belgian and German cities.
94 The Habsburg Monarchy collapsed in 1918 and, at that time, constituted the following present-day territories: Austria, Croatia, the Czech Republic, Hungary, Slovakia, Slovenia, Galician Poland, western Ukraine, the Südtirol in Italy and Transylvania in Romania.

As for a more modern perspective on sex matters in general, and on prostitution in particular, one needs to bear in mind that the Czechs enjoyed only a short period of independent democracy between 1918 and 1938 before they fell into the hands of Hitler and his henchmen first and then – in post-war Europe – into the hands of communist regime. Interestingly, under all three powerful authorities, whether Austrian, German or Russian, prostitution was either somehow regulated, or – on other occasions – somewhat restricted. It seems that this longer period of Germanic influence (Communism lasted approximately forty years) has left a permanent trace in the overall attitude of the Czechs to sexual matters and – in particular – sex for sale. This may be observed, according to Ember and Ember (2003:380), in the fact that *since the end of Communism in 1989, Czech society is once again approximating Western European patterns*, although – from the point of view of today – the statement must be qualified as understatement. For example, homosexuality was illegal at the time of Austrian rule and Communist influence. Afterwards, however, gay and lesbian communities began to be more and more visible,[95] and some cities have developed their own – relatively large – gay communities. Although there have been some, so far, unsuccessful attempts to legalize same-sex registered partnerships, Prague has gained a reputation as a famous gay tourists destination. Let us quote Ember and Ember (2003:387) who say:

> [...] prostitution is outside the law and therefore effectively legal for both males and females over 18 years of age. Since the end of Communism, the Czech Republic has become a destination for sex tourists, both heterosexual and homosexual, especially from neighbouring Germany and Austria.

The German and Austrian directly pronounced interest in the Czech sex industry is seen today especially in the large number of brothels located beside country roads leading to the neighbouring countries, and a great number of Erotic Centres located in every city and town. It may seem that only European Union rules prevent the Czech government from introducing full legalization of prostitution, and its taxation and regulation.

Apparently, the situation of sex workers should be somewhat different in the Ukrainian culture as it has always been – unlike Czech – more influenced by religion and Communists, being part of the Soviet Union from 1917 (east and central Ukraine) and 1939 (west Ukraine) to 1991. Similarly to most other religious countries, there is a two-faced approach to sex for sale in Ukraine; that is the official one and the factual. Officially and formally prostitution is illegal in this country but it is, in fact, largely ignored, hence tolerated. The long-lasting

---

95 It is estimated that, as Ember and Ember (2003:386) put it, discreet gay establishments had operated in larger Czech cities since the early 20th century.

ignorance of the issue of sex for sale has turned Ukraine into one of the largest, now frequently internet-mediated, "exporters" of women to the international sex industry and sex-partner seeking clientelle. Suffice it to take Odessa as an illustrative example of the overall situation of commercial sex in Ukraine. Only ten years after the collapse of the Soviet Union Odessa became one of the centres of international prostitution, mainly because of its favourable conditions as a port city and thus a gateway to the western world. In addition, the attitude of the police was one of the ignorance-through-corruption one, hence pushing young girls into the trade. Initially, that is in the 1990s, a considerable percentage of girls were tricked into the sex business through promises of lucrative job opportunities abroad, and then forced into prostitution, but these days most sex workers are joining the trade voluntarily. It seems that the efforts made by the Ukrainian authorities in the late 1990s to prevent women trafficking have brought poor results as *Natashas* are still present on the streets in major European cities.

As for the legal status of prostitution in Poland, the last of the three representatives of the Slavonic cultural zone, it is by all means closer to the Ukranian model rather than the Czech one. It needs to be stressed, however, that it is extremely difficult – if at all possible – to draw a uniform historical account of the legal approach to the issue of sex for sale in Poland. This is mainly, but not exclusively, due to the political history of Poland as a state, which was wiped out from the map of Europe for almost two hundred years at the close of the 18th century only to gain full political independence in 1989 when the era of Communist regime came to a definite end. Throughout the two centuries, the territory of present-day Poland was variously divided into three areas of political sovereignty, that is German, Austrian and Russian. The overall result of this prolonged political and administrative rule of neighbouring powers over the Polish territory, nation and society was the implementation of German, Austrian or Russian legal regulations and social expectations over the areas the respective governments controlled. It may thus be assumed that what was legally binding about the status of prostitution in Germany was also true for northern and western parts of present-day Poland. In turn, the laws executed within the limits of Habsburg Monarchy, and later Austria-Hungary, were also at work in the south-east part of present-day Poland, and as such were similar to – if not the same as – the ones to be found in the Czech Republic and western Ukraine in the 19th and 20th centuries.

Finally, the north-east and central parts were under the laws and regulations of Russia, and later the USSR, and the issue of prostitution must have been treated in accordance with the same procedures as in Russia. To illustrate the situation of prostitutes in the central and north-east parts of present-day Poland, let us take pre-Second World War Lublin as an example, which – according to

Rodak (2007:189) – may be treated as a representative Polish town with the Russian control on its historical record. The town shows certain tendencies that were observable in other municipal areas in the territory in question. For example, female prostitution before the Second World War was legal for women who registered themselves as prostitutes, and went for medical check-ups twice a week. Obviously, many prostitutes ignored the obligation of medical examinations, as well as there were women working in the sex business at that time, but illegally, without being registered, and this group, as argued by Rodak (2007:191), constituted the vast majority of sex workers at that time. Another particularly typical characteristic feature of the Slavonic cultural zone in that period was the illegal status of any form of male prostitution. As for the legal status of brothels, they have been illegal since 1922 as has been soliciting in the streets, though with the advent of capitalism those in control of organized prostitution have found lee ways to escape the danger of facing the letter of law.

As with various forms of publicity, the hard and fast line of distinction between open encouragement and any form of forced soliciting is frequently difficult to draw and, hence, one can speak about a peculiar form of soliciting, which – though officially illegal – has acquired a specifically Polish taste, which in its flavour is much akin to Amsterdam window-soliciting by sharing the visual element, and restraining from involving any form of verbal publicity. Obviously, the road-soliciting discussed here is not an exclusively Polish phenomenon, and it is there to be seen in other European countries. In Poland, a specific group of prostitutes called *tirówki* (lit. 'lorry-girls') stand by the main roads which lead out of major cities, usually in close proximity of forest and solicit silently lorry drivers, or drivers in general, by wearing scanty apparel and producing ever same-looking smiles on their heavy painted faces. Although recent statistics show that this form of prostitution is *passé* now and, according to *Newsweek* reports, only 20% of Polish sex workers may be referred to as *tirówki* (lit. 'lorry-girls'),[96] the phenomenon itself seems to represent a kind of compromise between what is legal and what is illegal, and what is socially run-down and, simultaneously, accepted. All in all, the legal status of prostitution in Poland is of the abolitionist type, that is prostituting oneself is not criminalized, though socially stigmatized, but – at least in the face of law – any form of making money on someone else's prostitution is illegal and criminalized. This legal situation, however, fails to stop escort agencies and massage parlours from veiling the real business behind their doors, and the institution of private clubbing boosts the business to a great extent.

96　Statistics taken from an article on prostitution in *polska.newsweek.pl* (available at polska.newsweek.pl/nagie-fakty-o-polskiej-prostytucji, 52908,1,1.html)

2.3.5 Non-Indo-European

The representatives that have been selected for the non-Indo-European cultural zone are Hungarian and Israeli, and – in what follows – their non-Indo-European approaches to the sex business will be discussed and contrasted with those of the European cultural areas. Although both cultures are members of a non-Indo-European family of languages they have relatively strong ties with the European continent and its trends. For Hungary, it is its east central geographical position that links it tightly to the European tradition. For Israelis, it is their long history of wandering all over Europe and the New World which makes them perfectly familiarized with western traditions and ways of life.

Historically, Hungary, like other members of the Habsburg monarchy, made use of its police forces to control prostitution, in which the proper hygienic conditions had to be ensured, and taxes had to be paid. In turn, Israeli tradition perceived any kind of extramarital sex as adultery, a situation that is still observable in orthodox Jewish communities. As Faraone and McClure (2006:42) report, *[...] in Israel's moral code, a woman's sexuality belonged to her husband alone, for whom it was reserved both before marriage as well as after.* As a result the institution of prostitution, especially stemming from beyond the Israeli community, has been perceived as a means of saving the purity of another man's wife or wife-to-be. Today, the Israeli legislative system accepts prostitution with the exclusion of brothels and pimping. The greatest percentage of prostitutes working in Israel comprises guest sex workers from Russia and former Soviet republics.

As for Hungary, according to Ember and Ember (2003:482), *sexuality is a difficult subject for most Hungarians to discuss openly due to a number of historical factors: conservative cultural traditions, Catholicism, and socialist morality.* However, there are certain facts that seem to contradict these generally accepted assumptions, for example legalization of homosexuality in 1961, which led to same-sex couples gaining most of the same rights as heterosexual married couples.[97] Furthermore, in 1999 the Hungarian government legalized and, in this way, regulated prostitution. Taken together, these two aspects of the Hungarian legislative system make Hungary one of the most liberal countries in Europe, and the most liberal nation in central east Europe. Recently, another step has been taken towards treating prostitution like any other profession or occupation, namely the introduction of entrepreneur's permits which prostitutes are sup-

---

97 According to Ember and Ember (2003:482), Hungary has one of the most liberal domestic partner laws in the world together with Scandinavia and the Netherlands.

posed to apply for, and which have been designed to generate profits for the government.

2.4 Concluding remarks

The general picture that emerges from the discussion proposed in the sections above is that the issue of sex for sale is omnipresent both historically and culturally. We may thus ask the question why prostitution is so high on the social agenda regardless of the period of time and corner of the world. A partial answer may be sought in the very much sexual nature of human beings which – for different reasons and to different extent – has been restricted, trivialised and criticised, and through sex trade you-name-them sexual needs could be satisfied on a financial basis. Needless to say, the overall situation of sex workers in today's cultures largely depends on the historical approach to prostitution in a given cultural zone. From the contemporary perspective, the tackling of the issue of prostitution may generally be divided into three groups of legislative approach:

1. legal and accepted,
2. not illegal, but regulated,
3. illegal, but illicitly present.

The first group comprises the Netherlands, Germany and Hungary, where it is legal to exchange sexual services for money, with hardly any serious restrictions. Secondly, the biggest group is made up of countries where sex work is not illegal, but somehow regulated and tolerated. These are Italy, France, the Czech Republic, Poland, Israel, the USA and the UK. Last but not least, there is Ukraine, where prostitution underground flourishes with the police force turning a blind eye to it being corrupted not to take legal actions against women of the streets.

Panchronic Developments of the Lexical Items Linked to the Conceptual Category FALLEN WOMAN

3.1 On the internal organisation of the conceptual category FALLEN WOMAN

The analysis that follows is aimed to be yet another brick in the burgeoning walls of the *Rzeszów School of Diachronic Semantics*. A number of scholars have already contributed a body of research tasks in the conceptual macrocategory **HUMAN BEING,** including the founder of the School Professor Kleparski (1990, 1997, 2008), Kiełtyka (2008), Kochman-Haładyj and Kleparski (2011), Cymbalista (2008), Kopecka (2009, 2011), Kudła (2010), Górecka-Smolińska (2011) and Więcławska (2011).

Most traditionally, the analysis of particular subfields that have been attempted begins with the introduction of the internal arrangement of the targeted conceptual categories and the lexical items linked to them (see, among others, Kiełtyka 2008, Kudła 2010, Górecka-Smolińska 2011 and Więcławska 2011). Here, we shall introduce the inner structure of the conceptual macrocategory **HUMAN BEING** with due attention to the position of the microcategory **FALLEN WOMAN** as its hyponym. According to the *Longman Lexicon of Contemporary English* (McArthur 1984), the conceptual subcategory **FALLEN WOMAN** has its place in the larger macrocategory **PEOPLE AND THE FAMILY**. Apart from the category targeted here there are other conceptual subcategories that stand to attention, among others:

1. **PEOPLE** e.g. **PARENT AND CHILD** (*guardian, child, ward*),
2. **FRIENDSHIP AND ENMITY** e.g. **NEIGHBOURS AND PARTNERS** (*companion, colleague, accomplice*),
3. **DEATH AND BURIAL** e.g. **BURYING AND CREMATING** (*burial, funeral, ashes*),
4. **SOCIAL ORGANIZATION IN GROUPS AND PLACES** e.g. **PEOPLE AND POPULATIONS, GROUPS AND PARTIES** (*humanity, folk, party, clique*),
5. **GOVERNMENT** e.g. **KINGS AND EMPERORS** (*ruler, viceroy, sheikh*),

6. **POLITICS AND ELECTIONS** e.g. **POLITICAL MOVEMENT AND PARTIES** (*Maoism, imperialism, neo-*),
7. **POLITICAL TENSION AND TROUBLE** e.g. **PERSONS PLOTTTING AND SPYING** (*ringleader, traitor, quisling*),
8. **SOCIAL CLASSIFICATIONS AND SITUATIONS** e.g. **LEVELS IN SOCIETIES** (*establishment, nobility, proletariat*).

When we narrow down our perspective to the macrocategory **PEOPLE AND THE FAMILY** we see that the following subcategories may be identified.

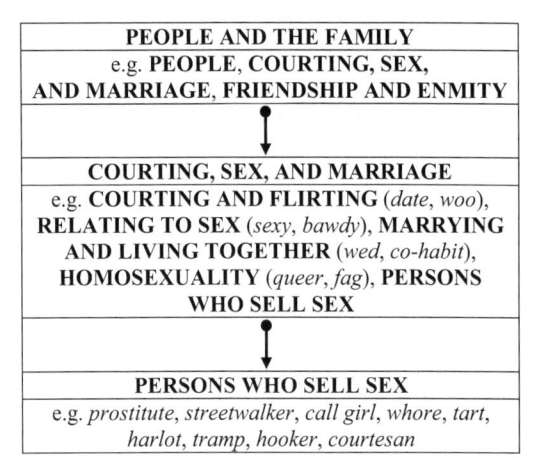

PEOPLE AND THE FAMILY
e.g. **PEOPLE, COURTING, SEX, AND MARRIAGE, FRIENDSHIP AND ENMITY**
↓
COURTING, SEX, AND MARRIAGE
e.g. **COURTING AND FLIRTING** (*date, woo*), **RELATING TO SEX** (*sexy, bawdy*), **MARRYING AND LIVING TOGETHER** (*wed, co-habit*), **HOMOSEXUALITY** (*queer, fag*), **PERSONS WHO SELL SEX**
↓
PERSONS WHO SELL SEX
e.g. *prostitute, streetwalker, call girl, whore, tart, harlot, tramp, hooker, courtesan*

*Fig. 3.1:   The organisation of the macrocategory **PEOPLE AND THE FAMILY**.*

Surprisingly, in McArthur (1984) the microcategory **PERSONS WHO SELL SEX** comprises a group of merely 10 constitutive elements, which stands in sharp quantitative contrast to other lexicographic sources (Ayto 2007 – around 60 elements, Spears 1991 – around 530 elements), and analytic sources (Schulz 1975 – around 80 elements). One of the common features of the lexical items listed is that they either currently or used to belong to Standard English with the exception of *tart* and *hooker* which are marked as slang in McArthur (1984).

3.1.1 Historical foundations of the intricacies in the structure of the conceptual category FALLEN WOMAN

Anyone who has ever conducted research into semantic changes in the conceptual domain **HUMAN BEING** is bound to conclude that the conceptual category **FEMALE HUMAN BEING** tops the list of the most pejoration-afflicted human-specific macrocategories. As Schulz (1975:72) observed almost 40 years ago, there are roughly one thousand terms to refer to a woman in sexually derogatory ways. When we take into account that around five hundred lexical items in the history of the English language are synonyms of *prostitute*,[98] what strikes us most is the yet unanswered question of *why have language users needed so many words to express one and the same notion*. The analysis that follows will make an attempt to provide at least a partial answer to this question. The first natural step to take seems to account for the inner organisation of the conceptual category **FALLEN WOMAN**.

According to the *EPSW*, members of the conceptual category **FALLEN WOMAN** can be further classified according to their economic and social status and how they are perceived. Apparently, the division is based on the original ancient Greek classification of prostitutes into two broad types, that is **PORNÊ** (from the Greek verb *pornêmi* 'sell'), and **HETAERA** (feminine form of Greek *hetairos* 'male friend', hence *hetaera* 'female friend, companion'), which may be referred to as basic level items (see, for example, Łozowski 1994:161) that organise and structure the category **FALLEN WOMAN**. The basis for the distinction between the two types is sought in the number and the anonymity of partners. The *EPSW* maintains that the concept HETAERA includes the meaning 'woman maintained by one or, occasionally, two men in exchange for his/their exclusive sexual access to her', whereas the notion PORNÊ encodes the sense 'woman who could not choose partners and sold herself to anyone who wished her'. Another distinctive conceptual element linked to the latter kind is that only HETAERA followed the Greek army on their campaigns and the relationships with the partners could be relatively long. PORNÊ, on the other hand, lived in a public place that men patronised and offered herself for hire on city streets, pacing the dark alleys near the marketplace or by the city walls. Interestingly, as the *EPSW* elucidates further, HETAERA started her career as a slave and the notion could include a flute player, as well as a brothel worker or, even, a streetwalker. Yet, there are numerous cases when ancient authors employed the two terms *pornê* and *hetaera* interchangeably – even with reference to the same woman within the canvas of a single literary work, which makes the line of distinction between the two vague and obliterated.

What is more, although a clear-cut demarcation line between the two concepts is difficult to draw the *EPSW* lists further subtypes which may contribute substantially to the genesis of the multitude of historical synonyms of *prostitute* in English. And so, within the concept PORNÊ we may differentiate between two conceptually very much related notions, namely STREETWALKER and BROTHEL WORKER, with the latter being slightly higher on the status ladder

---

[98] The data based on Farmer and Heleny (1965) in Schulz (1975) and Spears (1991).

and public perception scale. It is noteworthy that there existed an intermediate subtype, namely the concept OIKEMA WORKER, which was employed to refer to a prostitute who accepted her partners in small houses (Gr. *oikema* 'little house').[99] Yet another subtype was the concept TRAINED PROFESSIONAL MUSICIAN which included a variety of singers, flute players (Gr. *auletrides*), harp players (Gr. *psaltrias*) and lyre players (Gr. *kitharistrias*). Trained professional musicians – both male and female – were invited to dinner parties in order to entertain the guests with music and the accompanying sexual pleasures. Rather unsurprisingly, there were times, as the *EPSW* notes, when the concepts of HETAERA and TRAINED PROFESSIONAL MUSICIAN overlapped. The highest rank in the typology of prostitute types – higher than HETAERA – is the concept MEGALOMISTHO which foregrounded the element of financial welfare, as it was used in the sense 'high priced prostitute'.

STATUS	TYPE	FEATURES
<HIGH[POS]>	Gr. MEGALOMISTHO	*megalomistho* 'high priced prostitute'
both <MALE[NEU]> and <FEMALE[NEU]>	Gr. HETAERA	better educated, a certain degree of economic autonomy, sometimes long-term engagements
	TRAINED PROFESSIONAL MUSICIANS	*singer*, Gr. *auletride* 'flute player', Gr. *psaltria* 'harp player', Gr. *kitharistria* 'lyre player'
	BROTHEL WORKER	
	OIKEMA WORKER	Gr. *oikema* 'little house'; male prostitutes found there
	STREETWALKER	
<LOW[NEG]>	Gr. PORNÊ	common whores working in the streets or brothels

Fig. 3.2: Towards a typology of prostitution – the Greek standpoint.

As for the Roman perspective, the stress is normally placed on the various conceptual elements related to aspects of transacting business though a certain basic division exists. According to the *EPSW,* the distinction made in ancient Rome was between the concept MERETRIX, which was a neutral term employed in the sense 'woman who earned', and was used to refer to a named prostitute, and the concept SCORTUM (Gr. 'leather bag'), which was a highly derogatory term for a nameless participant of dinner parties. What strikes us most is a seemingly obvious parallel to the Greek differentiation between PORNÊ and HETAERA in which the level of anonymity plays a similarly crucial role. The other two

---

99 Curiously enough, it was oikema, not a brothel, which male prostitutes used as their working place.

concepts found in the Roman world of prostitution, namely LUPAE and MULIER SECUTULEIA, are lower in social status. The former, that is Lat. *lupae* 'she-wolf', was zoosemically used to refer to a prostitute of ferocious or rapacious disposition and the latter, that is Lat. *mulier secutuleia* 'chasing woman', meant a nymphomaniac who was as desperate as ready to pay for sexual pleasures. It seems, however, that the last concept MULIER SECUTULEIA should rather be included in the conceptual microcategory **PROSTITUTE'S PARTNER**. Its mention in the division of prostitute types that were found in ancient Rome may point to the perception of female partners of male prostitutes as prostitute-like.

STATUS	TYPE	FEATURES
<HIGH[POS]>	Lat. MERETRIX	'woman who earned'; a neutral term used with reference to a named prostitute, often an object of romantic intrigue
both <MALE[NEU]> and <FEMALE[NEU]>	Lat. SCORTUM	'leather bag'; a derogatory, insulting term for a nameless participant of dinner parties
<LOW[NEG]>	Lat. LUPAE	'she-wolf'
	Lat. MULIER SECUTULEIA	'chasing woman'; a woman so desperate for sex as to pay for it

Fig. 3.3.   Towards a typology of prostitution – the Roman basis.

Taking now the features of each human activity as a group of constitutive elements, each of them may be said to relate either to the very nature of the activity performed or to the rest of the inherent features that – although relate directly to the quality, action or feature – may be successfully conceptually detached from the core elements of the notion described. And so, for example, the concept DRIVING involves the tempo of driving, the frequency of usage of gear levels and the use of the rear mirror. These conceptual elements characterise the action of driving itself. However, such features as being careful, preference for nocturnal driving and the mode of sitting behind the steering wheel are only contextually related to the notion DRIVING. Aggression, the nocturnal nature of the work performed, and the type of sitting position assumed may also be attributed to a great number of other human occupations and activities, not only drivers. And so, for example, some police officers prefer night shifts, porters tend to spend a substantial part of their lives in a sitting position, and some office clerks tend to behave more aggressively than others.

When we narrow our perspective to the occupation targeted here we notice that some sex workers – either for objective or subjective reasons – choose to lure their prospective clients during the hours of the night. Some are characterised by a pendulum movement while others are staged within the limited canvas of window frames to lure their potential customers. Therefore, one can speak about intrinsic non-sex-worker-specific mentions, such as physical location, movement, type of behaviour and attitude, or time of activity. Faraone and McClure (2006:8) provide a clear-cut taxonomy of Roman sex workers with regards to the varying aspects of transacting their business.

TYPE	FEATURES
Lat. PROSEDA/Lat. PROSTABULUM	'sitting/standing before the brothel'
Lat. CIRCULATRIX	'streetwalking'
Lat. PETULCA	'aggressive soliciting'
Lat. NONARIA	'time at which their liaisons occur'
Lat. PUELLA	'girl'; established euphemism

Fig. 3.4:   Taxonomy of Roman sex workers.

Furthermore, one observes yet another parallel between the oldest profession in Rome and Greece, which stems from the parameter of locations referred to as *cellae* (Lat. 'cribs'), which were small houses consisting of a room with a stone bed. Such cribs spread throughout the city, and they apparently correspond to Greek *oikemata* that performed the sense function 'small houses'. Interestingly, the *EPSW* informs us that archaeological evidence points to the absence of the so-called "red light" districts, and prostitutes were there to find and see all over the cities: on the streets, in graveyards, brothels (Lat. *lupanaria, fornices*), cribs, inns, baths and circuses. As to the financial side of gratification for sexual services, the usual price for hiring a *meretrix* was two asses (1 Roman **as** corresponds to 1 English **penny**), which was the price of a loaf of bread, and it was well beyond the reach of the average urban worker.

3.2 Historical growth of the lexical items linked to the conceptual category FALLEN WOMAN

It is common knowledge to say that in the history of natural languages words, like people, come and go leaving behind them the stories of their lives, and these stories are written by those who live on. Some of these stories are long and dull, some momentous but eventful, while the existence of other words is full of sudden ups and downs and frequently inexplicable controversies. Yet, they all have one thing in common; that is they are all worthy of discussion and the effort made in uncovering their stories. Obviously, the older the word, the more difficult it may be to fully unearth its history in a reliable fashion, without an overreliance on supposition. In order to make the analysis of the words selected clearer and easier to follow, the material will be pigeon holed within clearly defined timeframes. The periods in the history of the English language reflect the taxonomy proposed by Fisiak (2000).[100]

PERIOD	TIMELINE
Old English (O.E.)	450–1150
Early Middle English (E.M.E.)	1150–1300
Late Middle English (L.M.E)	1300–1450
Early Modern English (E.Mod.E)	1450–1650
Late Modern English (L.Mod.E)	1650–1800
Present-day English (Pres.E.)	1800–

Fig. 3.5: *The taxonomy of the periods in the history of English.*

For each historical period specified, the angle that will be taken is that of surveying the etymological roots, and the spectrum of structural, semantic and rhetorical processes involved in the formation of the body of synonyms panchronically related to the conceptual category **FALLEN WOMAN**.

3.2.1 Formative mechanisms employed in the coinage of lexical items linked to the conceptual category FALLEN WOMAN

The tables below are based on the material itemised in the *HTE* in the section labelled PROSTITUTION. Of 148 lexical items listed, 93 have been selected for the analysis of mechanisms that have been put to work in the formation of X-phemisms. Yet, a thorough analysis of the material gathered in other lexicographic sources – with the *OED* taking pride of place – and the research carried out thus far provides us with compelling reasons to include other lexical items, the body of which amounts to 61 words related historically to the conceptual category **FALLEN WOMAN**,[101] which will be treated on an equal basis with the historical lexical items listed in the *HTE*. Those lexical items (40) that are

---

100 Note that scholars differ as to the demarcation lines of the historical periods in the English language. Baugh and Cable (2002), for example, give the year 1500 as the approximate boundary line between Middle English and Modern English. Wełna (1996), in turn, treats the year 1100 as the closure of Old English and the commencement of Middle English.
101 Out of 61 lexical items added to the *HTE* list 40 are words also included in the *HTE*, but under the label UNCHASTITY. The *OED* data, however, confirmed the presence of 'prostitute' as one of the senses recorded for these lexical items.

not labelled as historical synonyms of *prostitute* in the *HTE*, but have been evidenced in the sense 'prostitute' at one point in their historical development have been put in the brackets, and those lexical items (21) that were added to the analysis as the outcome of library search in such lexicographic historical sources as Partridge (1984), Rawson (1981, 1989), Spears (1991) and Ayto (2007) have been underlined. Additionally, those words which, at a certain point in their semantic evolution, were used in the female-specific sense 'prostitute' and later started to be applied in the male-specific sense 'male prostitute' have been highlighted. Such problems of distinction are by no means a rarity in the literature of the subject. For example, Kleparski (1997) is evidently not entirely certain in all cases whether a given lexical item the semantic evolution of which he traces in his study deserves the label of historical synonym of *prostitute*.

The tools employed fall into the following categories: structural, semantic and rhetorical. As for syntactic/grammatical tools, the only instance that has been found is the superlative Pres.E. expression *the oldest profession*, which simultaneously is an example of the mechanism of circumlocution. Let us commence our discussion with the category of structural tools.

To start with, the data analysed seems to point to the overwhelming productivity of the mechanism of compounding, which – historically speaking – has triggered the formation of a good number of cover terms for *prostitute* throughout the ages. Interestingly, up to Late Modern English only four processes were clearly at work, that is 23 cases of compounding (e.g. *portcwene, common woman, polecat, fling-dust, laced mutton*), 11 cases of derivation (e.g. *hackster, waistcoateer, occupant, harlotry*), 3 cases of clipping (*bawd, miss, wench*) and 1 case of remodelling (*hackster*). Similarly, throughout the Late Modern English and Present-day English periods the productivity of compounding was relatively stable with the total of 14 cases found in Late Modern English (e.g. *nightwalker, doll-common, town-miss, mobbed-head*), and 18 cases in Present-day English so far (e.g. *loose fish, horse-breaker, brass-nail, pavement princess*). In turn, the productivity of morphological derivation may be said to have been on the decline with merely two cases recorded for Late Modern English (*molly, trully*), and 6 cases for Present-day English (e.g. *tartlet, prossie, prosty*). With regards to the productivity of clipping, it has clearly shown a tendency to grow in a slow if not steady fashion, with only 2 cases in Late Modern English (*strum, hack*), and 4 cases in Present-day English (e.g. *pros, pross, pro, bim*). Alphabetisms, reduplication, blending, rhyming slang together with remodelling emerge as the least productive mechanisms in the formation of historical synonyms of *prostitute*. Note that the least productive mechanisms – with the exception of remodelling – have only been at work since the beginning of Present-day English, which may point to an emerging shift in the use of structural tools in the formation of cover terms which are semantically linked to the conceptual category **FALLEN WOMAN**.

The material analysed here leaves no doubt as to the nature of the morphological processes at work. Yet, the only lexical item that retains its misty origins is the alphabetism *B-girl*, which some lexicographic sources – such as the *UrbanDictionary*, Ayto (2007) and Green (2003) – label as the Present-day English synonym for *prostitute*. The *OED*, however, informs us only of one sense of the word *B-girl*, that is 'woman employed to encourage customers to buy drinks at a bar'. In the *OED* the alphabetism *B-girl* is treated as a shortened form of *bar girl*, but – alternately – Ayto (2007) suggests that it may be treated as the short of *bad girl*.

No.	STRUCTURAL TOOLS			
	Old English			
	Compounding	Derivation		
1	*forligerwif*	*mylt-estre*		
2	*portcwene*	*be-þæc-estre*		
3	*horcwene*	*for-ligerwif*		

	Middle English			
	Compounding	Clipping		
1	*common woman*	?? *bawd* < *bawdstrot*		
2	*tickle-tail*	*wench* < *wenchel*		

	Early Modern English			
	Compounding	Derivation	Clipping	Remodelling
1	*strange woman*	*hack-ster*	*miss*	*hackster*
2	*public woman*	*twigg-er*		
3	*streetwalker*	*waistcoat-eer*		
4	*polecat*	*mar-tail*		
5	*walk-street*	*occup-ant*		
6	*night-shade*	*commun-ity*		
7	*hackney-woman*	*dox-y* < *dock+y*		
8	*mar-tail*	*(harlot-ry)*		
9	*fling-dust*			
10	*night-trader*			
11	*hackney-wench*			
12	*hell-moth*			
13	*public commoner*			
14	*night-worm*			
15	*Winchester goose*			
16	*(stewed strumpet)*			
17	*(laced mutton)*			
18	*(wagtail)*			

Late Modern English

	Compounding	Derivation	Clipping	Remodelling
1	night-walker	moll-y	strum < strumpet	(jilt) < gillot
2	marmalade-madam	(trull-y)	hack < hackney	
3	town-woman			
4	hackney-lady			
5	doll-common			
6	high-flyer			
7	market dame			
8	barber's chair			
9	town-miss			
10	kennel-nymph			
11	(tomrig)			
12	(buttered bun)			
13	(mobbed-head)			
14	(Cousin Betty)			

Present-day English

	Compounding	Derivation	Clipping	Remodelling
1	loose fish	(tart-let)	pros	(hooer)
2	receiver-general	pross-ie	pross	
3	dolly-mops	pross-y	pro	
4	horse-breaker	prozz-y	(bim) < bimbo	
5	queen's woman	prost-ie		
6	soiled dove	prost-y		
7	white slave			
8	brass nail			
9	twopenny upright	**Quasi-reduplication**		**Blending**
10	yum-yum girl	yum-yum girl		prostisciutto
11	working girl			
12	pavement princess	**Alphabetisms/Acronyms**		**Rhyming Slang**
13	street girl	?? B-girl		brass
14	bad girl			brass nail
15	call girl			
16	sex worker			
17	(scarlet woman)			
18	(fly girl)			

Fig. 3.6:   Historical synonyms of prostitute formed by means of structural tools.

In terms of the working of semantic tools in the formation of historical synonyms linked to the conceptual category **FALLEN WOMAN**, it is worth noting that the mechanisms of forming technical jargon and – otherwise frequently employed – human flippancy are either difficult to acknowledge or are hardly ever found at work. As for the process of one-for-one substitution, it must be pointed out that all one-word lexical items – regardless of their classification here – are instances of its employment. The tables given below clearly show that the process of borrowing has the highest level of productivity (31 lexical items). Interestingly, it is the mechanism of circumlocution that demonstrates an increasing level of productivity with the passage of time, which may prove the ongoing trend of political correctness and testify to Rawson's (1981) rule that the longer the euphemism, the more effective it is.

There are, however, several doubts as to the ultimate origin of the lexical items in question, especially and naturally the origin of those that belong to the days long gone. For instance, in most etymological reference books the word *strumpet* is said to be of obscure origin, though certain possible etymological conjectures are provided as well. It may be concluded that they all point to the mechanism of borrowing as the most likely source behind the appearance of the word *strumpet* in English. As Rawson (1989) and Partridge (1984) suggest, the source language was L.Lat. and its form *strumpum* used in the sense 'dishonor, violation'. Alternately, Rawson (1989) also highlights the possibility of borrowing the form *strumpet* from M.Du. *strompe* 'stocking', in which case we are faced with the working of the mechanism of metonymy coupled with borrowing. Similarly, Rawson (1989) points to the French origin of the form *bawd* developed from O.Fr. *baude* 'lively, bold'. The author also suggests that *bawd* may have originated as a clipped form of *bawdstrot*, and, more importantly, its meaning was originally associated with the conceptual value <MALE$_{[NEU]}$> as the word was used in the sense 'procurer'[102] only to incorporate the conceptual element <FEMALE$_{[NEU]}$> in the 18th century.[103] Although the lexical item *bawd* occurs in the *HTE* as a M.E. acquisition, here it is included as a L.Mod.E. borrowing as the word developed the sense 'prostitute' during that period of the history of English.

Likewise, the remaining two lexical items – that is *punk* and *croshabell* – are of obscure etymology. As to the word *punk*, it is suggested in Partridge (1984) that the lexical item in question may have been borrowed from Lat. *punctum* 'small hole, especially one caused by pricking', whereas both the *OED* and Rawson (1989) fail to formulate any hypothesis regarding the rise of the sense 'prostitute'. The most difficult etymological problem seems to be involved in uncovering the etymological roots of the word *croshabell*. There are hardly any traces which could lead us to at least a plausible etymology of the word. Having no definite lexicographic assistance, the only possible method to employ here is deduction, and

---

102 Consider the following *OED* quotation: 1386 He was A theef, and eek a somnour, and a *baude* [v.r. *bawde*].
103 See: 1706 *Bawd*, a leud Woman that makes it her Business to debauch others for Gain; a Procuress.

thus, it seems that the word *croshabell* might have been of foreign origin as its phonological original layout fails to meet the Anglo-Saxon phonotactic restrictions.

No.	SEMANTIC TOOLS		
	Old English		
	Borrowing		Circumlocution
1	*hóre* (O.N.)		*bepæcestre*
2			*firenhicgend*
3			*portcwene*
4			*synnecge*
	Middle English		
	Borrowing		
1	*pute* (Fr.)		
2	*putain* (Fr.)		
3	?? *strumpet* (Lat./Du.)		
4	*(harlot)* (Fr.)		
5	*common* (Fr.)		
6	?? *bawd* (Fr.)		

	Early Modern English		
	Borrowing	Eponymy	Circumlocution
1	*drab* (Ir.)	*(Tib)*	*lady of pleasure*
2	*putanie* (Fr.)	*(hiren)*	*(light of love)*
3	*courtesan* (Fr.)	*moll*	*sisters of the bank*
4	*(trull)* (G.)	*hackney*	
5	*(callet)* (Fr. or Gael.)		
6	*(pucelle)* (Fr.)		
7	*(succubus)* (Lat.)		
8	*(amorosa)* (Sp./It.)		
9	?? *croshabell*		
10	?? *punk* (Lat.)		
11	*prostitute* (Lat.)		
12	*hackney* (Fr.)		

	Late Modern English		
	Borrowing	Eponymy	Circumlocution
1	*fille de joie* (Fr.)	*doll-common*	*lady of easy virtue*
2	*frow* (Du.)	*(tomrig)*	*fille de joie*
3	?? *bawd* (Fr.)		

	Present-day English		
	Borrowing	Eponymy	Circumlocution
1	*horizontal* (Fr.)	*tom*	*the oldest profession*
2	*geisha* (Jap.)	*dolly-mop*	*lady of the evening/night*
3	*shawl* (Anglo-Ir.)	*molly*	*white slave*
4	*poule de luxe* (Fr.)		*working girl*

5	*escort* (Fr.)		*pavement princess*
6	*puta* (It.)		*sex worker*
7	*bimbo* (It.)		*moonlighter*
8	*trug* (It. *trucca*)		*queen's woman*
9	*(shickster)* (Yid.)		

Fig. 3.7   Historical synonyms of prostitute coined by means of semantic tools.

Most of the lexical items tabled here are of relatively unambiguous etymology, but – as was the case in the previous category of formative mechanisms – neither is the category of rhetorical tools devoid of cases of etymological doubts and uncertainties, for example, in the case of the lexical item *slut*, which – as Partridge (1984) and Rawson (1989) argue – is ultimately related to the form *slattern* and its basic etymological sense 'idleness'. Partridge (1984) also points to the likely relation of *slut* to O.N. *slota* 'droop, flag'.

Another controversy seems to be hidden behind the origin of the lexical item *twigger*, which – according to Rawson (1989) – may be etymologically related either to *twig* 'do anything vigorously or strenuously' or to *twigle* 'copulate'. There is, however, another plausible path of the origin of this word, which may be classified as a case of a zoosemic metaphorical extension from *twigger* in the sense 'breeder' – when used of a ewe – to the sense 'prostitute'.

Last but not least, the form *barber's chair* which – although no lexicographic sources confirm the supposition advanced here – may be treated as an instance of a metonymic extension based on an item used by a prostitute for the purpose of displaying her charms, if any, usually on a window display, and transferred to mean simply 'prostitute'.

No.	RHETORICAL TOOLS		
	Old English		
	Understatement	Metaphor/Foodsemy	Metonymy
1	*quean* < *cwéne*	*myltestre*	*bepæcestre*
2	*firenhicgend*	*?? scylcen*	*forligerwif*
3	*synnecge*		*portcwene*
4	*scand*		
5	*portcwene*		

Middle English		
	Understatement	Metaphor	Metonymy/Synecdoche
1	*common woman*	*?? slut*	*?? strumpet*
2	*common*	*(filth)*	
3	*wenchel/wench*		

Panchronic Developments of the Lexical Items

Early Modern English				
Understatement	Metonymy/ Synecdoche	Metaphor		
		Zoosemy	Metaphor	
1	public commoner	stew	cat	sisters of the bank
2	strange woman	walk-street	hackney	(succubus)
3	public woman	night-shade	hackney-woman	aunt
4	streetwalker	waistcoateer	hackney-wench	
5	walk-street	fling-dust/-stink	polecat	
6	night-shade	night-trader	?? twigger	
7	fling-dust/-stink	streetwalker	(yaud)	
8	night-trader	(baggage)	(wagtail)	
9	miss		mermaid	**Foodsemy**
10	(loon)		(cockatrice)	(laced mutton)
11	(limmer)		hell-moth	meat
12	(mort)		night-worm	
13			Winchester goose	
14			bat	
15			quail	
16			plover	

Late Modern English				
	Understatement	Metonymy/ Synecdoche	Metaphor	
			Zoosemy	Metaphor
1	night-walker	nocturnal	mouse	aunt
2	town-woman	market dame	harridan	(cousin)
3	girl (about/of the town)	kennel-nymph	hackney-lady	(Cousin Betty)
4	town-miss	(vizard) (syn)		nun
5	woman of the town	(crack)		
6	lady of easy virtue	(mobbed-head)		
7	(mot/mott)	?? barber's chair		
8				
9		**Alliteration**	**Hyperbole**	
10		marmalade-madam	high-flyer	

Present-day English					
	Hyperbole	Understatement	Metonymy/ Synecdoche	Metaphor	
1	(fly-girl)	professional	receiver-general	hooker	
2		model	tail (syn)	horse breaker	
3		street girl	twopenny upright	flagger	
4		bad girl	scrubber	hustler	
5		call girl	(scarlet woman)	**Zoosemy**	**Foodsemy**
6		gay	(pick-up)	cow	prostisciutto
7		unfortunate		scrubber	(tart)
8				loose fish	(tartlet)
9				soiled dove	

10				*moth*	
11				*poule-de-luxe*	
12				*(chippy)*	
13				*(scrub)*	

Fig. 3.8:   Historical synonyms of prostitute formed by means of rhetorical tools.

3.3 Methodology contour

The end goal set to the analytical part of the study is to scrutinise the lexical items panchronically and onomasiologically linked to the conceptual microcategory **FALLEN WOMAN**, or – to phrase it more precisely – to account for the etymology and semantic development of historical synonyms of *prostitute*, with due attention devoted to the mechanisms employed in their formation and – last but not least – to the illocutionary force the targeted synonyms evoke. In the most general terms, the apparatus adopted for our data analysis draws on the various elements of the cognitive framework and its selected principles will be briefly discussed in this section. Naturally, we shall confine our methodological outline only to those notions, mechanisms and processes that may somehow be involved in the practical part of this work. In limiting our presentation to such an indispensable degree the author of this monographic study has been guided by the fact that the task of presenting the elements of cognitive linguistics employed specifically for the purposes of analysing the semantic diachrony of lexical items has been performed on numerous occasions by, among others, such *RSDS* research workers as Grygiel (2005), Kiełtyka (2006), Cymbalista (2008), Kopecka (2009) and Więcławska (2011). All these works that propose accounts of the methodology employed have found their way to the published world (Grygiel and Kleparski 2007, Kiełtyka 2008, Cymbalista and Kleparski 2013, Kopecka 2011 and Więcławska 2012).[104]

To start with, let us concentrate on the issue of lexical relations, some of which are more topical in the type of diachronic analysis offered here. It seems that such notions as **homonymy** and **polysemy**[105] are an inherent part of any task involving the analysis of semantic changes in a well-defined conceptual micro- and macrocategory. The notion of homonymy – customarily defined as a relation based on *the fact that two words of different origin have the same form* (Dirven and Verspoor 1998:27) – proves crucial in any analytical task. Take, for example, the lexical item *tart* which has two unrelated etymological paths. On

---

104   For a recent comparative account of cognitive and classical approaches to semantic analysis, see, among others, Murphy (2010) and Crespo (2013).
105   For the discussion of the relation between homonymy and polysemy, see, for example, Łozowski (2000) and Murphy (2010).

the one hand, *tart* – when employed in the adjectival sense 'severe, sour, bitter' – derives ultimately from the P.I.E. root **der* while, on the other, *tart* used in the nominal sense 'dish of baked pastry with different ingredients' is evidenced to have been adopted from Fr. *tarte* 'open tart' in the 13th century. It is the latter *tart* that underwent the foodsemic metaphorical extension in the second half of the 19th century, and started to be applied in the sense 'girl, woman' and 'prostitute'. In turn, the notion of polysemy understood here as *the fact that a word may have two or more related senses* (Dirven and Verspoor 1998:27) occurs everywhere as evidenced by all the research workers in the field.

In the context of our well-defined research task, let us narrow the focus of our attention down to the notion of **synonymy** which is described by Ullmann (1957:108) as *one sense with several names*, which may be said to represent an onomasiological approach to defining the lexical relation which is typically explained by means of the phrase *sameness or similarity of meaning* (see Palmer 1981, Aitchison 1994 and Dirven and Verspoor 1998). For example, Cruse (1986:267) defines synonyms as *lexical items whose senses are identical in respect of 'central' semantic traits, but differ, if at all, only in respect of what we may provisionally describe as 'minor' or 'peripheral' traits*. Significantly, Cruse (1986:265) also introduces the notion of **cognitive synonymy** which the author defines along the following lines:

> X is a cognitive synonym of Y if (i) X and Y are syntactically identical, and (ii) any grammatical declarative sentence S containing X has equivalent truth conditions to another S^1, which is identical to S except that X is replaced by Y. (Cruse 1986:88)

Cruse (1986:265) informs us that cognitive synonymy is one type or degree of synonymy in general and postulates a scale of synonymity from **absolute synonymy** to **non-synonymy**, whereby cognitive synonymy lies somewhere in between the two notions. What most – if not all – semanticists seem to agree on (see, for example, Murphy 2010:110) is that it is virtually impossible to find absolute synonyms in a natural language because when there exist two lexical items with exactly the same meaning and application, naturally, one of them either falls into oblivion or develops different semantic values with the flow of time. Apart from the notion of absolute and cognitive synonymy, Murphy (2010:110) postulates the notion of **sense synonyms** which the author defines as those lexical items that *have one sense that means the same as one of the other word's senses*. To illustrate his point, the author explains the contextual difference between the adjectives *funny, peculiar* and *comical*. For example, when we say *My tummy feels a bit funny whenever I eat fish* we may use *peculiar* instead of *funny*, but not *comical*. In turn, in the context of describing jokes *funny* may be substituted with *comical* rather than *peculiar*. The choice of substitutes depends on the polysemous nature of the adjective *funny* different senses of which *match up semantically with different sets of words* (Murphy 2010:110).

As for cognitive synonyms, according to Cruse (1986:270-285), they do share certain semantic properties, but they differ semantically in some respects. Palmer (1981:89-91) discusses five ways in which synonyms may differ, and his classification corresponds roughly to the one proposed by Cruse (1986:270-285). First of all, cognitive synonyms may differ in respect of *inherent expressive traits* as is the case with such pairs of lexical items as *father/daddy*, *infant/baby* and *cat/pussy*. It is the second lexical item in each pair of cognitive synonyms that is capable of conveying emotive expressive elements while the first item in each pair tends to be rather neutral as to the presence or absence of expressive load. Simultaneously, it may be argued that the first lexical item in each pair of cognitive synonyms belongs to a more formal style of language whereas the second item is rather more characteristic of an informal style.

This distinction drawn above brings us to another difference that may exist between the members of a pair of cognitive synonyms, namely that of different registers or varieties of language employed by individual speakers according to a given occasion or context of use. Cruse (1986:283) argues that one may speak about three interacting dimensions of variation within register, namely field, mode and style. Field variation, or – in other words – the difference in the topic or field of discourse involves the occurrence of synonymous words in technical or subject-specific texts or utterances, such as legal discourse, scientific discourse, advertising language, sales talk, political speeches, football commentaries, cooking recipes, etc. The cognitive synonyms that illustrate field-specific synonymy are, for example, *matrimony/wedlock*, the former of which is frequently employed in legalese while the latter is more likely to be encountered in a religious context.

As for mode as a dimension of register, its function is to differentiate between various channels of transmission of a linguistic message, whether it is written, spoken, telegraphed or such like. Take, for example, the use of *about* which is chiefly restricted to spoken language and, on the other hand, *concerning* may be labelled as belonging to the written register. Finally, style which is the dimension of register concerned with different relations between participants involved in the act of a linguistic exchange of information. As Cruse (1986:284) stresses, the dimension of style is often described in terms of formality-informality, but – in fact – the parameter in question is much more intricate than that because the relations between participants depend on a number of factors, such as roles in a situation, familiarity, social positions, mutual hostility, indifference or friendliness. It must be stressed at this point that it is this dimension of register, and synonymy variation – more generally – that triggers the multiplication of cognitive synonyms in such areas of experience as death, excretory functions, money, religion, power relations and sex, the last of which is of particular interest for the on-going analysis. For each of these areas, take death as an exemplifier, a number of subtly differentiated lexical items may be found, such as *kick the bucket, snuff it, cop it, pop off, peg out, expire, perish, pass away, decease* and many others (see Kleparski 1990:26). Each of the terms enables the speaker to tune in finely and adequately to a given context of use.

Significantly, none of the authoritative works that discuss the problem of synonymy points to the importance of the taboo-and-euphemisation dimension in both synchronic and historical rise of synonyms. Suffice it to mention the abundance of body part names which are used euphemistically to replace the direct tabooed words. For example, *pussy, beaver, keyhole, pudendum, apricot, cauliflower, muffin, cookie, scar, wound* are but a few instances of euphemistic or dysphemistic names used to refer to female genitalia.

Like different registers that exist within one natural language, different dialects also contribute greatly to the discourse cohesion, and hence have a direct communicative role to play. The dialectal variation is another means of differentiating between cognitive synonyms. Cruse (1986:282) distinguishes between geographical, temporal and social dialectal variation, but stresses a certain level of inseparability between the categories in question. To illustrate the point, let us take the following pairs of cognitive synonyms: *sofa/couch, autumn/fall* and *wee/small* result from geographical variation, *scullery/kitchen* and *serviettes/napkins* exemplify the social dimension of dialectal variation and, last but not least, *wireless/radio* and *swimming-bath/swimming-pool* reflect the temporal dimension of dialectal variation.

Another difference one may observe between cognitive synonyms is collocational restriction, or – as Cruse (1986:279) defines it – *arbitrary co-occurrence that is irrelevant to truth-conditions*. The author distinguishes between three subtypes or degrees of collocational restriction, namely systematic, semi-systematic and idiosyncratic. In the case of systematic collocational restrictions, cognitive synonyms share semantic traits in the choice of their collocates. For example, both *kick the bucket* and *die* – despite their major difference in style – systematically collocate with the lexical items marked by the semantic marking <HUMAN$_{[NEU]}$>. In turn, semi-systematic collocational restrictions are observed when cognitive synonyms share only certain semantic traits and each of the cognitive synonyms has a particular expectation as to the choice of their collocates. To illustrate the point, Cruse (1986:281) provides an example of a pair of synonyms *customer* and *client* which are collocationally restricted in that the referent of the former usually receives something material in return for money while the person labelled with the latter form is given professional or technical service. Last but not least, idiosyncratic collocational restrictions can be defined as synonyms the collocates of which may only be identified by a set list of possible matches. For instance, the synonymous adjectives *spotless*, *flawless*, *immaculate* and *impeccable* – though roughly corresponding to the same quality – tend to have different nominal collocates, and so while *performance* may be qualified as *flawless*, *immaculate* or *impeccable*, *kitchen* is qualified as either *spotless* or *immaculate* and *behaviour* may only be qualified as *impeccable*.

The last of the five differences is concerned with what Cruse (1986:285) defines as **plesionyms**, that is synonyms which are no longer cognitive in nature. In turn, Palmer (1981:91) describes this difference as closeness in meaning, a loose type of synonymy. According to Cruse (1986:285), plesionyms, or a loose type of synonymy, are the final and extreme stage on the scale of synonymity before non-synonymy. It is crucial to note at this point that the line of distinction between plesionymy and non-synonymy is difficult, if at all possible, to draw while the difference between plesionyms and cognitive synonyms lies in the fact that plesionyms *yield sentences with different truth-conditions* (Cruse 1986:285). For example, such pairs as *pretty/handsome*, *hill/mountain*, *laugh/giggle* and *murder/execute* may be provided to illustrate the point.

As shown by the rich literature on the subject (see, for example, Kleparski 1996, 1997, Geeraerts 1997, Dirven and Verspoor 1998, Blank 2001 and Crespo 2013) the notion of synonymy is inherently linked with the onomasiological approach to any analysis of lexical resources. Hence, we shall now proceed to discussing the distinction between **semasiology** and **onomasiology**. Generally speaking, the focus of the former lies in analysing all senses of a given form; namely that semasiology (< Gr. *séma* 'sign') deals with the polysemous nature of lexical items, while the latter concentrates on the possible lexical realisations available for a given concept in a language; meaning that onomasiology (< Gr. *ónoma* 'name') deals with synonymy. To be more precise, let us quote Kleparski (1997:64) at this point who specifies the distinction in question along the following lines:

> While a typical semasiological study addresses the question of what the senses of expressions are, onomasiology-oriented analysis seeks to answer the question of what names are linked with a particular concept, i.e., the relation holding between the concept and synonymous expressions associated with this concept. The expressions relating to a given concept form the onomasiological structure, while the polysemous items form the semasiological structure.

In order to illustrate the difference between the two analytical approaches to the lexicon the following diagram may be proposed:[106]

---

106 Based on the schema proposed by Blank (2001:7).

semasiological perspective ⎯⎯⎯⎯⎯⎯⎯⎯⎯⎯→

    LEXICAL ITEMS   SENSES

                                                   'take hold of suddenly'

        seize   'take into custody'

    comprehend   'perceive the meaning of'

    understand

                           ←⎯⎯⎯⎯⎯⎯⎯⎯⎯⎯ **onomasiological perspective**

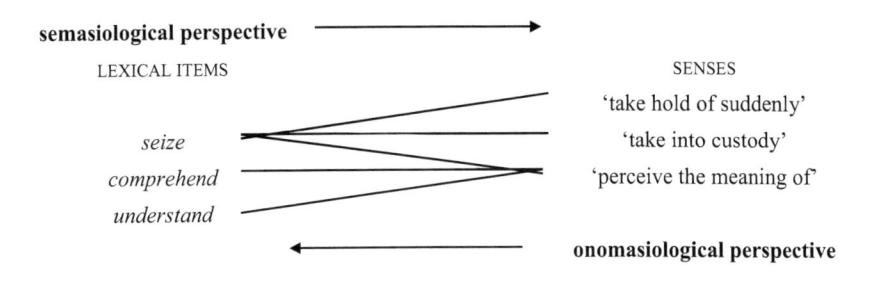

It needs to be stressed at this point that the cognitive analysis to be conducted in the ongoing sections is largely semasio-onomasiological in nature. As Blank (2001:11) argues, the cognitive approach to onomasiology equips a linguist with an adequate tool for linguistic analysis as it provides one with a deeper understanding of human conceptualisation patterns. Blank (2001:11) accounts for the necessity to incorporate cognitive onomasiology into a diachronic study of language in the following way:

> Combining diachronic lexicology with onomasiology and applying it to more than only one or a few languages can enable us to show empirically which conceptualisations are proper to a single or very few speech communities [...]. Cognitive onomasiology then procure us deeper insight into the way our mind works.

Yet another distinction requires some attention from the viewpoint of the ongoing analysis, namely the notions of **synchrony**, **diachrony** and **panchrony**. The traditional Saussurian dichotomy into synchrony and diachrony has been evidenced to be very much defective by cognitive linguists who argue that one can hardly speak about a clear-cut boundary between the two in a linguistic investigation. Significantly, Saussure (1916:138) himself postulated the term **panchrony** as a possible means of accounting for language regularities, but – at the same time – claimed that *[...] from the panchronic point of view, one cannot reach individual facts of language*. In turn, cognitive linguists believe that only a combination of synchrony and diachrony, as well as semasiology and onomasiology, contributes greatly to a truthful, deeper and fact-revealing linguistic investigation. Geeraerts (2010:237) explains that the notion of the so-called lexicogenesis provides cognitive linguists with a tool for analysing the onomasiological inventory of a language across time along the following lines:

> 'Lexicogenesis' [...] involves the mechanisms for introducing new pairs of word forms and word meanings – all the traditional mechanisms, in other words, like word formation, word creation, borrowing, blending, truncation, ellipsis, and folk etymology, that introduce new items into the onomasiological inventory of a lan-

guage. Crucially, semasiological change is a major mechanism of lexicogenesis [...].

Similarly, Łozowski (1999:32) perceives panchrony as a combination of diachrony and cognition or, in other words, as language change analysed in the wider context of human understanding. In turn, Kleparski (1996, 1997) goes somewhat further and argues that panchrony, as a mixture of synchrony and diachrony, is indispensable in any linguistic investigation. As the author explains further, *this standpoint is at least partly justified on the grounds that history frequently accompanies the present day* (Kleparski 1996:79).

Since the data corpus subject to our analysis comes from different periods of the history of English, the author feels justified to talk about lexical items targeted in our analysis as forming a panchronic onomasiological dictionary related to the internally complex conceptual microcategory **FALLEN WOMAN**. The internal structure of the conceptual microcategory in question may be represented graphically in the following way:

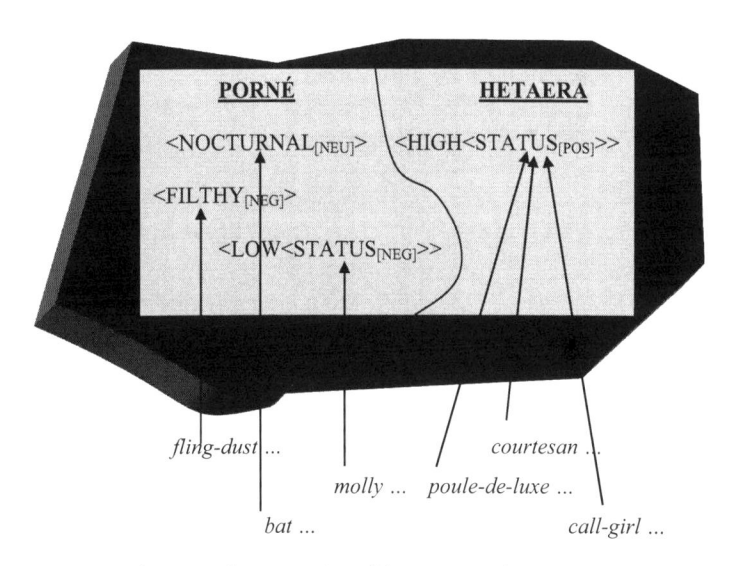

Fig. 3.11: *The internal organisation of the conceptual microcategory **FALLEN WOMAN**.*

Any link to the conceptual microcategory **FALLEN WOMAN** necessitates at least a cursory account of the axiological load that may be present in the semantics of lexical items. It is worth noting at this point that in order to account for the varied axiological charge with which lexical items may associate, Kleparski (1990) introduced four types of pejoration, namely **moral, behav-**

ioural, aesthetic and **social pejoration**.[107] The author provides ample evidence that there seems to obtain a certain order of appearance of these individual types of pejorative load in the diachronic development of the semantics of evaluatively loaded lexical items. As Kleparski (1990:46-47) elucidates, the most frequent order of the stages of pejoration is the following:
1. social pejoration (e.g. *Jasper* 'man/fellow' > 'rustic simpleton'),
2. behavioural pejoration (e.g. *ass* 'long-eared equine smaller than a horse' > 'ignorant fellow, perverse fool, conceited dolt'),
3. aesthetic pejoration (e.g. *crock* 'broken down horse' > 'physically debilitated person'),
4. moral pejoration (e.g. *minx* 'pet dog' > 'pert or hussy/lewd, wanton woman').

As we shall soon see the words analysed in what follows most frequently involve the lowest type of pejorative downfall, that is moral pejoration, as being immoral, unchaste and engaging in mercenary sex according to various orders and commandments – including the Decalogue – are all types of behaviour held in very low esteem, if not downright despicable. Additionally, as we shall presently see, the conceptual microcategory **FALLEN WOMAN** is so internally multifaceted that any adequate account of its internal complexity would involve, among other things, extending the concept of **illocutionary force** viewed here as the amount of emotional and affective potential linked to a given word or expression.

Thus, the panchronic onomasiological dictionary related to the conceptual microcategory **FALLEN WOMAN** shall be analysed with the aid of selected elements of cognitive model of language analysis, as developed by Langacker (1987), Taylor (1995) and Kleparski (1997). More precisely, the following elements employed in the earlier *RSDS*-oriented analyses shall be put to practice. First of all, the notion of **conceptual category** is understood here – following Wittgenstein (1953), Rosch (1978), Lakoff (1987) and Taylor (1995) – as embodied in our conceptual systems, which in turn *grow out of bodily experience and make sense in terms of it; moreover, the core of our conceptual systems is directly grounded in perception, body movement, and experience of a physical and social character* (Lakoff 1987:xiv). The general interest of our analysis is the conceptual category **HUMAN BEING**, which – regarding its scope – we shall refer to as a **macrocategory**, and the particular focus is the subtype of the

---

107 This does not mean that the various types of evaluative elements must necessarily appear and thus be taken into account in any case of historical semantic analysis. For a recent study of English material involving aesthetic evaluation, see, for example, Sylwanowicz (2012).

conceptual macrocategory **HUMAN BEING** or, in other words, what shall be referred to as the conceptual **microcategory FALLEN WOMAN**.

As established in the earlier research conducted by Rosch (1978), conceptual categories are characterised by a centrality or salience effect, as well as family resemblance. In a nutshell, the **centre** of the conceptual category comprises the best, that is most salient examples or members of the category, which have a special cognitive status of being prototypical, while the **periphery** of the category include the less representative, and thus, less salient members. And so, for example, as the analysis will reveal, such lexical items as *call-girl* and *courtesan* are best representatives of the subcategory **HETAERA** within the microcategory **FALLEN WOMAN** while *poule-de-luxe* and *grande horizontale* may be said to be less salient exemplars of the species. The theory of **prototypes**, which is employed to a limited degree in the analysis that follows, is the one that dealt the fatal blow to the hitherto prevailng understanding of conceptual structures (see Łozowski 1994).

In offering individual etymological and semantic accounts of category members, here the members of the conceptual microcategory **FALLEN WOMAN**, we shall incorporate the cognitive model of analysis which, as Kleparski (1997:36) puts it, *stresses that semantic structures at all levels may be characterised relative to cognitive domains* or, in the works of *RSDS*, **conceptual domains (CDs)**. To be more specific, the notion of conceptual domains – following Kleparski (1997:36-37) – shall be understood here as *an open set of attributive [here: conceptual] values (or elements), which are specified for different locations within the attributive paths of CDs*. And hence – to visualise the notion with an illustrative example – in the construal of the sense 'streetwalker' of the compound *fling-dust* such **CDs** as **DOMAIN OF SEX [...], DOMAIN OF MORALITY [...]** and **DOMAIN OF SOCIAL STATUS [...]** may be said to be involved for which the following conceptual values are respectively activated, namely <FEMALE$_{[NEU]}$>, <COMMERCIALLY UNCHASTE$_{[NEG]}$> and <LOW$_{[NEG]}$>. In turn, the notion of attributive paths specified for conceptual domains is *viewed as conceptual dimensions along which the meanings of lexical categories are regarded as similar or different* (Kleparski 1997:36).

Yet another part and parcel of the cognitive apparatus employed here is the notion of **entrenchment** which, as specified in Kleparski (1997:37), is understood as the relation or linking of a lexical category to certain locations within conceptual dimensions of a given conceptual domain. The meaning of lexical items in question will be accounted for in terms of **activation** or **highlighting** of certain conceptual values/ elements specifiable for attributive paths within certain conceptual domains. Moreover, for some senses of a word certain conceptual values/

elements are rendered as being **foregrounded**, that is come to be more or the most important, whereas others are or become **backgrounded**, that is are less salient. Take, for example, the semantics of the lexical item *slut* which may be rendered in terms of activating and highlighting of the conceptual element <FILTHY_[NEG]> presupposed for the attributive path of **DOMAIN OF PHYSICAL CHARACTERISTICS AND APPEARANCE [...]** throughout the course of its existence in English, as the word has always been used in the sense 'woman of dirty or untidy appearance'. Additionally, the semantics of *slut* (1450>1881 'woman of a low or loose character; a bold or impudent girl') may be described in terms of necessitating an entrenchment link to **DOMAIN OF CHARACTER AND BEHAVIOUR [...]** for which such negatively charged conceptual values as <BOLD_[NEG]> ^ <IMPUDENT_[NEG]> ^ <LOOSE_[NEG]> are clearly foregrounded. Note that in Present-day English *slut* is used either in the sense 'woman whose sexual behaviour is immoral' or 'woman who looks dirty or untidy', and hence its semantics is accountable in terms of activating and highlighting of the conceptual values <FILTHY_[NEG]>, <LOW_[NEG]> and <IMMORAL_[NEG]> presupposed for the attributive paths of **DOMAIN OF PHYSICAL CHARACTERISTICS AND APPEARANCE [...], DOMAIN OF SOCIAL STATUS [...]** and **DOMAIN OF CHARACTER AND BEHAVIOUR [...]** respectively. Simultaneously, one may speak of backgrounding of the conceptual elements <BOLD_[NEG]> ^ <IMPUDENT_[NEG]> ^ <LOOSE_[NEG]> specifiable for the attributive path of **DOMAIN OF CHARACTER AND BEHAVIOUR [...]**.

3.4 Old English X-phemisms linked to the conceptual category FALLEN WOMAN

The *HTE* records the total of twelve lexical items that were formed in the course of Old English as synonyms variously linked to the conceptual category **FALLEN WOMAN** the body of which comprises *forligerwif, myltestre, portcwene, hóre, beþæcestre, horcwene, firenhicgend, scand, scrætte, scylcen, synnecge* and *cwéne* that are tabled below.

Old English	
Structural Tools	
Compounding	Derivation
forligerwif	*mylt-estre*
portcwene	*be-þæc-estre*
horcwene	*for-ligerwif*
Semantic Tools	
Borrowing	Circumlocution
hóre (O.N.)	*beþæcestre*

		firenhicgend
		portcwene
		synnecge
Rhetorical Tools		
Understatement	Metaphor	Metonymy
quean < cwéne	*myltestre*	*bepæcestre*
firenhicgend	*??scylcen*	*forligerwif*
synnecge		*portcwene*
scand		
portcwene		

Fig. 3.12: Old English synonyms of prostitute.

All those lexical items are – to a varying degree – continued both in form and substance today, either fully as in the case of *hóre*, *portcwene* and *cwéne* or partially, as in the case of *forligerwif*, *myltestre* and *synnecge*. On the other hand, the body of lexical items analysed here includes several O.E. items, the currency of which may be said to have terminated before the advent of Modern English (*scrætte*, *bepæcestre*, *firenhicgend*, *scand* and *scylcen*). From the morphological point of view, the structural tools involved in the process of the formation of synonyms were – most visibly – compounding (O.E. *forligerwif* – Pres.E. 'woman in a lying position',[108] O.E. *portcwene* – a potential form in Pres.E. *portqueen*, and O.E. *horcwene* – Pres.E. lit. 'woman whore') and derivation (O.E. *myltestre* the meaning of which may be defined as 'woman that consumes or is consumed', *bepæcestre* that may be rendered as 'woman that is under a roof', *forligerwif*), which corresponds to the high productivity of these two word-formation processes in the Anglo-Saxon times.

As for semantic tools, we find instances of lexical borrowing, represented by the synonym *hóre*, and circumlocution seen in the rise of such O.E. lexical items as *bepæcestre*, *firenhicgend* (Pres.E. 'person who intends a wicked deed'), *portcwene* and *synnecge* (Pres.E. 'sinner, sinful woman'). Last but not least, rhetorical tools have been involved in the formation of O.E synonyms of *prostitute* in the form of understatement (*quean*, *firenhicgend*, *synnecge* and *scand* Pres.E. 'shame'), metonymy (*bepæcestre*, *forligerwif* and *portcwene*) and what may be labelled as a case of foodsemic metaphor (*myltestre*).

To begin with, the analysis of the morphological structure of the three O.E. compounds, namely *forligerwif*, *portcwene* and *horcwene*, shows that the heads of the compounds are O.E. lexical items linked to the conceptual category **FEMALE HUMAN BEING** since both *wif* and *cwéne* meant, among other senses,

---

[108] The present-day interpretation of O.E *forligerwif* is based on the analysis of the morphological elements involved in the formation of the whole X-phemism.

'woman' at that time. Similarly, in the case of derivation the feminine suffix -*estre* is attached to the roots *mylt* and *bepæc*.

Diachronically, the pejorative development of the words originally used in the sense 'woman' has been evidenced by various historical semanticists, such as Schreuder (1929), Schulz (1975), Kleparski (1990), Kochman-Haładyj (2007a, 2007b) and Kochman-Haładyj and Kleparski (2011). Synchronically, however, one may claim that both the modifiers and the roots employed, that is *forliger*, *port*, *hor*, *mylt* and *bepæc*, contributed to a less negatively-loaded illocutionary force of the whole composite determinants. Let us now concentrate on the sense developments of the modifiers and the roots in question to get the full picture. With regards to any construal of the sense 'prostitute' – for the sake of avoiding redundancy – we shall ignore the fact that any involvement of the conceptual value <FEMALE[NEU]> specified for the attributive path of **DOMAIN OF SEX [...]** presupposes the highlighting of the attributive element <HUMAN[NEU]> for the **DOMAIN OF BEING [...]** because each of the lexical items analysed remains within the limits of the higher-order conceptual category **HUMAN BEING**.

To start with, the lexical item *forligerwif* may be treated as a result of the employment of two structural tools, namely derivation *for-liger* and the process of compounding *forliger-wif*. As to the meaning of the elements involved in the formation of the compound, according to *An Anglo-Saxon Dictionary* (henceforth: the *ASD*), O.E. *forliger* was used in the sense 'fornication'.[109] Hence, the resulting sense of the *forligerwif* compound may be defined as 'woman fornicator' or 'adulteress'. In this manner the form *forligerwif* started to associate diagnostically with the conceptual value <COMMERCIALLY UNCHASTE[NEG]> presupposed for the attributive path of **DOMAIN OF MORALITY [...]**. Interestingly, when we analyse the structure of *forliger* it turns out that the morphemes involved are the prefix *for-* and the root *liger*. As for the former, it is an O.E. prefix which – as Baugh and Cable (2002:181) point out – was employed to intensify the verb or add the element of either destruction or prejudice. The form *leger*, in turn, meant 'lying' or 'place to lie in'. This gives us some ground to assume, with a fair amount of certainty, that the semantics of *forligerwif* may be interpreted as 'woman who is in a lying position, which is destructive' employed in the sense 'prostitute'. As such the word constitutes a historical example of an X-phemism formed by means of a metonymic extension based on a \\POSITION FOR PROFESSION\\ contiguity pattern.

---

109 This sense of *forliger* is evidenced by the following *ASD* quotations:
Se óðer heáfodleahter is gecweden *forliger*. Mod.E. 'The second chief sin is called fornication.'
Ascúnige man swiðe fúle *forligra*. Mod.E. 'Let a man earnestly shun foul fornications.'

The lexical item *cwéne* (Pres.E. *quean*) deserves to be singled out for special attention since it not only came to be employed as a historical synonym of *prostitute* itself, but it also entered two composite determinants, that is *portcwene* and *horcwene* that have also joined the body of lexical items used in the sense 'prostitute' in the history of English. The etymological roots of *cwéne* point to its historically primary sense 'woman' apparently descended from the P.I.E root *$g^u en$-, whose traces are found in many languages of the Indo-European family. Take, for example Gr. *gyne* that may be found in both *gynecology* and *misogynist*, and in the Celtic proper female names *Guinevere* and *Gwendolyn*. The body of descendant forms in other languages includes Pol. *żoná*, Russ. *žená*, Cz. *žena*, Sw. *kvinna*, Da. *kvinde*, Ir.G. *bean*, Per. *zan*, Alb. *zonjë*, which once meant or they still mean 'woman'. Then – in a relatively short span of time – the word *cwéne* deteriorated in meaning, and in Early Middle English started to be used unfavourably with reference to the female kind. The further downfall on the evaluative scale – according to the *OED* – led to the rise of the M.E. sense 'jade, hussy'. In the 16th and 17th centuries the phonologically and morphologically modified form *queane*[110] started to be applied in the sense 'harlot, strumpet'.

As elucidated by Kleparski (1990), both *quean* and *queen* have Germanic roots with O.H.G *quena* and Gothic *kwino* both employed in the sense 'woman'. The representative context to illustrate the differentiation in meaning between the two forms is – following the interpretation by Skeat (2005) – in the text of *P. Plowman* C. ix. 46, where it is said that *in grave all are alike; you cannot there tell a knight from a knave, or a queen from a quean*. The historical co-existence of the two similar forms and the accelerated pejoration of the semantics of *quean* may have contributed to the ultimate evaluative downfall of one of the senses of *queen*, which – at the beginning of the 20th century – started to be employed in slang register in the sense 'the effeminate partner in a homosexual relationship', which meant that the word was associated contextually with the conceptual element <HOMOSEXUAL_{[NEU]}>.

For a better understanding of the involvement of euphemisation processes in the semantic evolution of *quean*, let us outline the stages of its sense development with more precision providing contextual evidence from the *OED* to make the picture complete. The historically primary sense of O.E. *cwéne* 'woman' is

---

110 As the *OED* informs us, in the course of M.E. the phonological outline of the word *quene* changed in order to differentiate it from the pronunciation of the form *queen*. The distinctive element of the pronunciation of M.E. *quene* was its open *e* denoted by the spelling *ei* or *ey*, and later by *ea*.

first recorded in the *OED* at the beginning of the 11th century and is evidenced with the following quotes:

a1000 Ic wæs fæmne ʒeong, feaxhar *cwene*.[111]
a1023 þæt..ane *cwenan* ʒ emænum ceape bicʒað..and wið þa ane fylðe andreoʒað.[112]

During the Middle English period the original meaning of *quean* 'woman' started to link with the conceptual elements <BOLD[NEG]> ^ <ILL-BEHAVED[NEG]>. These values specifiable for **DOMAIN OF CHARACTER AND BEHAVIOUR [...]** became prominent already in Early Middle English. This led to the rise of the restricted sense 'jade, hussy', which is documented in the following *OED* material:

c1205 Whær swa heo funden æine mon..þa *quenen* [c1275 *cwenes*] lude loʒen.[113]
c1290 An olde *quene* þare was biside, strong hore and baudestrote.[114]
↕
1969 Nora (an old *quean* who thinks she's an old queen).

The next stage in the semantic evolution of *quean* may – after Kleparski (1990:100) – be referred to as the phase of moral pejoration since the lexical item came to be used in the sense 'harlot, strumpet' in the second half of the 16th century. Here, one observes the activation of the conceptual element <COMMERCIALLY UNCHASTE[NEG]> presupposed for the attributive path of **DOMAIN OF MORALITY [...]**. This period in the semantic history of *quean* is of particular interest to us as – with a fair degree of certainty – we may postulate that it was at that time that the form *quean* became a euphemistic synonym of *prostitute* resultant from the application of the mechanism of understatement. Somewhat speculatively, one may conjecture that, for a period of time, language users tended to employ the form *quean* in its earlier sense 'bold, impudent woman' to refer to a prostitute, refraining from calling a spade a spade, and then extralinguistic hypocrisy acted as a gentlewoman in the rise of euphemistic *quean* 'prostitute'.

The semantic story of the word *quean* does not end at the outset of the Early Modern English period, but rather the word undergoes further sense modification in the early 20th century when it starts to be employed in the sense 'male homosexual of effeminate appearance'. The rise of this novel sense may be pictured in terms of activation of the conceptual elements <MALE[NEU]> as well as <HOMOSEXUAL[NEU]> and, hence one may speak of a radical change as to the set of attributive values within **DOMAIN OF SEX [...]** and **DOMAIN OF**

---

111 Mod.E. 'I was a young woman, a hoary-headed prostitute.'
112 Mod.E. 'that...a common prostitute they buy cheap and with her then commit impurity.'
113 Mod.E. 'wherever they found a man, there were prostitutes put up loudly.'
114 Mod.E. 'An old prostitute was there besides, a strong whore and madam.'

SEXUALITY [...] respectively. This shift of meaning is evidenced by the following *OED* quotations:

> 1935 We did hear startling tales... of 'family' life, of marriage ceremonies, of fights with knives for the favor of some *'quean'*, as the perverts are called in prison.
> 1968 I did not want him to think me 'queer' and himself a part of homosexuality, a term I disliked as it included prostitutes, pansies, pouffs and *queans*.

Furthermore, it needs to be stressed that in the case of this sense of *quean* one can also speak of activation of the conceptual elements <EFFEMINATE$_{[NEG]}$> ^ <GIRLISH$_{[NEU]}$> presupposed for the attributive path of **DOMAIN OF CHARACTER AND BEHAVIOUR [...]**. Interestingly, the sense 'homosexual' became restricted when, according to Partridge (1984), the word *quean* was employed in the sense 'ageing passive homosexual' in prison slang in the second half of the 20th century. In order to account for this sense-thread of the word, apart from the activation of such conceptually central elements as <MALE$_{[NEU]}$> and <HOMOSEXUAL$_{[NEU]}$> presupposed for the attributive paths of **DOMAIN OF SEX [...]** and **DOMAIN OF SEXUALITY [...]** we may speak of an entrenchment link to the attributive paths of the peripheral **DOMAIN OF CHARACTER AND BEHAVIOUR [...]** and **DOMAIN OF AGE [...]** for which the values <PASSIVE$_{[NEG]}$> and <AGEING$_{[NEG]}$> respectively are brought to the fore.

When we scrutinise the semantics of the O.E. compound ***portcwene***, the **CD**s that seem to be cognitively central for the construal of its sense are those of **DOMAIN OF SEX [...]** and **DOMAIN OF LOCATION [...]** for which such evaluatively neutral values as <FEMALE$_{[NEU]}$> and <PORT$_{[NEU]}$> are activated. The resultant semantic interpretation of the compound is that of 'port woman', which only vaguely – given the extralinguistic reality of many European cities – suggests its negatively loaded O.E. sense 'prostitute'. However, only when we take into account the extralinguistic information that ports were – or rather have always been – harbouring places for all types of shady dealings and services, including those offered by the oldest profession, do we realise that O.E. *portcwene* may have been simply an auspicious term rather than a direct appellation. Hence, one may postulate that the compound euphemism *portcwene* is the result of the working of the mechanism of metonymy based on the \\LOCATION FOR PROFESSION\\ contiguity. Note that the same mechanism may have been to be at work in such cases as Pres.E. *nymph of the pavement* or Pol. *ulicznica* 'streetwalker'.[115]

---

115 Other names of professions outside the conceptual category **FALLEN WOMAN** that also represent the working of the metonymic extension \\LOCATION FOR PROFESSION\\ include such words as Pol. *rolnik* 'farmer' or *drogowiec* 'road worker'.

Finally, the last of the three O.E. compounds listed here, **horcwene**, is made up of two elements *hóre* and *cwéne*, the latter of which was discussed in the section above. As for the former, that is **hóre**, its etymological roots go back to the close of the Anglo-Saxon times when, according to the *OED*, *hóre* was adopted directly from O.N. *hóra*. It seems that – from the very beginning of the history of the word – its semantics has been associated with such a conceptual value as <COMMERCIALLY UNCHASTE[NEG]> since it was borrowed already appended with the sense 'prostitute', most probably together with other derivational formations such as O.N *hór* 'adultery' and O.N. *hórkona*. Surprisingly, however, the ultimate origin of O.E. *hóre* goes back to the P.I.E root **qār-* which gave rise to Lat. *cārus* 'dear',[116] O.Ir. *cara* 'friend' and *caraim* 'I love'. Hence, it seems that at one point in time – most probably at some pre-Anglo-Saxon stage – the form that became the historical synonym of *prostitute* was linked to the conceptual value <LOVING[POS]> presupposed for the attributive path of **DOMAIN OF CHARACTER AND BEHAVIOUR [...]**. The fact that the O.E. form *hóre* entered the Anglo-Saxon word stock with the sense 'prostitute' may imply that the process of euphemisation had already been completed and the euphemism had been lexicalised with the negatively loaded value <IMMORAL[NEG]>. This early sense of *hóre* is evidenced by the following *OED* material:

a1100 *Prostituta pellax*, i. meretrix quæ prostat, i. mendax, leas fyrnhicʒe, *hore*.
c1200 ʒef þu... best rumhanded and to glewmen and to *hores*.

At this point one may draw a tentative conclusion that the auspicious illocutionary force of the Latinate borrowing *cārus* may have as well stimulated the abundance of cognate forms in the whole Germanic world, exemplified by such words as G. *hure*, Du. *hoer*, Sw. *hora* and Da. *hore*, all of which evolved – according to Ayto (2005) – from the prehistoric Germanic form **khōrōn*. Obviously, from the present-day perspective the word *whore* has little – if anything – to do with positively sounding overtones and, thus, fails to meet the necessary conditions of a euphemism, but rather, it seems to be a perfect example of a dysphemism.

The next stage in the semantic development of *hóre* is marked by the generalization of meaning when, in the early 13th century, the word started to be applied in the sense 'unchaste, lewd woman'. This generalised meaning may be accounted for in terms of activation of the conceptual value <LEWD[NEG]> presupposed for the attributive path of **DOMAIN OF CHARACTER AND BEHAVIOUR [...]**. The *OED* also informs us that the use of the word *hóre*, employed in the generalised sense was accompanied by a possessive determiner *his*

---

116 According to Ayto (2005) and the *OED*, Lat. *cārus* is the source of Mod.E. *caress* and *charity*.

to refer to a concubine or a kept mistress, in a way strengthening the commodity-for-sale attitude towards the referents expressed by the prominence of <COMMERCIALLY UNCHASTE$_{[NEG]}$> attributive value. The following *OED* quotations provide historical evidence of this sense extension:

> c1205 Nes nan swa god wif i þon londe þe he walde... þet he ne makede *hore*.
> 1297 A fol womman in spousbruche he huld vnder is wif. Sein dunston him sede wel þat it was a luþer lif... Wroþ was þe king & is *hore* þat he *hor* folie wiþsede.
> ↕
> 1817 Calling a married woman or a single one a *whore* is not actionable, because fornication and adultery are subjects of spiritual not temporal censures.

Interestingly, the early-17th-century historical data points to the emergence of yet another sense of *hóre* based on an analogy of senses. The rise of the sense 'male prostitute' involves the replacement of the conceptual value <FEMALE$_{[NEU]}$> with the conceptual value <MALE$_{[NEU]}$> both of which are presupposed for the attributive path of **DOMAIN OF SEX [...]**. This historical sense is evidenced by the following *OED* material:[117]

> 1633 He that affronts Me, is the sonne of a Worme, and his father a *Whoore*.
> ↕
> 1906 Gig Young can play the top *whore* in 'The Killer Elite' because his sad eyes suggest that he has no expectations and no illusions left about anything.

The view that prevails in lexicographic sources is that the lexical item *whore* is one of few dysphemisms that has remained in full power over the ages. As Hughes (2006:493) observes, *[...] other strong terms like **bitch**, **bastard**, and **bugger** have all acquired humorous, ironic, or jocular tones, but **whore** remains powerfully condemning. [...] The emotive power of **whore** also explains the need for a steady supply of euphemisms [...]*. The tendency to avoid the heavily loaded term in question may, at least partially, answer the question of why about 500 terms have appeared in the history of the English language to serve as euphemistic or dysphemistic synonyms onomasiologically linked to the conceptual microcategory **FALLEN WOMAN**.

As for the employment of the mechanism of derivation, apart from the O.E. synonym *forligerwif* analysed in the foregoing, the remaining lexical items belonging to this category of tools are O.E. *myltestre* and O.E. *bepæcestre*. Both *myltestre* and *bepæcestre* are not only derivationally complex forms, but are also the products of rhetorical mechanisms, namely metaphor and metonymy respectively. Moreover, the form *bepæcestre* may be treated as an instance of circumlocution.

---

[117] It is worth noting at this point that the present-day spelling *wh-* has been in use, as observed by Ayto (2005) and the *OED*, since the 16th century.

Morphologically, ***myltestre*** is composed of a root followed by a suffix, which here takes the form of *mylt* followed by *-estre*. A closer inspection of the etymology of the O.E. suffix *-estre* reveals that – as the *ASD* informs us – it is, like *-istre* and *-ystre*, a feminine suffix added to nouns of action. Corresponding forms in other languages include Latin *-ix* and Pres.E. *-ess*. As to the O.E. base *mylt*, the *ASD* reports that the root is *meltan* used in the Anglo-Saxon times in the sense 'melt, become liquid, be consumed, dissolved'.[118]

Taking the characteristics of the O.E. suffix *-estre* into account, together with the sense of the base *mylt*, one may attempt the semantic analysis of the whole derivative in question. A rather straightforward interpretation of the semantics of O.E. *mylt-estre* is 'woman that consumes or is consumed', and thus the word may constitute a lexical representation of the very well evidenced conceptual metaphor SEX IS CONSUMPTION. This metaphorical sense of Anglo-Saxon *myltestre* is documented by the following *ASD* quotation:

ASD Ne læt ðu ðine dohtor beón *myltestre*.

The realisation of the conceptual metaphor verbalised as SEX IS CONSUMPTION in the Anglo-Saxon lexicon might constitute yet another proof for the universality of the cognitive mechanism of foodsemy recently discussed in Kleparski (2008, 2013). Yet, it is virtually impossible to decide whether the illocutionary force of O.E. *myltestre* was decisively positive or negative. Therefore, one is tempted to resort to employing the most general label introduced in *Chapter 1* – an X-phemism.

In turn, the O.E. ***beþæcestre*** seems to be internally more complex as its morphological structure involves both the prefix *be-* and the suffix *-estre* attached to the root *þæc*. The interpretation of the meaning of the O.E. prefix *be-* in the context of the derivative in question is far less obvious than the construal of the suffix *-estre*. According to the *ASD*, the most plausible meaning of the prefix *be-* here equals the sense of Pres.E. preposition *by* or – as Mitchell and Robinson (2012:58) interpret it – O.E. *be-* corresponds to Pres.E. *about*. The semantic value of both affixes present here coupled with the base *þæc* 'roof'[119] can be rendered in Pres.E. as 'woman that is about/under a roof'. Speculative as it may sound, it may be assumed that the employment of *þæc* 'roof' is an instance of a *pars pro toto* extension, whereby a roof is used as a representative part of the whole building.

One may risk a conjecture that O.E. *beþæcestre* in a way corresponds semantically to ancient Gr. *oikema worker* 'little house worker'. Note that this in-

---

118 This meaning is exemplified with the following *ASD* quotations:
Ne sceal ánes hwæt *meltan*. Mod.E. 'Be consumed on the pile'.
119 This sense is evidenced by the following *ASD* material:
Gé þearfum forwyrndon, ðæt hi under eówrum *þæce* mósten in gebúgan.

terpretation places the synonym *bepæcestre* among lexical realisations of the mechanism of metonymy based on a different type of contiguity; that is \\LOCATION FOR PROFESSION\\ type. Yet, one may pursue another way of tomographing the essence of O.E. *bepæcestre*, and treat it as a case of circumlocution. After all, hinting that a woman is located under a roof most certainly had no direct connotation with prostitution in Anglo-Saxon times. Only when a roofed location coincided with the appropriate context did it become clear that the activation of the conceptual value <COMMERCIALLY UNCHASTE$_{[NEG]}$> was there for all to see. Unfortunately, one is reduced to speculations as to the illocutionary force of O.E. synonym *bepæcestre*. On the one hand, it seems that – much in the same way as most synecdochic extensions – *bepæcestre* was linked to certain negative connotations. On the other hand, the possible involvement of the mechanism of circumlocution may suggest the presence of positive overtones attached to the use of *bepæcestre*.

Likewise, O.E. ***firenhicgend*** may have resulted from the process of circumlocution, judging by the semantics of the constitutive elements involved. As the *ASD* explains, O.E. *firen* was used primarily in the sense 'wicked deed, crime, sin'[120] while O.E. *hycgan* served to convey the sense 'direct the mind' or 'be intent upon'.[121] Hence, the sense of the morphologically complex *firenhicgend* may be interpreted as 'that who intends a wicked deed, a sin', and – as such – can hardly be qualified as a direct appellation. What is more, the fact that the sense of *firnhicgend* associated with the conceptual value <COMMERCIALLY UNCHASTE$_{[NEG]}$> makes it a suitable candidate for a representative of the mechanism of understatement. Here, like with several Anglo-Saxon synonyms of *prostitute*, it is difficult to say whether the concept of a wicked intention served euphemistic or dysphemistic purposes.

There is yet another O.E. synonym that bears a strong sense resemblance to the compound *firenhicgend*. According to the *ASD*, in Anglo-Saxon times **synnecge** was used in the sense 'sinner, sinful woman', which may be evidenced with the following quotation:

ASD Seó [Mary Magdalen] wæs ærest *synnecge*.

One has grounds to believe that the employment of O.E. *synnecge* in the sense 'prostitute' was an instance of a combination of the working of circumlocution on the one hand, and the mechanism of understatement on the other. Yet, the

---

120   The *ASD* exemplifies this sense of *firen* with the following quotation:
       Nú eft gewearþ flæsc *firena* leás. Mod.E. 'Flesh is again become void of sins'.
121   This meaning of *hycgan* is evidenced by the following *ASD* material:
       Hió *hogde* georne ðæt hire mægþhád clǽne geheólde. Mod.E. 'She earnestly determined to keep her maidenhood pure'.

question that remains to be answered is that of whether *synnecge* was used as an auspicious or rather an offensive term.

Likewise, the body of historical data featuring the mechanism of understatement includes O.E *scand* employed chiefly in the sense 'shame'. Yet, according to the *HTE*, the word is a representative of a body of historical synonyms onomasiologically related to the conceptual category **FALLEN WOMAN**. As the *ASD* reports, in Anglo-Saxon times *sceand* served to encode the sense 'shame, disgrace, infamy' and – as such – could be employed in the female-specific evaluatively pregnant sense 'prostitute'. However, the illocutionary force of the word remains somewhat blurry.

Last but not least, there are two synonyms recorded in the *HTE* files which are a problem to any analytic treatment. Firstly, there is O.E. *scylcen* used in the sense 'shield' that could also be employed in the secondary meaning 'prostitute', and this case is rather difficult to classify into any of the categories of X-phemism formation mechanisms. The only feasible path of interpretation is the hypothesis that – in the case at hand – a metaphoric extension was at work in the rise of this Anglo-Saxon synonym of *prostitute*. Here, one could venture forth the claim that the metaphorical schema SEX IS FIGHT/WAR stands behind the employment of *scylcen* 'shield' as a source for the sense 'prostitute'.

The discussion of conceptual metaphor (see section 1.2.3) shows that the working of the metaphor SEX IS FIGHT/WAR[122] is observable in the metaphorical employment of such words as *sword*, *weapon* and *pole* in the sense 'penis' and *wound*, *cut*, *scar* in the sense 'vagina'. Interestingly, the clear contrast seems to obtain here in the conceptualisation of male as the attacker (and hence victimizer), and female as the attacked (and hence victimised). The employment of the concept of SHIELD alters the traditional role in the conceptualisation schema discussed here, because the referent marked as female is no longer a victim, but rather turns into an armed defender. Finally, another problematic Anglo-Saxon lexical item is ***scrætte***, which is recorded in the body of *HTE* as a historical synonym

---

[122] The fact that the concepts WAR and FIGHT show a close conceptual link with the concept DEATH seems relatively obvious, but it might seem somewhat surprising that sex may be conceptualised in terms of death. However, the *OED* data provides evidence that in the late 16th century the verb *die* began to be employed in the sense 'experience a sexual orgasm', and hence constituted a lexical realisation of the conceptual metaphor SEX IS DYING. The following *OED* quotations testify to this sense of *die*:
1599 Claudio. Nay, but I know who loues him… and in despight of all, *dies* for him. Prince. Shee shall be buried with her face vpwards.
1673 Now *die*, my Alexis, and I will *die* too.
↕
1974 Come let me love you… let me *die* in your arms.

of *prostitute*. However, there is no such entry in the *ASD*, and thus no data or hints are available as to the interpretation of *scrætte* in terms of the processes involved in the formation of the O.E. *prostitute* synonym. What is somewhat surprising – when we take into account the entirety of the Old English data – is that out of twelve synonyms recorded in the *HTE* only *scrætte* is of utterly obscure origin, and thus can hardly be classified under any of the X-phemism formation labels.

In an attempt to draw a contrastive parallel, let us point to the fact that in Polish, there are synonyms of *prostitute* which are – to some extent – cognitive equivalents of O.E synonyms. Take, for example, the semantics of Pol. *nierządnica* (lit. 'she that goes against rules' > 'harlot'), which may be said to correspond to O.E. *firenhicgend* 'that who intends a wicked deed', and Pol. *mewka* (lit. 'seagull' > '(sea-resort) prostitute') conjures somewhat similar connotations as O.E. *portcwene* (lit. 'port woman'). In turn, Pol. archaisms *grzesznica* and *nałożnica* seem to be direct semantic equivalents of O.E. *synnecge* ('sinner' > 'erring sister') and *forligerwif* ('she that is in a lying position' > 'illicit bed companion') respectively. Finally, Pol. *bezwstydnica* (lit. 'without shame' > 'morally shameless woman'), to some extent, corresponds conceptually to O.E. *scand* 'shame'. The question that remains unanswered so far is whether the conceptualisation of prostitution in terms of foregrounding of such values as <PORT <CONNECTED[NEU]>>, <WRONGDOING[NEG]>, <SINFUL[NEG]>, <SHAMEFUL[NEG]> or <LYING[NEU]> is universally comprehensible. It goes without saying that in order to verify this one would have to engage in the task of analysing historical female specific data from various subgroups of Indo-European family of languages.

3.5 Middle English X-phemisms linked to the conceptual category FALLEN WOMAN

Although, as shown by a number of studies dedicated to the problem of moral pejoration in the history of English, such as Kleparski (1990, 1997), Kochman-Haładyj and Kleparski (2011), there has been a particular growth of female-specific negatively loaded words, it is surprising to unearth the fact that throughout the Middle English period only a few synonyms enriched the body of lexical items linked to the conceptual category **FALLEN WOMAN**. Quantitatively speaking, the resemblance between the Old English and Middle English periods is relatively strong. However, the types of mechanisms involved in the formation of the synonyms are slightly different, which is shown in *Figure 3.13* given below.

Middle English
Structural Tools

Compounding	Clipping
common woman	?? bawd < bawdstrot
tickle-tail	wench < wenchel
Semantic Tools	
Borrowing	
pute (Fr.)	
putain (Fr.)	
?? strumpet (Lat./ Du.)	
(harlot) (Fr.)	
common (Fr.)	
?? bawd (Fr.)	
Rhetorical Tools		
Understatement	Metaphor	Metonymy
common woman	?? slut	?? strumpet
common	(filth)	
wenchel/ wench		

Fig. 3.13: Middle English synonyms of prostitute.

The analysis of the material tabled above shows that out of the corpus of eleven synonyms arising during the Middle English period six were incorporated into the English word stock through the process of borrowing (*strumpet* from Latin), mostly from French (*pute, putain, harlot, common, bawd*). Two of them were formed by means of the process of compounding (*common woman, tickle-tail*), another two with the help of the mechanism of back-clipping (*wench < wenchel, bawd < bawdstrot*), and two more by means of the mechanism of metaphor (*slut, filth*). It is worth mentioning that the rise of several M.E. synonyms of *prostitute* can be attributed to more than one category of formation mechanisms. Thus, for instance in the case of M.E. *common woman* one may speak about the working of the process of compounding coupled with the mechanism of understatement and borrowing. Likewise, M.E. *strumpet* can be treated as a combined lexical realisation of the working of the mechanisms of borrowing and metonymy.

3.5.1 Middle English synonyms and structural tools

Let us start with the semantic history of M.E. **common woman**, the origins of which go back to the very beginning of the 14th century when – as the *OED* reports – the form *co(m)mun* was adopted from O.Fr. *comun*[123] employed in the

---

[123] According to the *OED*, O.Fr. *comun* was formed from *com-* 'together' and *-mūnis* 'bound, under obligation' and, as Ayto (2005) observes, apart from developing into O.E. *co(m)mun*, either Lat. *commūnis* or O.Fr. *comun* gave the basis for a number of

sense 'of general, public, or non-private nature'. This historically original sense of *common* is exemplified by the following *OED* material:

> 1300 To pastur *commun* þei laght þe lend.
> ↓
> 1543-4 The greate Turke, *common* enemy of all christendome.
> 1875 [They] have no *common* ground.

Significantly, though somewhat surprisingly, the *OED* data shows that – at exactly the same time – the O.E. adjective *commun* started to collocate habitually with the noun *woman*, and the combination of both served to express the sense 'harlot'. As the *OED* elucidates, this sense of the whole composite determinant may have developed from the application of the adjective *common* employed in the sense 'existing for the use of the public'. Hence, the one who was referred to by the syntagma a *common woman* was the one who was available to any man that wanted her – in other words publicly available – and not the property of one man only. One may therefore assume, with a decent amount of certainty, that the application of the adjective *commun* in the sense 'harlot', may – in fact – have served some sort of concealing purposes, and formed a euphemistic synonym of *whore* through the mechanism of understatement. From the cognitive perspective, the employment of the M.E. form *commun* in the sense 'harlot' may be handled in terms of the activation of the evaluatively laden conceptual value <COMMERCIALLY UNCHASTE_{[NEG]}> presupposed for the attributive path of **DOMAIN OF MORALITY [...]**. The euphemistic use of the compound is evidenced by the following *OED* quotations:

> 1300 Siþen [Sampson] went vntil a tun Til a wijf þat was *commun*.
> c1440 There she was a *Comyn woman*, and toke all that wolde come.
> ↕
> 1875 The *common prostitute* rarely has any offspring.

Interestingly, according to the *HTE*, it took merely three decades for the second element of the discussed syntagma, *woman*, to be disposed of and for *common* to acquire – on its own – the sense 'prostitute'. However, as modern lexicographic sources, such as the *ODE*, *Longman Dictionary of Contemporary English* (henceforth: *LDCE*), *Oxford Dictionaries Online* (henceforth: *ODO*) and *Macmillan English Dictionary* (henceforth: *MED*) report, neither the adjective nor the noun *common* are currently employed in the sense 'prostitute'.

Most dictionaries that have been consulted stress another dominant feature of the sense of a *common woman*, namely its position on the social ladder and social perception scale. The conceptual value that seems to be clearly fore-

---

Mod.E. lexical items, such as *community*, *communion*, *communicate*, *commune* or *communism*.

grounded is the value <LOW_{[NEG]}> presupposed for the attributive path of **DOMAIN OF SOCIAL STATUS [...]**. As *The Slang of Sin* (henceforth: *SS*) informs us, Shakespeare coined the modified form ***commoner*** specialised in the sense 'low prostitute'. The *OED* evidences the development of this modified form and its sense at the turn of the 16th and 17th centuries and provides the following quotations as the evidence:

1601 O behold this ring... He gaue it to a *Commoner* a'th Campe If I be one.
↕
1695 What think you of that noble *commoner* Mrs. Drab?

Curiously enough, the inventiveness of language users went much further as the original form was modified into ***public commoner*** and ***community***, which were first employed – according to the *HTE* – at the start of the 17th century (1604 Oh, thou publicke *Commoner*; 1606 One of these painted *communities*, that are ravisht with Coaches and upper hands). Like in the previous cases, the rise of the 17th-century synonyms of *prostitute* may – among others – be characterised in terms of activation of the conceptual value <LOW_{[NEG]}> presupposed for the attributive path of **DOMAIN OF SOCIAL STATUS [...]**.

Another M.E. synonym of *prostitute* which underwent a number of structural modifications is the compound ***tickle-tail***. It was first recorded in the first half of the 15th century (see the *OED*) in the sense 'loose or wanton woman', and its rise involves the activation of the conceptual value <LOOSE_{[NEG]}> presupposed for the attributive path of **DOMAIN OF MORALITY [...]**. The following *OED* quotation testifies to this short-lived sense of *tickle-tail*:

1430 Canst thou no better come to holynesse, Than lese thiself al for a *tikel~taylle*?

Interestingly, neither the *OED* nor the *HTE* treats *tickle-tail* as a historical synonym of *prostitute*, but there are other sources, such as Schulz (1975), Partridge (1984) and Green (2003), which portray the rise of the discussed sense of *tickle-tail* in terms of activation of the conceptual value <COMMERCIALLY UNCHASTE_{[NEG]}> presupposed for the attributive path of **DOMAIN OF MORALITY [...]**. The rise and semantic development of this early compound, as well as its later modified E.Mod.E. variants, such as *wagtail, tub-tail,*[124] *open-tail,*[125]

---

[124] As the *OED* reports, the form *tub-tail* was used in the late 16th century in the contemptuous sense 'one who wears a farthingale or a hooped skirt', and the *HTE* places *tub-tail* under the label UNCHASTITY. As a result, through the mechanism of metonymy based on the \\ITEM OF CLOTHING FOR A PERSON\\ contiguity pattern *tub-tail* was used in the sense 'unchaste woman'. Unfortunately, no other lexicographic sources seem to confirm the employment of *tub-tail* as a historical synonym of *prostitute*.

mar-tail and *tail* itself most of which are characterised by the presence of the conceptual value <COMMERCIALLY UNCHASTE[NEG]> need all be explained in terms of the semantic evolution of *tail*. This is due to the fact that in each case – that is in the semantics of all the lexical coinages enumerated above – the sense of *tail* forms the semantic core of the resultant meaning.

First things first, the etymological roots of *tail* go back to the early 9th century when – as the *OED* reports – the word was employed in the sense 'the posterior extremity of an animal, forming a flexible appendage to the trunk, or the continuation of the trunk'. This original sense extended metaphorically at the outset of the 14th century to yield the sense 'the lower and hinder part of the human body' or 'the fundament, buttocks, backside'. The extension of meaning discussed here seems to be the outcome of the application of a highly general conceptual metaphor, namely A HUMAN BEING IS AN ANIMAL, through which a conceptual mapping is made between **DOMAIN OF ANIMAL BODY PART [...]** and **DOMAIN OF HUMAN BODY PART [...]**.[126]

One may suppose that the metaphorically extended meaning of *tail* formed the basis for the later employment of the word *tail* in isolation, or as the head of composite formations (*wagtail* and *mar-tail*) in the sense either 'loose woman' or 'prostitute'. To be more precise, however, it needs to be acknowledged that the mechanism of *pars pro toto* metonymic extension may have been at work in the formation of *tail* and its derivatives as historical synonyms of *prostitute*, whereby the name of a body part was used to refer to a person as a whole.[127] Interestingly, from the chronological point of view, morphologically complex forms, such as *wagtail* and *mar-tail*, were in use by the end of the 16th and at the beginning of the 17th centuries respectively, though it was not until the middle of the 19th century that the form *tail* itself started to be employed in the evaluatively tinted sense 'prostitute'. A number of lexicographic sources, such as Partridge (1984), Green (2003) and Holder (2008), seem to agree on the derogatory overtones linked to the form *tail* and its various historical derivatives, thus confirming the dysphemistic status of most metonymically triggered lexical items. It is worth noting that modern lexicographic sources that have been consulted, such

---

125 According to the *OED*, the form *open-tail* was a rare 17th century application of the sense 'light, indelicate or unchaste woman', and thus in fact failed to function as a historical synonym of *prostitute*.
126 The metaphorical schema A HUMAN BEING IS AN ANIMAL forms the axis of a number of analyses of such authors as Kiełtyka (2007, 2008, 2011) and Kleparski (2008, 2013).
127 For a recent analysis of this issue, see among others, Kopecka (2011) and Więcławska (2012).

as *LDCE*, *ODO* and *MED*, include in their macrostructure *tail* with the sense 'women collectively regarded in sexual terms'.

As for the two clipped forms coined in the Middle English period, let us start with **bawd** as an instance of lexical borrowing coupled with the mechanism of clipping. First of all, it needs to be stressed that the process of pejoration of the word was relatively slow. Although *bawd* had already surfaced in the Middle English period in the sense 'one employed in pandering to sexual debauchery; go-between, pander', the word acquired the status of a historical synonym of *prostitute* only in Late Modern English. As the *OED* informs us, the origin of the form *bawd* lies in obscurity, but has little or nothing to do with O.Fr. *baud*, *baude* 'lively, gay, merry'. However, both Rawson (1989) and Ayto (2005) provide the O.Fr. adjective *baud(e)* as a possible root for M.E. *bawd* borrowed from French. Moreover, both authors trace the origin of the lexical item further back to O.H.G *bald* which may have been the source of Pres.E. *bald*. Interestingly, Holder (2008) argues that the original meaning of *bawd* was 'dirty', but fails to account for the source or the time frames of this meaning development.

Yet, another etymological hypothesis ventured by both the *OED* and Rawson (1989) is the claim that M.E. *bawd* originated as a clipped form from M.E. **bawdstrot** adopted from O.Fr. *baudetrot*. These early occurrences of *bawdstrot* and *bawd* are evidenced by the following *OED* quotations:

1362 And eke be þi *Bawde*, and Bere wel þin ernde.
1483 Thenne Vago his *bawde* wente in to his preuy chamber.
↕
1842 A vile, shameless *bawd*, Whose craft was to deceive the young and fair.

However, as most lexicographic sources seem to confirm, the M.E. nominal form *bawd* was originally employed mainly with reference to male procurers, and thus its original semantics must be accounted for in terms of activation of the conceptual value <MALE$_{[NEG]}$> presupposed for the attributive path of **DOMAIN OF SEX [...]**. The second quotation listed above shows that the conceptual value <FEMALE$_{[NEU]}$> gained prominence in certain contexts featuring the sense 'procuress'. According to the *OED*, Schulz (1975), Rawson (1989) and Hughes (2006), the form *bawd* underwent the process of feminization as after 1700 the word has appeared with almost exclusively female applications. Likewise, Schulz (1975) and Rawson (1989) report that from the 18th century onwards *bawd* was used in the sense either 'female prostitute' or 'female keeper of a brothel'. However, neither *MED* nor *LDCE* confirms the existence of the form *bawd* and the sense 'female prostitute' in the Pres.E. word stock and the only reminder present in English today is the adjective *bawdy* currently employed in the sense 'about sex' present in such collocations as *bawdy jokes* or *bawdy* *songs*. In turn, *ODO* lists the entry *bawd*, which is labelled as *archaic*, and the definition of the sense associated with the word is 'female keeper of a brothel'.

As for the illocutionary force evoked by *bawd*, it appears that from the very beginning of its existence in the English lexicon it has had a commercially sexual connotation, and thus one may stipulate that it may be labelled as an orthophemism with neither positive nor negative illocutionary potential. This might imply that it was the form *bawd* that triggered the formation of cover terms which either had more auspicious or more derogatory overtones linked to them.

In turn, the clipped form **wench**, as well as its original base **wenchel** can boast a more classic history of female-specific semantic degeneration. The form *wenchel* – the earlier of the two – came into being in the 9th century when it was used in the sense 'child of either sex', but it soon developed a novel historical meaning, that is 'servant, slave'; the semantic change discussed here exemplifies what Kleparski (1990) calls social pejoration. During its later history in English the semantics of *wenchel* evolved further, and the 14th-century quotation provides tangible evidence that moral pejoration was the next stage in the meaning evolution of *wenchel*; then the word started to be employed in the morally evaluatively loaded sense 'prostitute':

> c1300 His Cardynals were þeraȝen þat he his dignete gan reue Wiþ *wenclen* [*S. Eng. Leg.* 89/96 fole wummen] forto go.

Likewise, the semantics of the clipped derivative *wench* may be said to have undergone semantic downfall on the evaluative scale over time. Its historically original sense 'girl, young woman' suffered both social and moral pejoration and the following *OED* quotations exemplify the historically original sense of *wench*:

> c1290 Nou is þis… gret schame…to sende a-boute…After þe gretteste Maistres, forto despuyti a-ȝen a fol *wenche*.
> a1450 The cryed þe fende and sayde: 'Alas,… al my myȝt ys lorne, now such a ȝeong *wench* hath ouercomen me'.
> ↕
> 1895 For she was ever the most spirity *wench* in the world.

Significantly, the stage of moral pejoration occurred in a relatively short span of time, because already in the middle of the 14th century *wench* had started to be employed in the sense 'wanton woman, mistress', especially in such M.E. collocations as *a common wench, a light wench, a wanton wench* or *a wench of the stews*. For this sense development one may thus speak of an entrenchment link to **DOMAIN OF MORALITY [...]** for which the conceptual value <COM-

MERCIALLY UNCHASTE[NEG]> is brought to the fore. The following *OED* quotations testify to this sense-thread of *wench* and *wench*-based collocations:

1362 Ermytes on an hep wiþ hoteide staues, Wenten to Walsyngham & here *wenchis* aftir.
1377 *Wenches of þe stuwes.*
c1386 I am a gentil womman and no *wenche*.
1390 Envie... Is of the Court the *comun wenche*.
1590 Nay, she is worse, she is the diuels dam: And here she comes in the habit of a *light wench*.
↕
1781 8 May, Chief Justice -, who loved a *wench*, summed up favourably, and she was acquitted.

Seemingly of primary importance, though, is the fact that the *OED* account fails to include the sense 'prostitute' in the polysemous structure of M.E. *wench*. However, both Schulz (1975) and Rawson (1989) place *wench* among historical synonyms of *prostitute*. This is justified on morphological and phraseological grounds because *wench*, like *woman*, entered a number of historical compounds (*common wench, wanton wench*), as well as phraseological formations (*wench of the stews*, and later *wench of the game*[128]), the semantics of which evoked clearly commercial connotations linked to female sexual conduct. One may thus assume – with a fair degree of certainty – that M.E. *wench* with the sense 'girl/woman of low morals' was in fact contextually employed as a euphemism, through the mechanism of understatement, in the sense 'prostitute'. The euphemistic nature of *wench* is also evidenced by such modern lexicographic sources as *MED* and *ODO*, which inform us that the word is a historical synonym of *prostitute*, but place the label *archaic* next to the evaluatively loaded sense.

3.5.2 Middle English synonyms and semantic tools

Let us now turn to the semantic tools employed in the formation of M.E. synonyms, among which one may discern only one process at work, namely borrowing. An example by all means worth scrutinising is the history of M.E. ***putain*** and its later variants realised as ***pute, putanie*** and ***puta***. According to the *OED*, the word goes back ultimately to the Latin form *pūtida* which meant 'stinking, disgusting'. The sense shift from the concept FILTH to the concept PROSTITUTION to which the word became onomasiologically linked makes all the

---

128 According to Green (2003), *wench of the game* is a 17th century term for 'prostitute in a brothel' as from the late 17th century up to the early 19th century *game* meant 'group of prostitutes, especially in a brothel' or, according to the *OED*, 'prostitution' in general (1606 Set them downe For sluttish spoyles of opportunitie; and daughters of the *game*).

forms plausible candidates for dysphemisms whose formation is cognitively based on the conceptual metaphor PROSTITUTION IS FILTH. The dysphemistic nature of M.E. *putain* and *pute* is evidenced by the following *OED* historical material:

a1300 'Fiz a *putaines*',[129] he said, 'quat er ȝe?'
c1380 Puplicans and *puteyns* trowiden to him.
c1380 Þei ben foule *putis*.
↓
1603 Fals *pewtene*, hes scho playit that sport, Hes scho me handlit in this sort?

Let us point to the fact that this somewhat immediate rise of the sense 'prostitute' viewed as activation of the evaluatively negative value <COMMERCIALLY UNCHASTE$_{[NEG]}$> constitutes a convincing item of evidence of the dysphemistic function of *putain* and its derivatives.

Chamizo Dominguez (2007), on the one hand, apparently acknowledges the disparaging nature of the word, but – on the other hand – searches for the origin of cognate terms in various Romance languages in Vulgar Latin *putto/putta* meaning 'boy' and 'girl' respectively. The author stresses that such forms as Fr. *pute*, Sp. and Pr. *puta* and It. *putta(na)* were used with euphemistic intentions. If this is the case, then *putain*, *pute*, *putanie* and *puta* may be treated as instances of the employment of the mechanism of understatement. Whichever path we adopt, it remains certain that all forms of *putain* – either in the Middle English period or later – were employed as a type of X-phemism acquired by means of the process of lexical borrowing coupled with the working of either metaphor or understatement. Interestingly, out of the body of modern lexicographic sources that have been consulted, only *ODO* includes the entry *puta* as the only currently used variant of M.E. *putain*. Also, we are informed that the word is employed informally in Spanish-speaking countries or parts of America in the sense 'prostitute or promiscuous woman', but also as a term of general disparagement for the representatives of the female kind.

Another instance of the effect of lexical borrowing is M.E. **strumpet**, which – according to the *OED* – was clipped to **strum** in the 18th century. The sense of both forms given in the *OED* is 'harlot, prostitute', but only E.Mod.E. *strum* is placed under the lexicographic label PROSTITUTION in the *HTE*. English lexicographic sources of today, such as *MED*, *LDCE* and *ODO*, provide entries for the longer form *strumpet* as a synonym of *prostitute* with the register label *archaic* or *old-fashioned*. The following *OED* quotations testify to this historically documented sense of *strumpet* and *strum*:

---

129 As the *OED* clarifies, the M.E. form *fiz a putain* meant 'whoreson', and the form *fiz* was an Anglo-French word for 'son'.

a1327 Uch a *strumpet* that ther is such drahtes wl drawe.
c1440 Sho become þe moste common *strompyd* in all þe land.
↕
1889 This is a disease of childhood, and the only exception to this I have seen was in a very young *strumpet*.

a1700 *Strum, Rum-strum,...* a hansom Wench, or Strumpet.
↕
a1825 *Strum*, a battered prostitute.

The *OED* takes no definite stand as to the origin of *strumpet*, and only points to Skeat's (2005) work as a source of a plausible etymology of the word. In turn, Skeat (2005), and Rawson (1989), provide three likely paths of semantic development of M.E. *strumpet*. To start with, the etymological roots of the word may go back to Lat. *stuprum* 'dishonour, violation',[130] and if we accept this option it would be difficult – if at all possible – to determine whether the illocutionary force of the word was positive or negative. Far-fetched as it may sound, one may assume that the borrowing of Lat. *stuprum* may have been conditioned by the conceptual metaphor PROSTITUTION IS VIOLATING RULES/ WRONGDOING in which the concept PROSTITUTION is understood, among other ways, in terms of the activation of negatively loaded conceptual values <UNRULY$_{[NEG]}$> ^ <DISHONOURABLE$_{[NEG]}$>.

Yet another etymological hypothesis indicates that the ultimate roots of M.E. *strumpet* may be sought in M.Du. *stromfe* used in the sense 'stocking', though – as Skeat (2005) reports – there is no direct link between the M.Du and M.E. forms. This hypothesis may yield a relatively obvious interpretation of the employment of metonymy as the X-phemism formation tool. The possible metonymic extension alluded to here is based on the \\FEATURE FOR PERSON ADORNED WITH THIS FEATURE\\ contiguity. Last but not least, Skeat (2005) elucidates that M.E. *strumpet* may have developed from Nor. *strumpen* or L.G. *strumfen* which served to render the verbal sense 'stumble, stagger, trip'. Hence, the possible extension of the semantics of M.E. *strumpet* may be 'one who trips or makes a false step'. Whichever path of semantic development one considers plausible, one aspect of the semantics of M.E. *strumpet* seems to be common to all of them, that is the stigma of the loanword. As for the illocutionary force evoked, one may speculate that the category of X-phemism seems to be the safest resort in this case.

Our analysis of M.E. borrowings closes with the word **harlot** which entered the English word stock in the 13th century with the sense 'vagabond, beggar,

---

130 Note that, for the same original meaning 'dishonour, violation', Rawson (1989) provides the L.Lat form *strumpum* as the root for M.E. *strumpet*.

rascal, villain, knave', and thus the original semantics of *harlot* may be accounted for in terms of the activation of the conceptual value <MALE[NEU]> and <LOW[NEG]> presupposed for the attributive paths of **DOMAIN OF SEX [...]** and **DOMAIN OF SOCIAL STATUS [...]** respectively. The historically primary sense may be illustrated by means of the following *OED* extracts:

a1225 And beggen ase on *harlot*, ȝif hit neod is, his liueneð.
1377 He was vnhardy, þat *harlot* and hudde hym *in ferno*.
↕
1659 What should you do with such *Harlots* in your Service?

The change in the conceptual value to <FEMALE[NEU]> took place in the middle of the 15th century when the form *harlot* developed a novel female-specific sense 'unchaste woman, prostitute, strumpet'. Apart from the shift of the conceptual value within **DOMAIN OF SEX [...]**, one may speak of highlighting of the conceptual value <COMMERCIALLY UNCHASTE[NEG]> presupposed for the attributive path of **DOMAIN OF MORALITY [...]**. The following *OED* quotations testify to this sense development:

1432-50 The *Harlottes* at Rome were callede *nonariæ*.
1526 Thy sonne ... which hath devoured thy goodes with *harlootes*.
↕
1859 Tho' *harlots* paint their talk as well as face, With colours of the heart that are not theirs.

With respect to the illocutionary force of M.E. *harlot*, it may be concluded that most lexicographic sources concur that both the form *harlot* and the meaning 'vagabond, beggar' were adapted from O.Fr. *herlot/ (h)arlot*. Another far less feasible etymology of the word, as the *OED* notes, is the eponymical development from the name of William the Conqueror's mother, *Arlette* or *Herleva*. Interestingly, M.E. *harlot* seems to have been perceived as an auspicious term since – as Rawson (1989) observes – it was incorporated as a concealing device to be employed instead of the semantically contaminated term *whore* in the translation of the Bible, the Geneva Bible published in 1560. Most modern lexicographic sources that have been consulted, such as *MED*, *LDCE* and *ODO*, confirm the currency of the M.E. sense 'prostitute', though the word is normally qualified with such stylistic labels as *archaic* or *old use*.

3.5.3 Middle English rhetorical tools at work

The remaining two M.E. synonyms of *prostitute* may be said to constitute lexical realisations of the conceptual metaphorical schema PROSTITUTION IS FILTH. The semantic story of ***slut*** shows that the sense of the word has always been associated – either literally or metaphorically – with the conceptual value <FILTHY[NEG]> presupposed for the attributive path of **DOMAIN OF PHYSICAL CHARACTERISTICS AND APPEARANCE [...]**. Since the beginning of the 15th century the word has been employed in the aesthetically loaded sense 'woman of dirty, slovenly or untidy habits or appearance' often qualified by such adjectives as *foul*, *dirty*, etc.[131] This early sense of *slut* is evidenced by the following *OED* historical material:

> 1402 The foulest *slutte* of al a tovne.
> 1581 I haue noted often those dames which are so curious in their attire, to be verie *sluttes* in their houses.
> ↕
> 1883 She looked the part of a ragged, slatternly, dirty *slut*.

The results of further metaphorical extension became observable in the middle of the 15th century when *slut* started to convey the behaviourally and morally pregnant sense 'woman of a low or loose character; bold or impudent girl'. The conceptual values that are foregrounded in the transfer case at hand are <BOLD[NEG]> ^ <IMPUDENT[NEG]> ^ <LOOSE[NEG]>, as well as <LOW[NEG]> presupposed for the attributive paths of **DOMAIN OF CHARACTER AND BEHAVIOUR [...]** and **DOMAIN OF SOCIAL STATUS [...]** respectively. The following *OED* quotations testify to this historically novel sense of *slut*:

> c1450 Com forth, thou sloveyn! com for the thou *slutte*!
> 1577-82 To haunt the Tauernes late,... And swap ech *slut* vpon the lippes, that in the darke he meetes.
> ↕

---

131 Note that the problem was long ago noticed by such authors as Kleparski (1990:150), who argues that the role of context must inevitably have had an impact on the development of such a great number of lexical items which are used to refer to women in an inauspicious manner, and that the main *causa movens* behind it should be sought, among others, in the perception of women through the evaluatively tinted terms that are employed to describe them. In other words, the prolonged and frequent co-occurrence of female-specific terms and negatively loaded adjectives has resulted in the pejorative development of the senses of the female-specific nouns. Kleparski (1990:150), however, proposes another possible account of the tendency of female-specific terms to go down the evaluative scale. According to the author, it may be the case that female-specific nominal lexical items have some inherent pejoratively loaded values which, in a way, attract the negatively loaded adjectives to accompany them. Whichever way we believe is true, the role of context remains one of these challenges that awaits linguistic enquiry and it is the author's belief that it may prove crucial to many phenomena that affect female-specific vocabulary and euphemisation processes among other areas. See also Karczmarczyk (2012:261) for more recent discussion of the negatively loaded adjectives that modify the semantics of nominals (in this case M.E. *dragon*).

1881 My lord shall marry this extravagant *slut*.

Although the *OED* macrostructure does not include the sense 'prostitute' as one of the meanings of M.E. *slut*, such sources as Schulz (1975) and Rawson (1989) confirm the employment of the word as a historical synonym of *prostitute*. The highly unlikely origin of the word provides virtually no help in determining the illocutionary force of M.E. *slut*. However, the entrenchment link to the attributive path of **DOMAIN OF PHYSICAL CHARACTERISTICS AND APPEARANCE [...]** for which the conceptual value <FILTHY$_{[NEG]}$> is brought to the fore, allows one to speculate that M.E. *slut* served dysphemistic purposes of the epoch. In turn, both Partridge (1984) and Rawson (1989) point to the relation of *slut* to *slattern* and its basic abstract sense, namely 'idleness'. All in all, the assumption that *slut* has always been a dysphemism rather than a euphemism may be said to be confirmed in modern lexicographic sources, such as *LDCE*, *MED* and *ODO*, where the word is qualified with the label *derogatory* or *offensive*.

The story of *slut* is an example of reversed zoosemy as the word developed the sense 'female dog, bitch' in the first decades of the 19th century, which constituted a lexical representation of a zoosemic extension so frequent in the history of English. At the same time the word has continued to serve as a pejoratively pregnant female-specific lexical item, which is attested throughout the 19th century. The animal-specific sense of *slut* is evidenced by the following *OED* quotations:

1821 A large *Slut* Which belongs to the Party atacted the Bare.
↕
1893 *Sluts* were not so frequently used for shepherding purposes as dogs, being less tractable.

Note that this sense of *slut* is now obsolete and hence absent from the contents of modern lexicographic sources that have been consulted.

The other of the two lexical realisations of the conceptual schema PROSTITUTION IS FILTH is the history of the word ***filth*** which – etymologically speaking – ultimately derives from O.E. *fýlþ* employed in the sense 'foul matter, corruption, rottenness', and the word corresponds to such Germanic cognates as Du. *vuilte* or O.H.G. *fúlida*. According to the *OED*, M.E *filth* continued, to a great extent, the semantic range of its O.E. equivalent *fýlþ* because it was used in the sense 'uncleanly matter, dirt' evidenced from the end of the 13th century. The following *OED* quotations testify to this literal M.E. sense of *filth*:

c1290 Þare feol out of eiþer eiȝe *Fuylþe* ase þei it were slym.
c1430 Voydynge *fylthes* lowe into the grounde.
↕

1873 A palace with superb staircases reeking in *filth*.

As the *OED* informs us, starting from the beginning of the 13th century the lexical item in question has been applied in the evaluatively pregnant sense 'moral impurities' (c1200 Holi maiden of þanke, and clane of alle *felðes*). It may justifiably be assumed that the following path of conceptual mappings may have underpinned in the diachronic evolution of the semantics of *filth*:

DIRT → MORAL DIRT → PERSON MORALLY CORRUPTED

In short, the diachronic development of *filth* may be said to have involved two types of semantic change. First of all, one may speak of the process of narrowing through which the sense 'foul matter' became restricted to the sense 'moral impurities'. Secondly, it seems that the metonymic extension based on \\FEATURE FOR PERSON ADORNED WITH THIS FEATURE\\ contiguity took place when the historical sense 'moral impurities' formed the basis of the rise of the human-specific sense 'person accused of being morally corrupted'.

The human-specific sense of *filth* is first recorded in the middle of the 14th century and – as the *OED* data confirms – the word served to convey the epicene sense 'vile immoral creature; whore'. Hence, it seems that around that time language users began to apply *filth* as a dysphemistic appellation for both sexes. The metaphorical heavily loaded sense of *filth* is evidenced by the following *OED* material:

c1350 Lest þat foule *felþe* schuld have hem founde þere.
↓
1565 27 loan of Kent, that *filth*… was she a sister of yours?
↓
1871 O ugly *filth*, detested Trull.

As confirmed by reference sources of today, such as *MED*, *LDCE* and *ODO*, the sense 'prostitute' fails to be listed in modern lexicographic sources. In fact, under the entry *filth* the sense 'the police' is the only human-specific sense of the word in question that is in circulation today – though restricted to slang register.

The Middle English period seems to be particularly productive in terms of the number of well-rooted formations that entered the English word stock in order to veil – either positively or negatively – the morally contaminated O.E. form *hóre*. Out of a dozen of M.E. synonyms four have retained their synonymous nature up to date, and the forms *wench*, *strumpet*, *harlot* and *slut* may all be found as separate entries in modern lexicographic sources with the sense 'prostitute'. Significantly, other mostly historical dictionaries, such as the *OED*, employ *wench*, *strumpet*, *harlot* and *slut* in their definitional formula of other historical synonyms of *prostitute*.

3.6 Early Modern English X-phemisms linked to the conceptual category FALLEN WOMAN

A cursory look at the synonyms of *prostitute* originating during the Early Modern English period suffices to allow the judgement that during that historical period many more lexical items started to be used in the sense 'prostitute' than in the Middle English period previously discussed. One may go further and assert that the Early Modern English period was by all means more seminal in the formation of *prostitute* synonyms than either the Middle English or the Old English periods, or indeed both historical periods taken together. Secondly, the employment of other mechanisms, such as remodelling or eponymy, is yet another striking difference between the earlier periods and Early Modern English. Thirdly, from the quantitative point of view, the most productive processes in the formation of historical synonyms of *prostitute* during the historical period discussed here were metaphor (21 cases recorded among which 16 are zoosemic extensions, 2 are foodsemic metaphors and 3 are of other types), compounding (17 cases recorded), understatement (12 cases found) and borrowing (12 cases recorded). The detailed quantitative account of the distribution of formative tools involved in the rise of historical synonyms of *prostitute* is given in *Figure 3.14* below.

Early Modern English			
Structural Tools			
Compounding	**Derivation**	**Clipping**	**Remodelling**
strange woman	*hack-ster*	*miss*	*hackster*
public woman	*twigg-er*	*hack*	
streetwalker	*waistcoat-eer*		
polecat	*mar-tail*		
walk-street	*occup-ant*		
night-shade	*commun-ity*		
hackney-woman	*dox-y < dock+y*		
fling-dust	*(harlot-ry)*		
night-trader			
hackney-wench			
hell-moth			
public commoner			
night-worm			
Winchester goose			
(stewed strumpet)			
(laced mutton)			
(wagtail)			
Semantic Tools			
Borrowing	**Eponymy**	**Circumlocution**	
drab (Ir.)	*(Tib)*	*lady of pleasure*	
putanie (Fr.)	*(hiren)*	*(light of love)*	

courtesan (Fr.)	*moll*	*sisters of the bank*	
(trull) (G.)	*hackney*		
(callet) (Fr. or Gael.)			
(pucelle) (Fr.)			
(succubus) (Lat.)			
(amorosa) (Sp./ It.)			
?? *croshabell*			
?? ***punk*** (Lat.)			
prostitute			
hackney (Fr.)			
Rhetorical Tools			
Understatement	**Metonymy/Synecdoche**	**Metaphor**	
		Zoosemy	**Metaphor**
public commoner	*(baggage)*	*cat*	*sisters of the bank*
strange woman	*stew*	*polecat*	*(succubus)*
public woman	*walk-street*	*bat*	*aunt*
streetwalker	*night-shade*	*hackney*	
walk-street	*waistcoateer*	*hackney-woman*	
night-shade	*fling-dust/-stink*	*hackney-wench*	
fling-dust (-stink)	*night-trader*	?? *twigger*	
night-trader	*streetwalker*	*(yaud)*	**Foodsemy**
miss		*(wagtail)*	*(laced mutton)*
(loon)		*mermaid*	*meat*
(limmer)		*(cockatrice)*	
(mort)		*hell-moth*	
		night-worm	
		Winchester goose	
		quail	
		plover	

Fig. 3.14: Early Modern English historical synonyms of prostitute.

Unlike the aforementioned account, which commenced with the discussion of the cases of employment of structural tools, here the starting point shall be the lexical realisations of metaphor. This is mainly due to the fact that this cognitive process turns out to be the *causa movens* behind the rise of the largest group of *prostitute* synonyms in the Early Modern English period.

3.6.1 Early Modern English metaphorically based X-phemisms

Let us start our account with the lexical item ***bat*** which seems to be a prototypical representative of the conceptual metaphor based on a zoosemic extension, namely A PROSTITUTE IS A NOCTURNAL CREATURE. As *SS* puts it, *bat* is a synonym of *prostitute [...] because the prostitute, like a bat, is a creature of the night.*

One of many night images used in slang describing prostitutes. Let us mention at this point Paul's (1891) classification of types of similarity which may trigger metaphorical extensions, as adopted in Grygiel and Kleparski (2007:101):

> 1. similarity of shape, for example, head (of a cabbage), eye (of the needle),
> 2. similarity of position, for example, foot (of a page, of a mountain),
> 3. similarity of function and behaviour, for example, whip 'official in the British Parliament whose duty is to see that members were present at the voting',
> 4. similarity of colour, for example, orange, hazel.

The metaphorical shift of *bat* apparently geared by the conceptual metaphor A PROSTITUTE IS A NOCTURNAL CREATURE may serve as an item of evidence that Paul's (1891) classification should be complemented with at least one more type of similarity, namely that of time, because it is the temporal dimension that comes to the fore here.

Historically speaking, *bat* entered the English word stock in the early 14th century in its M.E. form *bakke*[132] to refer to a small mouse-like quadruped with thin membrane wings that enable it to fly. The original semantics of *bat* may be accounted for in terms of activation of the conceptual value <NOCTURNAL_{[NEU]}> that is foregrounded in **DOMAIN OF CHARACTER AND BEHAVIOUR [...]**. In fact, this conceptual value <NOCTURNAL_{[NEU]}> seems to have been mapped from the conceptual category **ANIMALS** to the conceptual category **FEMALE HUMAN BEING**. According to the *OED*, the transfer in question must have taken place at the outset of the 17th century when *bat* started to associate with the conceptual value <COMMERCIALLY UNCHASTE_{[NEG]}> presupposed for the attributive path of **DOMAIN OF MORALITY [...]** when employed with reference to women engaged in the oldest profession. The following *OED* quotations testify to this historical sense development of *bat*, the effects of which are still visible in current English:

> 1607 Synnes, that in the shapes of *Bats*, Skreech-owles, and such others ominous mid night-walkers, wasted the bawdy night in shameless and godlesse Reuilings.
> 1732 They're *bats*, who chase their Twilight Prey.
> ↕
> 2001 Prostitutes – '*bats*' in local speech – met them at the depot by the company store.

Interestingly – yet somewhat understandably – as the *OED* reports, this application of *bat* has become restricted with time and, currently, the word used in a female-specific sense is restricted to Am.E.. Note that the rise of the metaphori-

---

132 As the *OED* reports, the M.E. form *bakke* might have been incorporated from Scandinavian languages as it corresponds to such forms as Da. *aften-bakke* 'evening-bat', O.Da. *nath-bakkæ* and O.Sw. *natt-backa* 'night-bat'.

cal sense 'prostitute' coincided with the importation of the English language to the American continent. Once the word was taken to form part of the vocabulary resources of the rising variety of English it was gone – historically speaking – for good in the old country. Naturally, the lexical gap that was left behind was filled by its historical synonyms.

The modern lexicographic sources that have been consulted, such as *LDCE* or *ODO*, inform us that *bat*, usually modified by *old*, is now used informally in the sense 'woman regarded as unattractive and unpleasant'. And, hence, the history of the word is a case of a reversal on Kleparski's (1990) evaluative scale because one may speak of a certain degree of amelioration from moral pejoration to aesthetic pejoration while the prevailing historical tendency is to the contrary, that is from aesthetic to moral pejoration (see Kleparski 1990).

In turn, the etymology of another case of the conceptual metaphor formulated here as A PROSTITUTE IS A NOCTURNAL CREATURE is far from clear. The origin of *cat* lies in obscurity, but the *OED* provides evidence for the fact that the word is one of the most widespread forms across the languages of the Indo-European family (see, for example, Sw. *katt*, Da. *kat*, Wel. and Cor. *cath*, Pol. *kot*, Russ. *kot*, It. *gatto* and Sp. *gato*). The word in question has been with us since Anglo-Saxon times and its historically primary sense 'well-known carnivorous quadruped which has long been domesticated and has been kept to destroy mice, and as a pet' is well evidenced already in Anglo-Saxon times. As Ayto (2007) maintains, the O.E. form *cat* was a development from Germanic **kattuz*, later reinforced by Anglo-Norman *cat*, which itself was a dialectal variant of O.Fr. *chat*.

According to the *OED*, *cat* acquired a secondary human-specific sense, at the beginning of the 13th century, when the word started to be used with the derogatory sense 'spiteful or backbiting woman', and later, in the early 15th century, when it first surfaced with the sense 'prostitute'. The historical rise of this sense of *cat* may be accounted for in terms of activation of the evaluatively negatively loaded conceptual value <COMMERCIALLY UNCHASTE$_{[NEG]}$> presupposed for the attributive path of **DOMAIN OF MORALITY**. Furthermore, the conceptual value <NOCTURNAL$_{[NEU]}$> presupposed for the attributive path of **DOMAIN OF CHARACTER AND BEHAVIOUR [...]** may be treated as the conceptual element that provided a functional link for the metaphor to have arisen. On the other hand, in terms of the cognitive apparatus employed <NOCTURNAL$_{[NEU]}$> was the element that was mapped from the macrocategory **ANIMALS** to the macrocategory **FEMALE HUMAN BEING**. The following *OED* material seems to testify to the zoosemic development of *cat*:

1401 Be ware of Cristis curse, and of *cattis* tailis.
1535 Hay! As ane brydlit *cat*, I brank.

↑
1708 Wrigglers, Misses, *Cats*, Rigs.

The lexicographic sources that have been consulted seem to concur that the female-specific pejoratively loaded sense of *cat* is more likely to have developed from the 'animal' sense rather than from the sense 'woman's external genitals', which – according to Green (2003) – surfaced in the English language much later, that is in the middle of the 19th century. Interestingly, this sense fails to be recorded in the *OED* data corpus.

The further evolution of *cat* involves entering a number of composite determinants, such as *polecat* at the end of the 16th century, used contemptuously in the sense 'courtesan, prostitute',[133] *alley cat* in the early 20th century, employed in the sense 'promiscuous woman' or 'prostitute',[134] as well as *geycat*, which occurred in Am.E. in the 1930s with a historically novel sense 'tramp's younger, homosexual companion'.[135] However, only *polecat* and *alley cat*, may be treated as historical synonyms of *prostitute*, though sexuality is what they all have in common.

Yet another E.Mod.E. lexical item that represents the metaphorical schema A PROSTITUTE IS A NOCTURNAL CREATURE is **hell-moth**, which was clipped to **moth** at the end of the 19th century. The etymological roots of both go back to O.E. *moþþe/mohðe*, which corresponds to cognates in several Germanic languages, such as M.Du. *motte*, Mod.Du. *mot*, M.H.G and Mod.G. *mot*, as well as Sw. and Nor. *mott maggot*. As to its historically primary semantic range, according to the *OED*, its original sense was 'the larva of a small nocturnal lepidopterous insect of the genus Tinea' which – since the 16th century – was extended and the word started to be employed in the sense 'any nocturnal lepidopterous insect of similar appearance'.

The low-ranking frequency of the compound *hell-moth* must have been particularly marked as the *OED* records only one quotation that testifies to the emergence of a historically novel sense 'prostitute', quoted below:

> 1602 Is there not one appointed for the apprehending of such *hell-moths* [harlots and curtizans], that eat a man out of bodie and soule?

Apart from positing a well-pronounced entrenchment link to **DOMAIN OF SEX** [...] and **DOMAIN OF MORALITY** [...] for which such conceptual elements as <FEMALE[NEU]> and <COMMERCIALLY UNCHASTE[NEG]> are

---

133 Consider the *OED* quotation: 1598 Out of mu doore, you Witch, you Ragge, you Baggage, you *Poulcat*, you Runnion, out, out.
134 See: 1942 Ragamuffin... *alley cat*. Ibid. Slut, *alley cat*. Ibid. Prostitute, *alley cat*.
135 Consider the *OED* quotation: 1926 He must have been an awful *gay cat* to get into the end of a carload of planed lumber. It's suicide.

foregrounded, the semantics of the compound *hell-moth* may be accounted for in terms of activation of the conceptual value <SINFUL_{[NEG]}> as the concept HELL has been invariably, though variously, associated with such negatively loaded values as <EVIL_{[NEG]}> and <SINFUL_{[NEG]}>, regardless of the religious denomination. In turn, the late-19th-century abbreviated form *moth* is recorded in a number of sources, such as the *OED*, *SS*, Partridge (1984) and Green (2003) and may be proved to have been in general use up to the 1930s. The Pres.E. form *moth* is recorded in a dysphemistic sense 'prostitute', which is evidenced by the following *OED* quotation:

> 1935 *Moth*, a female of easy virtue.

As Partridge (1984) argues, the human-specific sense of *moth* may have developed either through the complex conceptual element <ATTRACTED BY NIGHT LIGHTS_{[NEU]}> characteristic for both *moths* as 'insects' and as 'women' or from the sense 'vermin', which emphasises even more the negative connotation the word *moth* could have been linked to. Curiously enough, there is a three-century gap in the semantic development of *moth*, which may obtain either due to the lack of records or a temporary disuse of this negatively loaded X-phemism for 'prostitute' (and the possible rise of other historical X-phemisms).

Finally, the least known E.Mod.E. lexical representative of the conceptual metaphor A PROSTITUTE IS A NOCTURNAL CREATURE is ***night-worm*** which is recorded only in the *OED* and the *HTE*. Interestingly, none of the other lexicographic sources or analytical works that have been consulted include *night-worm* as a historical synonym of *prostitute*. The following early-17th-century *OED* quotation exemplifies this sense of *night-worm*:

> 1605 Bed-Brokers, *Night-Worms* and Impressitors.

The fact that there is only one recorded use of the E.Mod.E compound *night-worm* employed in the sense 'prostitute' points to a relatively short-lived history the lexical item in question. As to the semantics of *night-worm*, apart from constituting one of the historical realisations of a zoosemic pattern A PROSTITUTE IS A NOCTURNAL CREATURE, one can also speak of the development of an entrenchment link to the attributive paths of such **CDs** as **DOMAIN OF SEX [...], DOMAIN OF MORALITY [...]** and **DOMAIN OF SOCIAL STATUS [...]** for which the conceptual values <FEMALE_{[NEU]}>, <COMMERCIALLY UNCHASTE_{[NEG]}> and <LOW_{[NEG]}> are activated. The conceptual value <LOW_{[NEG]}> accounts for the specific sense of the word; historical data shows that *night-worm* was used with reference to the lowest representative of the trade.

In addition, yet another realisation of the conceptual schema may be formulated, that is A PROSTITUTE IS A BIRD. Already Schulz (1975:74) observes that several bird names became lexical representatives of the conceptual metaphor A PROSTITUTE IS A BIRD at some point in their semantic history and the author enumerates in this context such bird names as *columbine, quail, flapper, bird, chicken, hen* and *sea gull*. In turn, Holder (2008) acknowledges the existence of, as the author puts it, *common avian imagery*, of which *goose* and *quail* are but a couple of examples. A number of other E.Mod.E. lexical items, such as *Winchester goose, wagtail, quail* and *plover* may be said to fit ideally here. As for the origin of the compound form **Winchester goose**, its etymological roots should be sought for in the semantic evolution of the head of this composite determinant, that is *goose*. As the name used in the sense 'large web-footed bird' *goose* originates in O.E. *gós* and the form corresponds to Mod.Du. and Mod.G. *Gans*, O.N. *gás* and Mod.Pol. *gęś*. The first human-specific sense of *goose* occurs relatively late in the history of English, that is in Elizabethan times, and – within the framework adopted – may be accounted for in terms of activation of the conceptual value <STUPID[NEG]> ^ <SIMPLE[NEG]> presupposed for the attributive path of **DOMAIN OF CHARACTER AND BEHAVIOUR [...]**. Although in the majority of Indo-European languages the metaphorical equivalents of English *goose* tend to be female-specific (Mod.Pol. *gęś* 'silly naive girl', Mod.G. *Gans* 'silly teen'), Rawson (1989) notes that English *goose* – as a symbol of stupidity – was, and still is, used with reference not only to women but feeble men as well. The following *OED* material testifies to the metaphorical sense of *goose* discussed here:

> 1547 Shall I stand still, like a *goose* or a fool, with my finger in my mouth?
> 1655 He did play the very *Goose* himselfe.
> ↓
> 1887 What a *goose* I was to leave my muff behind me.

In the early 17th century, as the *OED* reports, the form *goose* started to be employed in the sense 'venereal disorder' or 'prostitute', the former of which must have followed the rise of the sense 'prostitute' by means of the mechanism *pars pro toto*. In order to account for the latter human-specific sense of *goose* we may speak of activation of the pejoratively pregnant conceptual value <COMMERCIALLY UNCHASTE[NEG]> presupposed for the attributive path of **DOMAIN OF MORALITY [...]**, the operation that may have contributed to the rise of yet another historical synonym of *prostitute*. The following *OED* quotations illustrate these historically novel senses of *Winchester goose*:

> 1591 *Winch*. Gloster, thou wilt answere this before the Pope. *Glost*. *Winchester goose*, I cry, a Rope, a Rope.
> 1661 This Informer... had belike some private dealings with her, and there got a *Goose*... This fellow in revenge for this, informs against the Bawd that kept the house.
> ↕

1778 In the times of popery here were no less than 18 houses on the Bankside, licensed by the Bishop of Winchester... to keep whores, who were, therefore, commonly called *Winchester Geese*.

The extralinguistic explanation of the origin of the modifier *Winchester* is provided by Pearson (1942:94) who goes along the following lines:[136]

The Bishop of Winchester had his Palace between the London Bridge and the Globe Theatre and owned most of the land in that district, fattening himself on the rent of sin; for it was the region of brothels, the women of which were known as *Winchester geese*.

Those prostitutes that were referred to as *Winchester geese* tended to be afflicted with syphilis since it was the meaner selection of prostitutes that was to be found in the district of Winchester (see Holder 2008). Hence, the account of the semantics of *Winchester goose* requires activation of the conceptual value <LOW$_{[NEG]}$> presupposed for the attributive path of **DOMAIN OF SOCIAL STATUS [...]**. Note that in terms of Kleparski's (1990) typology of pejorative charges one may speak here of two types of pejoration because the semantics of *Winchester goose* may be said to associate with both socially negative elements, as well as morally tinted values.

The analysis of modern lexicographic works, such as *MED*, *LDCE* and *ODO*, confirms that the only human-specific sense to be found in Present-day English is 'foolish person', which is additionally labelled as either *old-fashioned* or *informal* as to its stylistic value. It may, therefore, be true that the inauspicious illocutionary force associated with *Winchester goose* had worn out well before the advent of Present-day English.

Similarly, the semantics of another bird term, that is **wagtail**, underwent the process of zoosemy-based moral pejoration across time. As the *OED* data confirms, the history of the word goes back to the early 16th century when the compound form – coined from the verb *wag* and the noun *tail* – started to be employed in the sense 'small bird belonging to the genus *Motacilla* characterised by the wagging motion of the tail'. Here, one should note that the working of the morphological process of compounding may have been coupled with the metonymic extension based on the \\FEATURE FOR PERSON/ENTITY ADORNED WITH THIS FEATURE\\ contiguity pattern. After all, a bird was named after a characteristic feature it was associated with, namely tail wagging.

The extralinguistically habitual feature of the bird may have provided a transmission channel for the shift to the conceptual category **FALLEN WOMAN**, the representatives of which are stereotypically associated with the tail-wagging movement. To be more precise, already towards the end of the 16th

---

136 Quoted after Hughes (2006:364).

century the word in question developed a human-specific sense 'harlot, courtesan'. Within the analytical framework adopted the semantics of *wagtail* is accountable in terms of activation of the conceptual value <COMMERCIALLY UNCHASTE$_{[NEG]}$> presupposed for the attributive path of **DOMAIN OF MORALITY [...]**. The human-specific sense of *wagtail* may be illustrated by the following *OED* quotations:

> 1592 If therefore thou make not thy mistress a goldfinch, thou mayst chance to find her a *wagtaile*.
> 1635 Join to make her Supple and pliant for the Duke: I hope We are not the first have been advanced by a *wagtail*.
> ↕
> 1710 Like Paris with his Gleek of *Wagtails* on Ida.

The *OED* also informs us that this historical synonym of *prostitute* was in common use only in the 17th century, which is confirmed by the absence of any human-specific senses of the word in any of the modern lexicographic sources that have been consulted.

The common avian imagery is also represented by the employment of ***quail*** as a historical synonym onomasiologically linked to the conceptual category **FALLEN WOMAN**. The word, according to the *OED*, was adopted from O.Fr. *quaille*. This is confirmed by Holder (2008), who – at the same time – rejects the etymological link between E.Mod.E. *quail* and Celtic *caile* 'young girl'. The historically original sense of *quail*, that is 'migratory bird allied to the partridge', surfaced in the 14th century, and – at the very beginning of the 17th century – *quail* developed the human-specific sense 'courtesan'. The rise of this historically novel sense may be rendered in terms of activation of such a conceptual value as <COMMERCIALLY UNCHASTE$_{[NEG]}$> presupposed for the attributive path of **DOMAIN OF MORALITY [...]**. The rise of human-specific sense of *quail* is evidenced by the following *OED* material:

> 1606 Heere's Agamemnon,... one that loues *Quails*.
> 1694 Several coated *Quails*, and lac'd Mutton.

Rawson (1989) alludes to the M.E. sense of *quail* which is absent in other lexicographic sources consulted. Namely, the author suggests that *quail* was also used in the epicene sense 'timid person' in Chaucer's time; however, the *OED* fails to include this sense. In turn, the further semantic development of *quail* – confirmed by most lexicographic sources – serves as ample evidence for the process of amelioration of which one has a truly rare occasion to speak in the case of human-and-female-specific analysis. Both the *OED* and Partridge (1984) report that *quail* started to be employed in – if not positively loaded than at least – neutral sense, that is 'girl, young woman' or 'girl student' in Am.E. slang in the second half of the 19th century. Evidently, the rise of this sense-thread stands in opposition to the generally prevalent **POSITIVE > NEGATIVE** or **NEUTRAL > NEGATIVE** developmental path of female-specific lexical items. The following *OED* quotations testify to this historical sense of *quail*:

> 1859 [The Freshman] heareth of *'Quails'*, he dresseth himself in fine linen, he seeketh to flirt with ye *'quails'*.
> 1904 Because she was hazed by the young woman students at Wesleyan, one *'quail'*, as the boys call them, who was a freshman here last year did not return to Wesleyan this fall.
> ↕
> 1970 For any woman... man has a strange conglomeration of terms:... *quail*, squab, [etc.]

Rawson (1989) claims that *[...] in our time,* [that is the end of the 20th century, the form *quail* meant] *usually a woman, often a young and attractive one [...]*. Yet, curiously enough, none of the modern lexicographic sources of the 21st century, such as *MED*, *LDCE* or *ODO*, registers any of the human-specific senses listed in the *OED*. At the same time, Rawson (1989) points out that other names of (game) birds, such as *bird, bird of the game, game hen, game pullet, lone dove, lone duck, partridge, pheasant* and *plover*, developed a secondary meaning 'prostitute' during the course of their semantic history. The development of this sense-thread constitutes yet another item of evidence of the existence of the conceptual metaphor SEX IS HUNTING within which one may observe another metaphorical schema; that is A PROSTITUTE IS A GAME BIRD. It seems fairly obvious that portraying a prostitute in terms of feathered prey[137] hunted by her clients must evoke negative associations and, thus, historical synonyms based on the metaphorical extension in question are most likely dysphemistic in nature.

Last but not least, the semantic history of E.Mod.E *plover*, which was adopted into English from O.Fr. *plovier* at the beginning of the 14th century, also represents the well-evidenced conceptual metaphor A PROSTITUTE IS A GAME BIRD. The historically original meaning 'the name of several gregarious birds of the genera *Charadrius* and *Squatarola*' provided the base for the rise of the zoosemic sense 'courtesan' or 'victim, dupe' that appeared in the early 17th century. The evolution of the semantics of E.Mod.E *plover* may respectively be associated with the process of activation of such a conceptual value as <COMMERCIALLY UNCHASTE$_{[NEG]}$> presupposed for the attributive path of **DOMAIN OF MORALITY [...]**. To account for the epicene sense, one may also speak about an entrenchment link to the attributive path of **DOMAIN OF**

---

137 Note that feathered nature of cheap entertainment, such as cabaret or down-stairs shows, seems to be associated in a way with the metaphorical schema in question.

CHARACTER AND BEHAVIOUR [...] for which the conceptual value <GULLIBLE[NEG]> is foregrounded. The following *OED* quotations testify to these human-specific senses of *plover*:

> 1614 Here will be Zekiell Edgworth, and three or foure gallants, with him at night, and I ha' neither *Plouer* nor Quaile for 'hem.
> 1626 Who's here?... what *Plouer*'s that They haue brought to pull? *Bra*. I know not, some green *Plouer*. I'le find him out.
> 1631 Thou art a most greene *Plouer* in policy, I Perceiue.

As the *OED* material quoted above shows, in this case the historical sense 'prostitute' was relatively short-lived and is now a relict of the past. More generally, there is not a single trace of the human-specific senses of *plover* in the modern lexicographic sources that have been consulted.

Within the zoosemic developmental path, one can speak of the existence of many well-evidenced metaphorical mappings between the conceptual categories **EQUIDAE** and **FALLEN WOMAN**, reflected lexically in the rise of a number of historical synonyms of *prostitute*. First of all, let us scrutinise the structurally productive case of *hackney*, which – on the one hand – entered several composite determinants, such as E.Mod.E. *hackney woman, hackney wench* and L.Mod.E. *hackney lady*. On the other hand, the word has undergone the process of clipping and is currently used in the form *hack*, and – on the other hand – has been subject to the mechanism of remodelling with the resultant lexical item being *hackster*. Interestingly, according to the *OED*, *hackster* is an instance of the process of derivation, whereby the suffix *-ster* was attached to the verb *hack*, and thus the semantic outcome is 'one that hacks, cutter'. Green (2003) places both forms *hackney* and *hackster* as alternative forms, which may suggest that *hackster* is treated as a modification of *hackney*. In this case, the semantic development of *hackster* may be expected to correspond roughly to that of *hackney*, that is it involves a metaphorical mapping from the conceptual category **EQUIDAE** to **FALLEN WOMAN**. Regardless of its structural origin, the ultimate human-specific sense 'prostitute' is recorded in the *OED* only twice at the close of the 16th and the beginning of the 17th century. The following *OED* quotations testify to this historical sense of *hackster*:

> 1594 Out whore, strumpet, six penie *hackster*.
> 1611 ... she hath bin a *hackster*, a twigger, a good one, in her time.

Let us now analyse in more detail the semantic history of *hackney*. The *OED* reports that the lexical item in question was adopted from O.Fr. *haquenée* in the first half of the 14th century in the animal-specific sense 'horse of a middle size used for riding as distinguished from a war-horse'. In turn, both Rawson (1989) and Ayto (2005) suggest that the name of this type of horse may have been an adoption of the proper name *Hackney*, which was once a village on the outskirts of London where horses were raised before they were either sold or hired. Therefore, in this case one may speak of the working of eponymy as a triggering force behind the emergence of the sense 'horse'. Note that the process was discerned in other cases discussed earlier, such as the employment of female proper names *lizzie*, *amy* or *molly* used in the sense 'homosexual'. The historically primary meaning of *hackney* may be illustrated with the following *OED* material:

> c1330 Tille oþer castels about þei sent tueye and tueye In aneus for doute, ilk on on his *hakneye*.
> c1440 A *hakeney* That ys swyft and ryght well ambling.
> ↕
> 1890 The farmer... mounted upon a stout, not over-refined *hackney*.

Significantly, already towards the end of the 14th century the conceptual values that started to associate with the semantics of *hackney* were <FOR HIRE$_{[NEU]}$> and <WORN-OUT$_{[NEG]}$>, and, hence, one may speak of an entrenchment link to the attributive path of such **CDs** as **DOMAIN OF SOCIAL STATUS [...]** and **DOMAIN OF PHYSICAL CHARACTERISTICS AND APPEARANCE [...]** respectively. The conceptual value <FOR HIRE$_{[NEU]}$> was mapped onto the secondary human-specific sense when the word *hackney* started to be employed in the epicene sense 'common drudge' in the middle of the 16th century. The following *OED* material testifies to this sense of *hackney*:

> 1546 Whan ought was to doo, I was common *hackney*.
> 1668 Which makes me mad that I should, by my place, become the *hackney* of this office, in perpetual trouble and vexation.
> ↕
> 1784 Such is all the mental food purvey'd By public *hacknies* in the schooling trade.

Curiously enough, it only took little less than half a century for *hackney* to associate with the gender-specific conceptual value <FEMALE$_{[NEU]}$> presupposed for the attributive path of **DOMAIN OF SEX [...]**, and the mapping may be said to have been the *causa movens* behind yet another historical zoosemic extension that comes under the label A PROSTITUTE IS A HORSE. In the case of the secondary sense 'prostitute' the conceptual value <FOR HIRE$_{[NEU]}$> was clearly foregrounded within the attributive path of **DOMAIN OF SOCIAL STATUS [...]**. Note at this point that the conceptual value in question is axiologically neutral in itself, but when it becomes human-specific, and – in particular – when it combines with the gender-specific conceptual value <FEMALE$_{[NEU]}$> it acquires pejorative overtones which are usually of moral and behavioural type. After all, there seems to be nothing improper or negative about hiring a piece of equipment or a horse. On the other hand, hiring a woman for sexual purposes has always been – openly or tacitly – socially condemned in most European cultures. Hence, the employment of *hackney* as a historical synonym of *prostitute* most plausibly triggered a fair amount of negative illocutionary force. This historical 16th-century sense of *hackney* is evidenced by the following *OED* data:

> 1579 Venus... that taught the women in Cyprus to set vp a Stewes too hyre out them selues as *hackneies* for gaine.
> 1593 When the *hackney* he hath payde for lyes by him.
> ↕
> 1679 She was so notoriously lewd that she was called an *Hackney*.

According to the *OED*, in the first decades of the 17th century *hackney* became a modifier in several composite determinants, such as E.Mod.E. *hackney woman*, *hackney wench* and L.Mod.E. *hackney lady* (1616 Olde *hackny women*, they hire out their jades; 1647 *Hackney-wenches*, that ith circus stand; 1678 No more than every Lover Does from his *Hackney-Lady* suffer). In turn, the abbreviated variant *hack* retains the majority of the senses of the longer base form *hackney*. The *OED* records show that the pejoratively loaded sense 'prostitute' was in use for over a century, which is evidenced by the following contexts of use:

> 1730-6 *Hack*, a common hackney Horse, Coach, or Strumpet.
> ↕
> 1864 *Hack*... a procuress.

The present-day lexicographic sources that have been consulted fail to record the female-specific sense of either *hackney* or *hack*, which confirms the rather short-lived nature of *hackney*-based historical synonyms onomasiologically linked to the conceptual category **FALLEN WOMAN**.

Another historical representative of the realisation of the metaphorical extension schema, formalised here as A PROSTITUTE IS A HORSE, is the case of E.Mod.E. **yaud**, which entered the English word stock at the outset of the 16th century to be employed in the sense 'mare, usually old and worn-out'. According to the *OED*, E.Mod.E. *yaud* corresponds etymologically to O.N. *jalda* and Mod.Sw. dialectal *jälda*, and the cognate forms were used in the sense 'mare' in poetic register. To account for the primary animal-specific historical sense of E.Mod.E. *yaud*, one may speak of an entrenchment link to such **CDs** as **DOMAIN OF SEX [...], DOMAIN OF AGE [...]** and **DOMAIN OF PHYSICAL CHARACTERISTICS AND APPEARANCE [...]** for which the conceptual values <FEMALE$_{[NEU]}$>, <OLD$_{[NEG]}$> and <WORN-OUT$_{[NEG]}$> are activated respectively. The following *OED* exemplary material testifies to the historically original sense of *yaud*:

> 1500-20 Schir, lett it nevir in toun be tald, That I sould be ane ȝuillis ȝald!

1641 Your *Yawdes* may take cold, and never be good after it.
↕
1866 [They] sneered at her as the 'grey *yaud* wha'd be better rode wi' martingal nor snaffle'.

Oddly enough, *yaud* in its secondary human-specific sense 'strumpet, whore' is first recorded in the *OED* at the beginning of the 15th century, which is around one hundred years prior to the emergence of its primary equine sense. In the context of the rise of the human-specific sense of *yaud* Kiełtyka (2008:172) argues along the following lines:

> [...] if one were not aware of the fact that **yaud** is etymologically related to the 14th century **jade** 'poor or worn-out horse, one would be tempted to conjecture that the analysed word may be said to represent a case where an animal receives its name from a lexical item originally used as a human term, the process earlier referred to as **reversed zoosemy**.

It is, however, worthy of note that the *HTE* records *yaud* in the sense 'prostitute' only in the middle of the 16th century, while the earlier record (the beginning of the 15th century) shows *yaud* as a modifier in a compound. According to the *OED*, the resulting composite determinant ʒ*aldson* was used as a term of abuse analogous to the already well-established *whoreson*. The secondary sense 'prostitute' may be described in terms of activation of the conceptual value <COMMERCIALLY UNCHASTE[NEG]> presupposed for the attributive path of **DOMAIN OF MORALITY [...]**. The following *OED* quotations provide samples of contextual evidence for the human-specific pejoratively loaded sense of *yaud*:

> 1400 ʒondire to ʒone ʒ*aldsones* he þat ʒeldes hyme ever... Be he neuer mo sauede.
> 1545 You leid that said Annapill Graheme wes ane freris get and freris *yawde*.

The *OED* also informs us that E.Mod.E. *yaud* enjoyed merely a regional currency in northern dialects of English, which may be taken as the grounds for the total absence of *yaud* in lexicographic works of today. The regional use of *yaud* is confirmed by *The Concise Scots Dialect Dictionary* (henceforth: *CSDD*) which records the lexical item *yad* in the senses 'old mare', 'old cow', 'contemptuous term for a slovenly or vicious woman' and 'jade'. Interestingly, there seems to be no trace of the employment of Sc. *yad* in the highly pejorative sense 'prostitute'.

Furthermore, E.Mod.E. **twigger** represents the working of the metaphorical zoosemic shift between the conceptual categories **OVIDAE** and **FALLEN WOMAN**. Structurally, this morphologically complex form is made up from the verb *twig* 'do anything vigorously and strenuously' and the derivational suffix -*er*. The construal of the historically primary sense of *twigger* 'vigorous, prolific breeder, especially a ewe', which dates back to the second half of the 16th century, involves the conceptual values <OVINE[NEU]> and <FEMALE[NEU]> presupposed for the attributive paths of **DOMAIN OF SPECIES [...]** and **DOMAIN OF SEX [...]** respectively. One may also speak of an entrenchment link to the attributive path of **DOMAIN OF CHARACTER AND BEHAVIOUR [...]** for which the conceptual value <VIGOROUS[POS]> is foregrounded. The following *OED* quotation illustrates the historically original sense of *twigger*:

> 1573 The lamb of such twinners for breeders go take, For twinlings be *twiggers*, encrease for to bring, Though som for their twigging Peccantem may sing.

The extralinguistic intensity of ewe's mating contacts may have provided the conceptual spark for the rise of the human-specific sense 'strumpet, harlot', in which the prolific nature of sexual contacts is far from being marginal. The metaphorically triggered human-specific sense of the lexical item in question may be described in terms of activation of such conceptually central values as <FEMALE[NEU]> and <COMMERCIALLY UNCHASTE[NEG]> presupposed for the attributive paths of **DOMAIN OF SEX [...]** and **DOMAIN OF MORALITY [...]** respectively. Consider the following *OED* quotations:

> 1594 Go, you wag! You'll be a *twigger* when you come to age.
> ↕
> 1694 Those whom Venus is said to Rule, as Punks, Jills, Flirts,... Whipsters, *Twiggers*, Harlots, Kept-wenches... will be famous this Year.

The scarcity of records in the usage of E.Mod.E. *twigger* in any of its historical senses seems to be only reinforced and confirmed by the virtual absence of the lexical item from the macrostructure of modern lexicographic sources.

The world of animals, which extends from the underwater depths up to the sky, comprises animals, both those that have actually accompanied human beings, and those the stereotypical images of which have accompanied human beings since time immemorial. Apart from horses, geese and elephants there are names of fairy-tale unicorns, mermaids and basilisks that – to a certain degree – may be said to form but a small and marginal fraction of the lexical items linked to the conceptual macrocategory **ANIMALS**. The three lexical items, namely *cockatrice*, *mermaid* and *laced mutton*, should be treated as borderline cases that may be placed within the frames of zoosemy since both *cockatrice* and *mermaid* are fictitious creatures that feature in legends and fairy-tales whereas *mutton* is used with reference to both food and an animal, especially the one intended for consumption. Despite being peripheral they all represent metaphorical extensions, and hence should be discussed here.

As for the history of E.Mod.E. ***cockatrice***, its etymological roots – as Ayto (2005:121) reports – go back to Lat. *calcātrix* originally used in the sense 'tracker, hunter', and the form was a direct translation of Gr. *ikhneúmōn* which, in turn, *was a name given to a mysterious Egyptian creature in ancient times which was said to prey on crocodiles*. At the close of the 14th century the lexical item *cockatrice* was incorporated into the English lexicon as an alternative to *basilisk* 'mythical serpent'. As Ayto (2005) defines it, the word was used to name a beast with the head, wings and body of a cock and the tail of a serpent, which is said to have been born from a cock's egg, and it can kill by its mere glance. The original animal-specific sense of *cockatrice* is evidenced in the following historical material taken from the *OED*:

> 1382 Vp on the eddere and the *kokatrice*.
> 1440 Ther is a *cocautrice* withe in the walle; and as ofte tyme as she hathe enye syght of youre men, þei bethe dede.
> ↕
> 1829 Till this dracontine *cockatrice* Should break its way to light.

The historically primary sense of *cockatrice* is documented to have undergone a zoosemic shift when – at the turn of the 16th and 17th centuries – the lexical item started to be applied as a name of reproach for a woman, and also – with the progression of pejoration – in the sense 'prostitute'. Hence, the metaphorical sense of *cockatrice* may be said to associate clearly with activation of such conceptual values as <FEMALE_[NEU]> and <COMMERCIALLY UNCHASTE_[NEG]> presupposed for the attributive paths of **DOMAIN OF SEX […]** and **DOMAIN OF MORALITY […]**. The following *OED* material testifies to the late-16th-century rise of the metaphorical sense of *cockatrice*:

> 1599 And withal calls me at his pleasure I know not how many *cockatrices* and things.
> 1687 Prithee let me see thy punk, thy *cockatrice*, thy harlot.
> ↕
> 1747 Where's your Aunt, you young *cockatrice*?… She's a base Woman, and you are –.

One has grounds to conjecture that the illocutionary force evoked by the use of *cockatrice* to convey the sense 'prostitute' was largely dysphemistic as the very image of a creature that kills with a mere look is far from being rose-coloured. The analysis of the data shows that the human-specific sense of *cockatrice* was current for over a century. The virtual non-existence of the lexical item in question in Present-day English is confirmed by various modern lexicographic sources of today; neither *LDCE* nor *MED* include the lexical item *cockatrice* in their word stock list, while *ODO* provides the entry of the noun in question only in the animal-specific sense.

Another name of a fictitious creature the semantics of which underwent a zoosemic shift is **mermaid**, which may be defined as 'imaginary creature with the head and trunk of a woman and the tail of a fish'. The word originally entered the English language as a M.E. compound made up of *mere* 'the sea' and *maid* 'young girl' towards the end of the 14th century. The historically primary sense was, as the *OED* and Maggio (1987) report, that of 'siren', especially in the early stage of the use of *mermaid*. Thus defined, the historically original sense of the lexical item may be illustrated by means of the following *OED* contexts:

> c1386 Chauntecleer so free Soong murier than the *Mermayde* in the see.
> 1432-50 Poetes feyne iij *meremaydes* [orig. *sirenes*] to be in parte virgines and in parte bryddes.
> ↕
> 1867 'Tis said a *mermaid* haunts yon water.

As borne out by the *OED* and Ayto (2005), towards the end of the 16th century *mermaid* developed a secondary human-specific sense 'prostitute', and hence one may speak here of an entrenchment link to **DOMAIN OF SEX [...]** and **DOMAIN OF MORALITY [...]** for which the evaluatively neutral conceptual value <FEMALE$_{[NEU]}$> and the pejoratively pregnant conceptual value <COMMERCIALLY UNCHASTE$_{[NEG]}$> are foregrounded. The metaphorical female-specific sense of *mermaid* is evidenced by the following *OED* quotations:

> 1590 Oh traine me not sweet *Mermaide* with thy note,... Sing Siren for thy selfe, and I will dote.
> 1602 A gentleman... shall not... sneake into a Tauerne with his *Mermaid*, but [etc.].
> ↓
> 1880 She had floated... semi-nude, with all the other *mermaids à la mode*.

The metaphoric quasi zoosemic female-specific sense 'prostitute' may be said to be based on the conceptual mapping of the conceptual value <SEDUCTIVE$_{[NEG]}$> which – in the process of semantic transfer – may have enabled the shift from the fringes of the conceptual macrocategory **ANIMALS** to the conceptual category **FALLEN WOMAN**. In extralinguistic terms, the conceptual event of seduction is realised vocally in the case of mermaids, while in the case of prostitutes it is realised both vocally and sensually and the two channels are frequently combined into what may be termed as "sex speak". With time, the commercially sexual connotations present in the sense of *mermaid* – like those of many other E.Mod.E. historical synonyms of *prostitute* – fell into oblivion and the only meaning that is recorded in the lexicographic sources of today is 'imaginary sea creature that has the upper body of a woman and a fish's tail' (see, for example, *MED, LDCE, ODO*).

The semantic history of the lexical item ***(laced) mutton*** may be said to constitute one of numerous lexical realisations of the conceptual metaphor that comes under the general label THE OBJECT OF SEX IS FOOD, such as, for example, *tart* and *meat* in English and *mięsko*, the diminutive form of *mięso* 'meat', *cielęcinka*, the diminutive form of *cielęcina* 'veal' in Polish.[138] At one point of its semantic evolution *mutton* extended its sense from 'the flesh of sheep' to 'sheep, especially one intended to be eaten', and then another shift took place with the resultant evaluatively loaded female-specific sense 'prostitute'. Here, we have reasons to conjecture that the metaphorical transfer proceeded either from the conceptual category **ANIMALS** to the conceptual category **FALLEN WOMAN** or – alternately – from the conceptual category **FOODSTUFFS** to the category **FALLEN WOMAN**.[139]

As for the etymological roots of *mutton*, the word was adopted from O.Fr. *moton* (rarely *molton*), and the lexical item corresponds both to such Romance forms as O.Sp. *moton* and It. *montone* and such Celtic forms as Wel. *mollt* and Bret. *maout*. The historically original sense of *mutton* 'the flesh of sheep' is evidenced by the following *OED* quotations:

> c1290 Huy nomen with heom in heore schip at þat hem was leof, Gies and hennes, craunes and swannes and porc, *motoun* and beof.
> c1420 Take fresshe brothe of *motene* clene.
> ↕
> 1897 The steaming dish of *mutton* and vegetables.

Significantly, when it comes to the illocutionary force of *mutton* let us stress that all names of meat that were incorporated into English as the linguistic consequence of the Norman Conquest were intended to serve as the better, more sophisticated, synonyms of the native – homely or somewhat crude – counterparts. As a result, the upper ranking social strata consumed Romance sounding *mutton*, *beef* and *poultry* whereas the commoners were reduced to eating Germanic-wise termed *sheep*, *cows* and *chicken*, if lucky enough to have any specimens of the species raised in their yards.

At the outset of the 16th century *mutton* developed a pejoratively pregnant human-specific collective sense 'loose women, prostitutes', which is additionally rendered in the *OED* in terms of cognitive metaphor *food for lust*. Similarly, Holder (2008) points to the common meat imagery evoked by the employment of *mutton* in the sense 'prostitutes'. The historically novel metaphorical sense of the word may thus be accounted for in terms of activating and foregrounding of the conceptual values <FEMALE$_{[NEU]}$> and <COMMERCIALLY UN-

---

138 For recent study of the problem, see Kleparski (2013).
139 As shown by Kleparski (2013), many types of meat products in various natural languages tend to develop negatively loaded senses, such as, for example Pol. *parówa*, the augmentative form of *parówka* 'frankfurter sausage' which, in prison slang means, 'inmate who is forced to pay sexual services to other inmates'.

CHASTE_[NEG]> presupposed for the attributive paths of **DOMAIN OF SEX** [...] and **DOMAIN OF MORALITY** [...].The following *OED* quotations testify to the early-16th-century development of this sense-thread of *mutton*:

a1518 And from thens to the halfe strete, To get vs there some freshe mete. Why, is there any store of rawe *motton*?
a1700 *Mutton-in long-coats*, Women.
↓
1973 They're aw cows hawkin' their *mutton*.

Interestingly, the *OED* records the pejoratively loaded sexual senses of *meat* at the end of the 16th century, which may suggest that the metaphorisation of the meat-specific lexical item *mutton* preceded historically the rise of the secondary sense of the general word *meat*. Holder (2008) reports that metaphorically *meat* stands for 'person viewed sexually, male or female, heterosexually or homosexually'; *a bit of meat* is used in the sense 'man's sexual partner', *fresh meat* is 'young prostitute' and *stale meat* is 'old prostitute'. Curiously enough, in many cases the mechanism of foodsemy is tightly interwoven with the metonymically conditioned transfer *pars pro toto* – or the other way round – as both *meat* and *mutton* may be proved to have developed the sense 'the male penis' and 'the female pudendum'. Furthermore, in such cases it is virtually impossible to resolve which of the two mechanisms, metaphor or metonymy, was at work first.

As for the modifier *laced* that makes a constitutive element of the compound *laced mutton*, it needs to be mentioned that – according to the *OED* – *laced* was employed to modify *mutton* as a symbol of a bodice typically worn by the members of the oldest profession. The compound *laced mutton* is a later acquisition, which is evidenced by the following late-16th-century quotations:

1578 And I smealt, he lou'd *lase mutton* well.
↕
1694 With several coated Quails, and *lac'd Mutton*.

The *OED* records show that the history of the compound *laced mutton* was relatively short-lived, especially when confronted with the long history of its head element *mutton*, which has been in common use since the beginning of the 16th century until quite recently. Present-day lexicographic sources, however, such as Green (2003) and *ODO*, provide the historical remains of the pejoratively loaded human-specific metaphorical sense of *mutton*, as the word still today forms part of a phrase *to hawk one's mutton* used in the sense 'work as a prostitute'.

Apart from the body of zoosemic and foodsemic extensions discussed in the foregoing, the conceptual category **FAMILY** seems to function as another source domain from which conceptual mappings take place to the conceptual microcategory **FALLEN WOMAN**. Hence, the schema that may be formulated is A PROSTITUTE IS A FAMILY MEMBER, for which Schulz (1975:66) provides such historical lexical realisations as L.Mod.E. *cousin* 'trull or strumpet' (19th-century cant),[140] E.Mod.E. *aunt* 'bawd or prostitute',[141] L.Mod.E. *mother* 'bawd'[142] and E.Mod.E. *sister* 'disguised whore'. The *HTE*, in turn, includes the entry **sisters of the bank** as a 16th-century synonym of *prostitute*.

The cognitive basis behind such a picturing of a prostitute is a specific kind of similarity that may be drawn between family and prostitutes, namely that both form a certain community that live, function together, and are – in a way – interdependent, at least to a certain degree. Out of all the body of synonyms of *prostitute* Schulz (1975:66) names only *sister* and *aunt* developed their secondary, pejoratively loaded sense in the course of the Early Modern English period. The roots of this metaphorically conditioned sense shift may be sought in the diachronic evolution of the lexical item in question.

The etymology of *sister* goes back to the Anglo-Saxon times when – according to the *OED* – the word was adopted from either Nor. and Sw. *syster* or Da. *søster*.[143] Cognates from other European languages are all used primarily in the sense 'female in relationship to another person having the same parents'. The historically original sense of *sister* is evidenced in the following *OED* contexts:

a900 Hæfde hine Penda adrifenne… forþon he his *swostor* anforlet.
a1100 Ða begann se cyngc… ʒyrnan his *sweostor* him to wife.
↕
1877 There was more than *sister* in my kiss, And so the saints were wroth.

Approximately at the same time, that is at the beginning of the 10th century, the lexical item *sister* underwent the process of meaning extension and – as the *OED* bears witness – the word started to be used in the broader sense 'one who is reckoned as, or fills the place of, a sister'. Furthermore, a note is made at this point that this extended sense of *sister* formed the basis for the metaphorical mappings into the conceptual category **COMMUNITY**, since current female-specific senses of *sister* are '(fellow) prostitute', '(fellow) feminist' and 'black woman' (used among blacks).

As for the E.Mod.E. collective expression *sisters of the bank*, its first occurrence is recorded in the *OED* in the middle of the 16th century. What is more important, however, is that the coinage of the expression *sisters of the bank* pre-

---

140 Consider the following *OED* quotation: a1700 One of my *Cosens*, a Wench.
141 As shown by the following *OED* material: 1607 She demanded of me whether I was your worships *aunt* or no. Out, out, out!
142 Consider the following *OED* context: 1785 *Mother* or the *Mother*, a bawd.
143 For a detailed analysis of the phonological evolution of O.E. *sweoster* as a result of the Scandinavian influence, see Wełna (1978).

ceded the rise of the compound *Winchester goose* by only several decades. In order to comprehend the connection between the two E.Mod.E. synonyms of *prostitute* targeted here one needs to delve into the etymology of the terminal part of the expression *sisters of the bank*.

As the *OED* data reveals, the lexical item *bank* underwent the process of specialisation of meaning at the beginning of the 14th century when – after approximately one century – its historically original sense 'raised shelf or ridge of ground' narrowed and this resulted in the rise of the sense 'the shelving or sloping margin of a river or a stream'. The historically novel sense became restricted further in the first half of the 16th century to convey the specific geographical localisation 'the south side of the Thames opposite London, and the brothel-quarter located there'. Incidentally, it is this very district of London, the so-called Bankside, which was in the hands of the Bishop of Winchester, the one who – through his notorious action of collecting rents from the bawdy houses of the area – contributed to the coinage of the other expression, namely *Winchester goose* discussed earlier. The following *OED* contexts testify to this very much specialised sense of *bank*:

> 1536 As moche shame for an honest man to come out of a tauerne… as it is here to come from the *banke*.
> 1548 *Sisters of the Bank*, the stumbling-blocks of all frail youth.
> ↕
> 1598 On this *Banke* was sometime the *Bordello* or Stewes.

Unlike the historical synonym *Winchester goose*, the expression *sisters of the bank* may be labelled as a one-time innovation that somehow never gained popularity and failed to spread; the *OED* provides only one 16th-century quotation in the entry for *sister* (1550 Immodeste and wanton gyrles haue hereby ben made *sisters of the Banck* (the stumbling stock of all frayle youth.), and the other one is given in the entry for *bank* (see quote 1548 above). Within the framework adopted, we may say that in the first half of the 16th century the semantics of *sister* when coupled with the semantics of *the bank* within one and the same phraseological syntagma developed an entrenchment link to **DOMAIN OF MORALITY** [...] for which such pejoratively pregnant conceptual value as <COMMERCIALLY UNCHASTE$_{[NEG]}$> is foregrounded to yield the sense 'prostitute'. As far as the question of the illocutionary force is concerned, the phrase *sisters of the bank* may have been an auspicious term since *sister* itself has been used in either neutral or positively coloured senses.

As for the etymological roots of ***aunt*** – another lexical realisation of the metaphorical schema A PROSTITUTE IS A FAMILY MEMBER – they go back to the late-13th-century form *aunte* adopted from Old French and used in the sense 'the sister of one's father or mother'. As the *OED*, Partridge (1984) and Green (2003) show, *aunt* developed a secondary metaphorical sense 'procuress, prostitute' in the early 17th century. Hence, to account for the semantics of *aunt*, apart from positing an entrenchment link to the attributive path of **DOMAIN OF SEX [...]** for which the evaluatively neutral conceptual element <FEMALE$_{[NEU]}$> is activated, we may speak of the foregounding of the pejoratively pregnant conceptual value <COMMERCIALLY UNCHASTE$_{[NEG]}$> presupposed for the attributive path of **DOMAIN OF MORALITY [...]**. This historically novel metaphorical evaluatively loaded sense of *aunt* is evidenced by the following *OED* material:

> 1607 She demanded of me whether I was your worships *aunt* or no. Out, out, out!
> ↕
> 1678 The easiest Fool I ever knew, next my *Naunt* of Fairies in the *Alchymist*.

As the *OED* data shows, this synonym of *prostitute* was relatively short-lived in the history of English and, currently, there are no traces of morally loaded sense of *aunt* in the lexicographic sources that have been consulted.

Another female-specific lexical item in the history of English that developed a secondary meaning 'prostitute' is ***succubus***, which entered the English word stock as a Late Latin borrowing towards the end of the 14th century. Ayto (2005) clarifies that Romance *succubus* (lit. 'one who lies down under another') was a feminine counterpart of the etymologically original Latin masculine form *incubāre* > *incubus* (lit. 'one who lies down on another'). While the former was employed in the sense 'demon in female form who has carnal intercourse with men in their sleep', the latter was used in the sense 'male demon who has carnal intercourse with women in their sleep'.

At the beginning of the 17th century *succubus* may be proved to have undergone the process of meaning widening when – according to the *OED* – the word started to be used in the more general sense 'demon, evil spirit'. From the diachronic perspective, this stage in the evolution of the semantics of *succubus* is the case of the metaphorical transfer. Already in the first half of the 17th century the conceptual mapping occurred between the conceptual categories **SPIRITUAL ENTITIES** and **FALLEN WOMAN** when the lexical item in question started to be used in the sense 'strumpet, whore; low woman'. For the rise of the historically novel metaphorical sense an entrenchment link may be traced to **DOMAIN OF SIN [...], DOMAIN OF MORALITY[...]** and **DOMAIN OF SOCIAL STATUS [...]** for which such pejoratively pregnant conceptual values as morally charged <EVIL$_{[NEG]}$>, <COMMERCIALLY UNCHASTE$_{[NEG]}$> and <LOW$_{[NEG]}$> are activated and brought to prominence. The following *OED* quotations testify to this metaphorical pejoratively loaded sense of *succubus*:

> 1622 A *Succubus*, a damned sinke of sinne.

1706 A flinching son of a *succubus*, to pretend to call for a looking glass and sneak away.
↕
1803 [A bed~maker] Like any fell *Succubus*, wrinkled and old, With the lip of the shrew, and the nose of a scold.

A closer inspection of the historical evolution of the semantics of *succubus* seems to point to the inauspicious illocutionary force of the word in question, and the historical prominence of such conceptual values as <SINFUL$_{[NEG]}$> and <EVIL$_{[NEG]}$> contributes to the dysphemistic nature of the semantics of *succubus*. Interestingly, although the lexicographic sources of today, such as *LDCE* and *ODO*, include the entry *succubus* there is no trace of its 'prostitute' synonymous sense, though the sense is very frequently implied in the contexts of use that are provided.

3.6.2 Early Modern English metonymy conditioned synonyms

The process that is frequently at work in the formation of historical synonyms of *prostitute* is metonymy. Here, the process in question was at work in the formation of such E.Mod.E. lexical items as *baggage, stew, walk-street, street-walker, night-shade, night-trader, fling-dust (-stink)* and *waistcoateer*. Obviously, the metonymic extensions are based on various types of contiguity, such as for instance:

- \\FEATURE FOR PERSON ADORNED WITH THIS FEATURE\\ (*baggage, fling-dust (-stink)*), *light of love* (discussed in the section on **circumlocution**),
- \\LOCATION FOR PROFESSION\\ (*stew, walk-street, streetwalker*),
- \\TIME OF ACTIVITY FOR PROFESSION\\ (*night-shade, night-trader*),
- \\POSSESSED FOR POSSESSOR\\ (*waistcoateer*).

To begin with, as the *OED* informs us, the lexical item **baggage** is an adaptation of either O.Fr. *bagage* 'property packed up for carriage' or O.Fr. *bagues* 'bundles, packs' and cognates of the former are found in Pr. *bagatge* or Sp. *bagage* while the corresponding forms of the latter are Pr. *bagua* and It. *baga*. Both Rawson (1989) and Ayto (2005) suggest there is an etymological link between *baggage* and *bag* although Partridge (1984) and Holder (2008) treat the two terms as separate entries. The *OED* explains further that the female-specific sense that developed in the late 16th century is believed to have originated in Fr. *bagasse*, which itself is of unknown etymology.

According to the *OED*, the historically original sense of *baggage* defined as 'portable property, luggage', present in English from the beginning of the 15th century underwent the process of meaning specialisation and – as a result of this

– the word started to be employed in the more restricted military sense 'the portable army equipment' already towards the end of the 15th century. This specialised sense shift is evidenced by the following *OED* contexts of use:

> 1489 *Baggage* and fardellages must be taken.
> 1591 Borne of the Boyes amongest other *Baggage*.
> ↕
> 1810 The *baggage* of the British army is always an embarrassment.

Furthermore, Rawson (1989) argues that it is this historical sense that gave rise to the development of the pejoratively pregnant female-specific sense. The word started to be used with reference to female kind mainly because – as Rawson (1989:31) puts it – ***baggage trains** of armies traditionally included loose-living camp followers*,[144] (1601 Every common soldier carrying with him his she-*baggage*).[145] The mid-16th century brought about the next stage in the semantic evolution of *baggage*. At this stage the shift in the semantics of the word necessitates the involvement of the conceptual value <FILTHY$_{[NEG]}$> presupposed for the attributive path of **DOMAIN OF PHYSICAL CHARACTERISTICS AND APPEARANCE [...]**. The 16th-century sense 'rubbish, refuse, dirt' may be illustrated by the following set of *OED* contexts:

> 1549 Nettles, Thistle... or suche lyke *baggage* grow.
> 1645 It runs out in weeds and *baggage*.
> ↕
> 1661 A mere Glut, Like loathed *Baggage* to the nauseous Gut.

There are good reasons to assume that this very sense underwent the process of meaning extension either through the mechanism of metaphor or metonymy. The sense development that is of primary interest to the on-going analysis is the late-16th-century rise of the sense 'woman of disreputable or immoral life, strumpet'. Here, the change in the semantics of *baggage* may be accounted for in terms of activation of such human-specific values as <FEMALE$_{[NEU]}$>, <COMMERCIALLY UNCHASTE$_{[NEG]}$> and <LOW$_{[NEG]}$> presupposed for the attributive paths of **DOMAIN OF SEX [...], DOMAIN OF MORALITY [...]** and **DOMAIN OF SOCIAL STATUS [...]** respectively. The historically novel female-specific sense of *baggage* is evidenced by the following selected *OED* contexts:

> 1596 Y'are a *baggage*, the Slies are no Rogues.
> 1693 A *baggage*, or Souldier's Punk, *Scortum Castrense*.
> ↓

---

144 Bold mine.
145 Quotation taken from Rawson (1989:31).

1851 She was a disreputable, daring, laughing, painted French *baggage*, that Comic Muse.

The question that remains unanswered is that of whether the female-specific sense of *baggage* constitutes a lexical realisation of the conceptual metaphor PROSTITUTION IS FILTH or rather should be attributed to the metonymic extension based on the \\FEATURE FOR PERSON ADORNED WITH THIS FEATURE\\ contiguity.

Curiously enough, approximately a century later, that is towards the end of the 17th century, the lexical item *baggage* was subject to the process of amelioration since the word started to be used playfully in the sense 'any young woman'. Some present-day lexicographic works, such as *ODO*, seem to confirm this sense development, as the dictionary defines *baggage* – among other things – as an evaluatively loaded word meaning 'cheeky, disagreeable girl or woman', with a note that this use is *archaic*.

As to the status of the E.Mod.E *prostitute* synonym **fling-dust (-stink)** one may say that this was yet another fleeting invention which failed to root in the English lexico-semantic system. Apparently, there is no trace of such a lexical item in modern lexicographic sources, such as *MED*, *LDCE* and *ODO*. From an extralinguistic perspective, the *raison d'etre* behind its origin – as Green (2003) conjectures – is the typical unintended action of stirring the dirt and dust while walking the streets. In cognitive terms, the semantics of the lexical item *fling-dust (-stink)* seems to be a historical realisation of the metonymic pattern \\FEATURE FOR PERSON ADORNED WITH THIS FEATURE\\, and its meaning may be rendered in terms of activation of the conceptual values <FEMALE$_{[NEU]}$> and <COMMERCIALLY UNCHASTE$_{[NEG]}$> presupposed for the attributive paths of **DOMAIN OF SEX [...]** and **DOMAIN OF MORALITY [...]**. This historically original sense of *fling-dust (-stink)* is evidenced by the following 17th-century *OED* contexts:

> 1621 She is an English whore, a kind of *fling-dust*, One of your London light-o'-loves.
> 1679 That he was not President of the Benedictines, his Lordship affirmed from the Testimony of three *Flingstinks*.

Additionally, to account for the 'streetwalker' sense of *fling-dust (-stink)* an entrenchment link to the attributive path of **DOMAIN OF SOCIAL STATUS [...]** may be expected for which the pejoratively pregnant value <LOW$_{[NEG]}$> is activated. This is meant to account for the non-definitional yet presupposed lower status of the streetwalking prostitutes referred to.

As for the second element of the composite determinant, that is *dust*, it may be assumed that the conceptual metaphor formulated as PROSTITUTION IS

FILTH may have played some role in the formation of this dysphemistic historical synonym of *prostitute*; this time again the conceptual picture of prostitute lying near the Greek *porné* order. After all, the concept of FILTH is inevitably linked to the activity of walking the streets, regardless of the purpose.

In turn, the metonymic extension based on the contiguity pattern \\LOCATION FOR PROFESSION\\ is realised lexically by, for example, the semantic evolution of *stew*, which originates, as Ayto (2005) clarifies, in the 14th-century adaptation of Vulgar Latin **extūfāre* via O.Fr. *estuve* 'vapour'. At the beginning of the 14th century, *stew* was linked to the conceptual category **CONTAINERS** as the word was used in the sense 'vessel for boiling', and – relatively soon – there developed the extended sense 'heated room used for hot air or vapour baths'. The following *OED* quotations testify to this diachronically original late-14th-century sense of *stew*:

> 1390 The bathes and the *stewes* bothe Thei schetten in be every weie.
> c1483 Natalye the wyf of the *stews* Kepeth a good *styewe*,… They goon thedyr to be stewed Alle the strangers.
> ↓
> 1865 Above the vaults the original Turkish bath, or '*stew*', remains in good preservation.

According to the *OED*, Partridge (1984) and Holder (2008), it is this very sense of *stew* that triggered the rise of the sense 'brothel'. As the lexicographic sources explain the extralinguistic reason for this sense development must have been the common underlying function of public hot-air bath-houses, which provided all types of sexual services for the needy and the wanting. Holder (2008) quotes Shakespeare at this point: *An I could get me but a wife in the stews*. This 14th-century evaluatively pejorative sense of *stew* is illustrated by the following *OED* material:

> 1362 lacke þe logelour And lonete of þe *stuyues*.
> c1460 Ye lanettys of the *stewys*, and lychoures on lofte.
> ↕
> 1873 Their ranks were filled by rogues and scare-crows from the styes and *stews*.

In the middle of the 16th century the sense 'brothel' may be said to have undergone a metonymically conditioned extension based on the contiguity pattern \\LOCATION FOR PROFESSION\\ through which the lexical item *stew* started to be used in the human-specific sense 'bawd, a prostitute'. Again the essence of the resultant sense may be accounted for in terms of activation of such conceptual values as <FEMALE[NEU]> and <COMMERCIALLY UNCHASTE[NEG]> presupposed for the attributive paths of **DOMAIN OF SEX […]** and **DOMAIN**

OF MORALITY [...]. The following *OED* contexts testify to this metonymic sense of *stew*:

1552 *Stew*, bavde, or merchaunt of whores, *leno*.
1639 I have matcht a *Stewes*; The notedst woman oth' Towne.
↕
1650 Instead of that beauty he had a notorious *Stew* sent him.

Another assumption that can be made is that the rise of the sense involves the development of an entrenchment link to the attributive path of **DOMAIN OF SOCIAL STATUS** [...] for which the pejoratively loaded conceptual value <LOW$_{[NEG]}$> becomes activated. As Partridge (1984) argues, the low social status of women working in stews must have been – at least partly – connected with the fact that the early-17th-century sense of *bagnio*, the synonym of *stew*, was '(high-class) brothel'. Interestingly, according to the *OED*, stew entered a compound together with *strumpet* or *whore* in the first half of the 16th century, and the resultant composite determinants **stewed strumpet/whore** – like *stew* alone – were used as opprobrious epithets imputing unchastity.[146]

As to the sexually explicit sense of *stew* in current lexicographic works, only *ODO* records the sexually-loaded sense 'brothel' with a label *archaic*. The other present-day lexicographic works consulted, such as *MED* or *LDCE*, fail to include any of the pejoratively pregnant senses of the past.

In turn, the next two E.Mod.E. synonyms, namely **streetwalker** and **walk-street**, have been in common use invariably since the 16th century.[147] The reason for this permanence may be the atemporal validity of the location (*street*) that became part of this composite determinant used with reference to the members of the oldest profession. After all, the daily practice of the trade has always been somewhat connected with street life, and all that goes with it, no matter what the geographical position, time of the day or night or historical time. To meet the referential needs, already in ancient Rome a specific term was coined for a prostitute working in the street (Lat. *circulatrix* lit. 'streetwalking'). Similarly, most European languages have corresponding terms in their word stocks, and all are counterparts of E.Mod.E. *streetwalker* or *walk-street*, such as Pol. *ulicznica*, Fr. *péripatéticienne*, Sp. *callejera/mujer de la calle*, It. *passeggiatrice*, G. *Straßenmädchen* and Sw. *gatflicka*. Hence, the rise of the metonymic extension

---

146 Consider the following *OED* quotations: 1532 This good scholer of Tindalle... findeth in his heart written by the spirit of God, yt freres & monkes... may... vnder the name of weddyng, make *stewed strumpettes* of nunnes. → 1575 Where is the strong *stued hore*?

147 As Rawson (1981) argues, the Pres.E. counterpart of E.Mod.E. *streetwalker* is *pavement princess* coined in CB lingo.

based on the contiguity schema \\LOCATION FOR PROFESSION\\, in the case of the semantics of the lexical items in question, is natural.

According to the *OED* data, the compound *streetwalker* started to be used in the sense 'common prostitute whose field of operations is the street' towards the end of the 16th century. This historically original sense of the compound may be rendered in terms of activation of such conceptual values as evaluatively neutral <FEMALE[NEU]> and pejoratively pregnant <COMMERCIALLY UN-CHASTE[NEG]> presupposed for the attributive paths of **DOMAIN OF SEX** [...] and **DOMAIN OF MORALITY** [...]. Additionally, an entrenchment link may be traced to **DOMAIN OF SOCIAL STATUS** [...] for which the conceptual value <LOW[NEG]> is evidently foregrounded. The following *OED* contexts testify to the sense of *streetwalker*:

> 1592 They shold see how these *street walkers* wil iet in rich garded gowns.
> 1762 Mr. Levet has married a *streetwalker*.
> ↕
> 1894 Where arbitrary power of arrest is given... the *streetwalker* proves a great revenue to the policeman.

The other 17th-century compound *walk-street* – though based on the same metonymic \\LOCATION FOR PROFESSION\\ contiguity pattern – has failed to survive for long (1611 *Bateur de pavez*, an idle or continuall **walke-street*... a lasciuious, or vnthrifty, night~walker). The fact that E.Mod.E. *streetwalker* has remained in common use – as confirmed by current lexicographic sources such as *ODO*, *LDCE* and *MED* – while its E.Mod.E. synonym *walk-street* became obsolete relatively quickly may be accounted for by the natural drive in most natural languages to avoid absolute synonymy.

What seems to be problematic is the cognitive nature of the other two E.Mod.E. synonyms of *prostitute*, namely **night-shade** and **night-trader**. They may be treated as either a pair of lexical realisations of the conceptual metaphor A PROSTITUTE IS A NOCTURNAL CREATURE/ENTITY or as the cases of the metonymic extension based on \\TIME OF ACTIVITY FOR PROFESSION\\ contiguity pattern. The temporal similarity that exists between the concept NIGHT and the conceptual category **PROSTITUTION** makes both cognitive mechanisms highly plausible as the operative forces behind the formation of such cover terms as *night-shade* and *night-trader*. Here, one may postulate a higher-level metaphor that comes under the label A PROSTITUTE IS A NOCTURNAL ENTITY, which encompasses the behavioural patterns and/or features of such entities as bats, cats, traders, girls and shades as well.

Another striking feature of the lexical items in question is their relatively short-lived nature as *prostitute* synonyms. Both *night-shade* and *night-trader* were recorded only in the *OED* in the 17th-century sense 'prostitute'. The semantics of both compounds may be accounted for in terms of activation of the conceptual values <FEMALE[NEU]> and <COMMERCIALLY UNCHASTE[NEG]> presupposed for the attributive paths of **DOMAIN OF SEX [...]** and **DOMAIN OF MORALITY [...]**. The sense 'prostitute' is illustrated below with one quotation for each lexical item:

> 1612 Here comes a *night-shade*. A gentlewoman-whore.
> 1629 All kinds of females, from the *night-trader l' the street... to the great lady in her cabinet.

Furthermore, in the case of *night-trader* it is only the sense 'the oldest profession' that is given in the *OED* records. In turn, the sense 'prostitute' of the lexical item *night-shade* may have developed from the earlier sense of the word, that is 'the shade or darkness of night' through the mechanism of personification. From the present-day perspective, neither of the two E.Mod.E. compound synonyms of *prostitute* discussed here has managed to withstand the test of time and lexicographic works of today fail to include either *night-shade* or *night-trader* in their macrostructure.

Last but not least, the pattern of the metonymic contiguity \\POSSESSED FOR POSSESSOR\\ has been realised lexically by the historical evolution of E.Mod.E. ***waistcoateer***. To be more specific – as suggested by Kopecka (2011:93) – the lexical item in question may be said to represent a lower level variant of \\POSSESSED FOR POSSESSOR\\ contiguity, that may be schematised as \\ARTICLE OF CLOTHING FOR PERSON WEARING IT\\. The historically original meaning of the base *waistcoat* 'garment of male attire, worn under an outer garment' dates back to the first half of the 16th century, and its original semantics may be rendered – among others – in terms of activation of the conceptual value <MASCULINE[NEU]> presupposed for the attributive paths of **DOMAIN OF GENDER [...]**. In the middle of the 16th century, however, the sense of *waistcoat* underwent the process of meaning extension through the development of an entrenchment link to **DOMAIN OF GENDER [...]** for which the conceptual value <FEMININE[NEU]> is activated as well. The following *OED* contexts testify to the 16th-century male- and female-specific senses of *waistcoat*:

> 1519 For makyng of a *waste cotte*. <MASCULINE[NEU]>
> 1649 The King... being in his *Wastcoat*, put his Cloak on again. <MASCULINE[NEU]>
> 1547 I cause a man to lye in his doublet, and a woman in her *waste cote*. <FEMININE[NEU]>
> 1688 *Wastcoat* or *Waistcoat*... is an Habit or Garment generally worn by the middle and lower sort of Women. <FEMININE[NEU]>

As evidenced by the *OED* contexts given above, the late 17th century brought about the semantic deterioration of *waistcoat* since, for some extralinguistic reasons, wearing one became a symbol of belonging to the lower strata of society. The *OED* sheds some light on the cultural background of the evaluative downfall of the article of clothing in question along the following lines:

> In the 16th and early 17th century the waistcoat was one of the normal garments of women, having superseded the **placard** and **stomacher**. Later in the 17th century (when going out of fashion), especially if worn without an upper gown, it appears to have been considered a mark of a low-class woman of ill-repute.

It seems that it was this new trend in female fashion that led to the formation of a derivative *waistcoateer* in the first half of the 17th century, which started to be employed in the socially and morally negatively tinted sense 'low-class prostitute'. Within the framework adopted here, the semantics of E.Mod.E. *waistcoateer* may be accounted for in terms of activation of the evaluatively neutral conceptual value <FEMALE$_{[NEU]}$> and the pejoratively pregnant conceptual value <COMMERCIALLY UNCHASTE$_{[NEG]}$> presupposed for the attributive paths of **DOMAIN OF SEX [...]** and **DOMAIN OF MORALITY [...]**. Additionally, one may speak here of an entrenchment link to **DOMAIN OF SOCIAL STATUS [...]** for which the conceptual value <LOW$_{[NEG]}$> seems to be foregrounded, to account for the low status of the sex workers referred to. The following *OED* contexts provide evidence for this sense of *waistcoateer*:

> 1616 Doe you thinke you are here sir amongst your *wastcoateers*, your base Weneches that scratch at such occasions?
> 1822 'I know the face of yonder *waistcoateer*', continued the guide.
> ↓
> 1916 The grave and mocking music of the lutenists or the frank laughter of *waistcoateers*.

Although the *OED* provides the last records of use of *waistcoateer* as late as the first half of the 20th century, Green (2003) treats the lexical item in question as a 17th-century synonym of *prostitute*. The fact that none of the modern lexicographic works that have been consulted, such as *MED*, *LDCE* and *ODO*, includes *waistcoateer* as an entry may suggest that the word may have become obsolete well before the advent of the 20th century.

To the modern eye there is nothing positive or negative about the semantics of *waistcoat*, and to the present-day reader the fact that it was somehow related to the idea of prostitution may be a fact belonging to curiosity shop realia rather than something to be taken for granted. Take, for example *high-heels*, the effect of which is, as Mills (1989:192) puts it *throw the weight of the wearer on the balls of the feet* and make walking fearsome trouble in itself, not to mention running – a suicidal act. Yet, today high-heels symbolically summon up all sorts of ideas of either female dominance or bondage and conspicuous sexuality, as well as male chivalry, as suggested by Kramarae and Treichler (1985). With other articles of clothing the ill repute, if not universally present, at least tends to go a long way. To take an example, the lexical item *apron* has for a long time in the history of English – as well as other languages, such as Polish – been associated with an idea of dependence on the female kind, if not unmanly sissiness not befitting the male species.

3.6.3 Early Modern English and the mechanism of understatement at work

Significantly, the operation of the mechanism of metonymy is not infrequently coupled with the mechanism of understatement in the formation of many E.Mod.E. synonyms onomasiologically linked to the conceptual category **FALLEN WOMAN**. Quantitatively, the mechanism of understatement is relatively productive for the period in question because as many as thirteen cover terms were formed in the course of Early Modern English to provide veils for the negatively loaded female-specific concept targeted here. Among the metonymically conditioned innovations, such words as, *streetwalker*, *walk-street*, *night-shade*, *night-trader* and *fling-dust* may be said to be lexical produce of the working of the mechanism of understatement.

Much in the same manner as M.E. *common woman* and, the truncated variant *common* (see section 3.5), the euphemistic employment of E.Mod.E. ***public woman*** is based on the idea of general (hence public) availability of women of the street. Interestingly, the *OED* treats both *common woman* and *public woman* as interchangeable syntagmas, which may testify to the conceptual proximity of the two historical synonyms of *prostitute*. As for the origin of *public* (M.E. *publike*) – which is the key element in the structure of the composite determinant in question – the word goes back to the end of the 15th century when – according to the *OED* – it was adopted from Fr. *public*, which, in turn, inherited the word from Early Lat. *poplicus* based on *poplus* meaning 'people'. The *OED* provides such synonyms of *publike* as *common*, *national* and *popular*, and the historically original sense of M.E. *publike* was 'of or pertaining to the people as a whole', as seen from the *OED*-quoted contexts below:

1484 *Public* administration.
1563 To… confound all, bayth priuat and *publict*, bayth hallowit and prophane.
↕
1977 The management of *public* corporations… was his particular field.

In the first half of the 16th century, *public* is evidenced to have undergone semantic development and the word started to be used in the more generalised sense, that is 'open to, may be used by, or may or must be shared by all members of the community, generally accessible or available'. Undoubtedly, it is this sense of *public* that – when combined with the notion FEMALE HUMAN BEING – gave rise to the formation of the compound *public woman* used auspiciously in the sense 'prostitute'. The semantics of the E.Mod.E. compound may be accounted for in terms of activation of such conceptual values as <FEMALE$_{[NEU]}$> and <COMMERCIALLY UNCHASTE$_{[NEG]}$> presupposed for the attributive paths of **DOMAIN OF SEX [...]** and **DOMAIN OF MORALITY [...]**. The rise of this historically novel late-16th-century syntagma is testified by the following *OED* material:

> 1585 [He] caused to be clothed two *publique* Turkish *women*, with very rich apparrell.
> 1662 To banish thence all the *publick Women*.
> ↓
> 1892 The houses of the '*public women*' (as they are still styled in modern places).

Yet another woman-headed compound that – in the history of English – came to be used euphemistically in the sense 'prostitute' is E.Mod.E *strange woman*. As to the etymology of *strange*, in the late-13th century, the adjective was adopted from O.Fr. *estrange* (1297 Þe king made him vroþ inou,... þat *strange* men in is owe lond dude a such trespas.), which corresponds to Fr. *étrange*, Sp. *estraño*, It. *strano*, all of which are rooted etymologically in Lat. *extrāneus* meaning 'external, foreign'.

At the outset of the 14th century there was a rise of the modified sense of *strange* whereby the lexical item in question started to be employed in the sense 'belonging to others, not of one's own kin or family'. As the editors of the *OED* conjecture, the syntagmatic consequence of the rise of this othering sense of *strange* was the formation of the compound *strange woman* in the first half of the 16th century, and the newly formed compound was, most probably, used auspiciously to convey the evaluatively pregnant sense 'prostitute'. Hence, for the semantics of *strange woman* one is justified in speaking about the rise of an entrenchment link to **DOMAIN OF SEX [...]** and **DOMAIN OF MORALITY [...]** for which the evaluatively neutral conceptual value <FEMALE$_{[NEU]}$> and the behaviourally and morally loaded conceptual value <COMMERCIALLY UNCHASTE$_{[NEG]}$> are clearly activated, as emerging from the following *OED* contexts:

> 1535 That thou mayest be delyuered also from the *straunge woman* [so later versions], and from her that is not thine owne.

1614 If I can... but rescue this youth, here out of the hands of the lewd man and the *strange woman*.
↓
1886 No fear of my being tempted by the *strange woman*, for was I not in love?

When we scrutinise the history of both E.Mod.E. woman-headed compounds, that is *public woman* and *strange woman*, we are tempted to formulate the conclusion that picturing of a prostitute as a woman either available to everyone or a woman who is not one's own wife,[148] (or both) forms suitable conceptual grounds for the formation of historical euphemisms. The rise of the euphemisms is either based on or largely conditioned by the mechanism of understatement. Hence, in the conceptualisation of PROSTITUTION we are dealing with activating and foregrounding of the conceptual values <HIGHLY AVAILABLE$_{[POS]}$> and <UNFAMILIAR$_{[NEG]}$> presupposed for the attributive paths of **DOMAIN OF AVAILABILITY [...]** and **DOMAIN OF KINSHIP AND FAMILIARITY [...]** respectively. From the present-day perspective, both euphemisms have been relegated to the past; neither of the two E.Mod.E compounds is recorded in the current lexicographic sources that have been consulted, such as, for example, *MED*, *LDCE* and *ODO*.

In turn, the E.Mod.E monosyllabic ***miss*** is the produce of the operation of understatement coupled with the application of the structural process of back-clipping. Most of the sources that have been consulted, such as the *OED*, Weekley (1921), Ayto (2005), Skeat (2005) and Holder (2008), acknowledge the clipped nature of *miss*, which is a shortened variant of M.E. *mistress* used most frequently in the sense 'woman who illicitly occupies the place of a wife'.[149] Rawson (1989) explains that M.E. *mistress* goes back to Fr. *maistre* 'master' and – as far as the semantics of *mistress* goes – *[...] its primary meanings revolve around the sense of a woman who has command over servants, children, a household, a territory, a state, or – getting to the issue at hand – a man's heart* (Rawson 1989:250). With the passage of time the negatively loaded sense 'kept lover' gained the upper hand and the positively loaded senses mentioned by Rawson (1989) were gradually overshadowed, and finally abandoned altogether. It is an interesting fact of language that the corresponding male-specific *mister* has never descended on the evaluative scale. Kleparski (1990), following Schulz (1975), refers to the process labelled as democratic levelling, through which lexical items whose semantics is accountable for in terms of activation of the con-

---

148 According to the *OED*, the English adjective *strange* corresponds semantically to two Heb. words *norkīyāh* and *zārāh* which stand for 'not one's own (wife)'.
149 The French word *maitresse* also had a short-lived career in 18th-and 19th-century Polish in which it was used in the sense 'kept woman', 'female lover'. Originally, as we are informed by Bańkowski (2000), it was employed in the sense 'teacher, tutor'.

ceptual values <HIGH$_{[POS]}$> and <FEMALE$_{[NEU]}$> presupposed for the attributive paths of **DOMAIN OF SOCIAL STATUS [...]** and **DOMAIN OF SEX [...]** tend to, with the passage of time, go down the social scale; a trend which hardly ever takes place in the case of lexical items whose semantics is accountable for in terms of activation of the conceptual value <MALE$_{[NEU]}$> presupposed for the attributive path of **DOMAIN OF SEX [...]**. The body of pairs of lexical items in English the female-specific item of which underwent the process of democratic levelling includes *marquis/marchioness*, *sultan/sultana*, *duke/duchess*, *governor/governess* and *courtier/courtesan*.[150]

The clipped form *miss* is first recorded in the *OED* in the first half of the 17th century as used in the evaluatively tinted sense 'kept mistress' or less commonly in the heavily pejoratively charged sense 'common prostitute'. On the contrary, Skeat (2005) provides the evaluatively neutral sense 'young woman, girl' as the historically original meaning of *miss* while Ayto (2005) conjectures that the 17th-century sense 'unmarried woman' was the female-specific etymological starting point of *miss*. Hence, it may be assumed that – in a relatively short period of time – the semantics of *miss* became linked to a new sense that is accountable in terms of an entrenchment link to the attributive path of **DOMAIN OF MORALITY [...]** for which the conceptual value <COMMERCIALLY UN-CHASTE$_{[NEG]}$> is foregrounded, as testified by the following *OED*-extracted quotations:

> 1645 The com'on *misses* [at Venice]... go abroad bare-fac'd.
> 1765 If one is a *Miss*, be a *Miss* to a gentleman I say.
> ↕
> 1826 Can you believe what the newspapers said that the parents connived at her being Colonel Barcley's *miss*?

Green (2003) informs us of a heavily ironic use of *miss* in the sense 'prostitute' in Standard British English. The use of the word in this sense started to fade away in the early 19th century, as confirmed by the *OED* quotations. From the present-day perspective, there is no trace of the ill-conceived sexuality in the semantics of *miss*, as evidenced by such current lexicographic works that have been consulted as *MED*, *LDCE* and *ODO*; the sense 'prostitute' is no longer

---

150 The effects of the process of democratic levelling are also visible in Polish where we find pairs of words with different secondary senses, and thus, for example while Polish *książę* 'prince' has never lost its high-brow connotations, perhaps with the exception of the descriptive phrase *książę ciemności* Eng. *prince of darkness*, Pol. *księżniczka*, a diminutive female-specific form of *księżna* is, to the present day, used in the evaluatively loaded sense 'good-for-nothing woman, young female who cannot be bothered to do any piece of creative work'.

linked to *miss* and the word most frequently appears in the sense 'unmarried woman (used before a family name)'.

The mechanism of understatement may have played some role in the formation of another E.Mod.E. synonym, that is ***loon***. It is important to note that there exists a homonymic form *loon* which – since the beginning of the 17th century – has been used in the sense 'any bird of the genus *Colymbus*, especially the Great Northern Diver, remarkable for its loud cry'. There are grounds to speak here about the mechanism of zoosemic extension given that the rise of the late-16th-century pejoratively loaded sense 'strumpet, concubine' had resulted from the conceptual mapping between the conceptual category **ANIMALS** and **FEMALE HUMAN BEING**. However, the lexicographic works that have been consulted, such as the *OED*, Weekley (1921), Rawson (1989) and Skeat (2005), argue that the E.Mod.E. sense 'strumpet' must have evolved from the 15th-century socially negatively loaded sense 'worthless person, rogue, scamp' with which the word was applied at that time. This case of semantic evolution provides further evidence for the existence of various types of pejorative load proposed in Kleparski (1990:167), who among others, goes along the following lines:

> [...] if an original evaluatively neutral or positive semantic structure begins to combine with evaluatively negative elements, these are most frequently socially negative components [...], and less frequently aesthetically or behaviourally negative components [...].

The example of *loon* seems to confirm the general tendency formulated by Kleparski (1990). According to the *OED*, the etymological roots of *loon* go back to the 15th-century northern – chiefly Scottish – form *lowen* used in the sense 'calm, quiet, serene',[151] which may have developed from O.N. *lúenn* 'beaten, weary, exhausted'. The historically primary sense of English *loon* 'worthless person' is accountable in terms of activating and foregrounding of such conceptual values as <WORTHLESS$_{[NEG]}$> and <LOW$_{[NEG]}$> presupposed for the attributive paths of **DOMAIN OF CHARACTER AND BEHAVIOUR [...]** and **DOMAIN OF SOCIAL STATUS [...]** respectively. The following *OED* contexts testify to this historically original sense of *loon*:

c1450 Þe clerkis þat were þare, leþir *lowens* [*rime chenouns*].
1590 For shame, subscribe, and let the *lowne* depart.
↕
1851 Out upon him, the lazy *loon*!

---

151 Interestingly, Warrack (1955) in his *Chamber's Scots Dictionary* defines the lexical item *loon* as a synonym of, among other things, *rascal, stupid fellow, servant, boy, loose woman* as well as *paramour*.

In the second half of the 16th century, one observes the rise of the pejoratively loaded female-specific sense 'strumpet', the account of which involves an entrenchment link to **DOMAIN OF SEX** [...] and **DOMAIN OF MORALITY** [...] for which such conceptual values as <FEMALE[NEU]> and <COMMERCIALLY UNCHASTE[NEG]> are clearly foregrounded, as seen from the following *OED*-extracted contexts:

> c1560 The gayest grittest *loun*.
> 1714 He ken'd the bawds and *louns* fou well.
> ↕
> 1828 Thou art too low to be their lawful love, and too high to be their unlawful *loon*.

Interestingly, in Present-day English the only human-specific sense recorded in such lexicographic works as *MED*, *LDCE* and *ODO* is 'silly, strange person' or 'crazy person',[152] which provides evidence for the disappearance of one of the two homonyms, that is *loon* used both in the historically original sense 'rascal, worthless person' and the later female-specific pejoratively loaded sense 'strumpet'.

Much in the same manner M.E. ***limmer***, which – according to the *OED* – is of Scottish or northern origin, followed the path of semantic evolution from the behaviourally negative sense 'rogue, scoundrel' to the evidently sexually specific sense 'strumpet' and, hence, the history of the word may justifiably be treated as the lexical manifestation of the working of the mechanism of understatement. The lexical item *limmer* appears in the middle of the 15th century, and it was originally used in the pejoratively coloured sense 'rogue, scoundrel', as evidenced by the following *OED*-quoted material:

> 1456 Ane unworthy *lymmare*, that settis nocht for honour bot for pillery.
> 1596 Adam Scot special bordirer and *limmer*, commounlie calit king of traytouris.
> ↓
> 1828 There have been a proper set of *limmers* about to scale your windows, father Simon.

In terms of the analytical apparatus employed in this study, for the historically original semantics of *limmer* one must postulate an entrenchment link to the attributive paths of **DOMAIN OF CHARACTER AND BEHAVIOUR** [...] and **DOMAIN OF SOCIAL STATUS** [...] for which, respectively, such negatively loaded conceptual values as <DISHONEST[NEG]> and <LOW[NEG]> are activated.

---

152 Note that, according to the *OED*, the survival of the word *loon* in the sense 'crazy person, simpleton' might have been influenced by the sense of the adjectival lexical item *loony* which derived as a shortened form from *lunatic* and was employed in the sense 'crazed, dazed, foolish'.

When, about a century later, *limmer* started to be applied in the specialised female-specific sense, the word may be said to have undergone yet another far-reaching stage of pejoration. As argued convincingly by Kleparski (1990), those lexical items that either start their historical existence with a female-gender conceptual value or – with time – acquire one, are almost inevitably bound to go down the evaluative scale, following the customary pattern of semantic development:

SOCIALLY/BEHAVIOURALLY NEGATIVE LOAD

↘ ↘ ↘ ↘

MORALLY NEGATIVE LOAD

Such was the case of the semantic evolution of *limmer*, which developed the female-specific morally negatively loaded sense 'strumpet' or 'jade, hussy' in the middle of the 16th century. The semantics of the novel sense may be rendered in terms of activation of the conceptual values <FEMALE[NEU]> and <COMMERCIALLY UNCHASTE[NEG]> presupposed for the attributive paths of **DOMAIN OF SEX [...]** and **DOMAIN OF MORALITY [...]**. The following *OED* contexts testify to this historically novel sense of *limmer*:

1566 In causa diffamacionis, viz. that his wyf was a *lymer*.
↓
1728 I wore nae frizzl'd *limmer*'s hair.
1897 'Oh – the *limmer* – how dared she', cried my mother, on fire instantly at the hint of an insult or rejection to her eldest son.

In the present-day lexico-semantic system of English, however, the lexical item *limmer* is practically non-existent and it must have faded into oblivion before the advent of the 20th century or shortly after. This is confirmed by such current lexicographic works that have been consulted as *MED*, *LDCE* and *ODO*, in which there are no records of *limmer*, in any of the senses that it was used throughout the centuries.

Last but not least, the history of E.Mod.E. ***mort***, with its L.Mod.E. variant ***mot/mott***, is – within the analysed body of lexical items – a 16th-century manifestation of the working of the mechanism of understatement. The historically original sense of *mort* 'girl or woman' is – as the *OED* editors argue – of obscure etymology.[153] Both Partridge (1984) and Green (2003) conjecture, however, that *mort* may be etymologically related to Du. *mot* as in *mot-huys* 'brothel'

---

153 Green (2003) points to the plausible etymological link of E.Mod.E. *mort* 'woman' with its 16th-century homonymic animal-specific sense 'salmon in its third year'. The author argues that women tend to be metaphorically conceptualised as FISH.

or – following Sampson (1928) – may be treated as a modification of Fr. *amourette* 'girlfriend'. The historically original semantics of E.Mod.E. *mort* necessitates positing an entrenchment link to **DOMAIN OF SEX** [...] for which the conceptual value <FEMALE$_{[NEG]}$> is activated, as evidenced by the following *OED* contexts below:

> 1561-75 A Kitchin *Mortes* [*sic*] is a Gyrle.
> 1621 Male Gipsies all, not a *Mort* among them.
> ↓
> 1969 'Look at them, two *mots*, Fergus.' Dan pointed at two mini-skirted girls.

Interestingly but not at all exceptionally, *mort* started to be used in the pejoratively pregnant female-specific sense 'harlot' relatively soon after – if not simultaneously with – the occurrence of the historically primary evaluatively neutral sense 'girl or woman' in the mid-16th century, which is confirmed by both the *OED* and Rawson (1981). Therefore, it is justifiable to assume that the process of moral pejoration must have taken place immediately afterwards. The historically novel sense 'harlot' may be accounted for in terms of activation of the negatively loaded conceptual value <COMMERCIALLY UNCHASTE$_{[NEG]}$> presupposed for the attributive path of **DOMAIN OF MORALITY** [...]. The following *OED* quotations illustrate the sense 'prostitute':

> 1567 Their harlots, whiche they terme *Mortes* and Doxes.
> 1622 Each man shall… enjoy His owne deare Dell, Doxy, or *Mort*, at night.
> ↕
> 1866 I! who had expected some swell *mot* or other, soon found myself seated beside the most beautiful young lady I ever beheld.

According to Partridge (1984), the L.Mod.E variant of *mort*, that is *mot*, was in common use from the late 18th to the 19th century, and then became obsolete with the exception of Irish English, in which the word in question has remained in slang register, surprisingly in the evaluatively neutral sense 'girl', not 'prostitute'.[154]

Another interesting development given in Partridge (1984) is that in the middle of the 20th century, *mott* became associated with the conceptual category **BODY PARTS** when the word started to be used in the sense 'female pudendum' in army slang. This sense development may be interpreted as a case of a metonymically conditioned extension from the sense 'prostitute' to the sense 'female pudendum', apparently based on the \\WHOLE FOR PART\\ contiguity pattern. It is worthy of note, however, that none of the current lexicographic

---

[154] Furthermore, Partridge (1984) informs us that the Dublin frequent orthographic variant form is *motte*.

works that have been consulted, that is *MED, LDCE* and *ODO*, includes either the lexical item *mort* or any of its historically recorded orthographic variants.

3.6.4 Early Modern English borrowing

Among the various semantic tools that contributed to the quantitative enlargement of the historical body of *prostitute* synonyms the most productive mechanism is the process of borrowing with a total of twelve lexical items recorded, out of which three have already been discussed in the foregoing (*putanie, succubus* and *hackney*). To begin with, let us scrutinse the etymological story of E.Mod.E. ***prostitute***, which – according to the *OED* – is evidenced to have been adopted into the English lexico-semantic system from Lat. *prōstitūt-us* 'expose publicly, offer for sale' in the second half of the 16th century. The historically original adjectival sense 'offered or exposed to lust' became specialised at the beginning of the 17th century when the word started to be used in the restricted historically novel female-specific meaning 'woman who offers her body for indiscriminate sexual intercourse, esp. for hire'. We are thus justified in saying that – at the historically primary stage – the semantics of *prostitute* may be accounted for in terms of activation of such conceptual values as evaluatively neutral <FEMALE$_{[NEU]}$> and negatively loaded <COMMERCIALLY UNCHASTE> presupposed for the attributive paths of **DOMAIN OF SEX […]** and **DOMAIN OF MORALITY […]** respectively, which is evidenced by the following *OED*-based historical contexts:

1613 I haue seene houses as full of such *prostitutes*, as the schooles in France are full of children.
1768 Your friendship as common as a *prostitute*'s favours.
↕
1840 A *prostitute*, seated on a chair of state in the chancel of Nôtre Dame.

Obviously, although the last quotation from the *OED* dates from the middle of the 19th century, the modern lexicographic works that have been consulted, such as *ODO, LDCE* and *MED*, confirm the continuous use of *prostitute* in its original human-specific sense up to Present-day English. Furthermore, the presence of *prostitute* in the macrostructure of lexicographic works of Standard English may serve as ample evidence that the lexical item in question has – at each stage of its existence in English – deserved the label of orthophemism with little or no negative illocutionary force associated with it.

Significantly, as the *OED* informs us, in the mid-17th century the lexical item *prostitute* is evidenced to have undergone the process of meaning shift whereby the change of conceptual values <FEMALE$_{[NEU]}$> into <MALE$_{[NEU]}$> and <HETEROSEXUAL$_{[NEU]}$> into <HOMOSEXUAL$_{[NEU]}$> may be proposed within the attributive paths of **DOMAIN OF SEX [...]** and **DOMAIN OF SEXUALITY [...]** respectively. At that time – somewhat fleetingly – *prostitute* was used in the pejoratively pregnant sparsely evidenced sense 'catamite' (1654 Her Brother Agathocles, a *prostitute* of an inspiring comeliness). Although the sense-thread disappeared from the lexico-semantic system of English as soon as it appeared, in the middle of the 20th century, the lexical item in question revived its male-specific application and started to be used in the slightly modified sense 'man who undertakes male homosexual acts for payment' (1958 A magnificent looking *male prostitute* whose oiled curls hung down his back and whose eyes and lips were heavily painted). For both male-specific 17th- and 20th-century sense-threads we may speak about the involvement of an entrenchment link to **DOMAIN OF MORALITY [...]** for which the negatively loaded conceptual value <COMMERCIALLY UNCHASTE$_{[NEG]}$> is activated and foregrounded.

Curiously enough, *prostitute* may be said to have undergone the process of widening of meaning soon after the word entered the English lexico-semantic system. According to the *OED*, since the mid-17th century the word was applied in a widened epicene sense 'one who debases oneself for the sake of gain' or 'corrupt and venal politician'. Hence, for this novel sense-thread we may speak about foregrounding of the negatively loaded conceptual value <COR-RUPT$_{[NEG]}$> presupposed for the attributive path of **DOMAIN OF CHARACTER AND BEHAVIOUR [...]**. The following *OED* historical material testifies to this sense of *prostitute*:

1647 To serve one man, a stranger, and a *prostitute* to all manner of licentiousness.
1760-72 The faithful and the perfidious, the *prostitute* and the patriot are confounded together.
↕
1980 You damned us... for turning scientists into military *prostitutes*.

The semantic developmental path of *prostitute* from 'one who undertakes sexual acts for payment' to 'one who debases oneself for the sake of gain' may be said to stand in opposition to the stages of pejoration proposed by Kleparski (1990). Instead of the most frequently evidenced behavioural to moral pejoration pattern we may speak here of the moral to behavioural direction, allowing for the historical co-existence of both senses.

Secondly, as the *OED* and Skeat (2005) elucidate, at the beginning of the 16th century ***drab*** was adopted into the English lexico-semantic system evidently from Ir. *drabog* with the evaluatively loaded female-specific sense 'dirty female, slattern'. In our terms, the semantics of the lexical item in question, apart from involving the activation of the conceptual value <FEMALE$_{[NEU]}$> presupposed for the attributive path of such a central **CD** as **DOMAIN OF SEX [...]**, is also accountable in terms of the involvement of an entrenchment link to **DOMAIN**

OF PHYSICAL CHARACTERISTICS AND APPEARANCE [...] for which the negatively loaded conceptual value <FILTHY[NEG]> is clearly foregrounded. The following *OED* extracts testify to this historically original sense of *drab*:

c1515 Sluttes, *drabbes*, and counseyll whystelers.
a1712 So at an Irish funeral appears a Train of *drabs* with mercenary tears.
↓
1872 Who ended by living up an entry with a *drab* and six children for their establishment.

As proved earlier in the semantic literature of the subject (see, for example, Schulz 1975, Kleparski 1997), the concept of PHYSICAL FILTH almost inevitably evolves into MORAL DIRT. This was shown in section 3.5 (see *slut, filth* and *putain*) and section 3.6.2 (see *baggage* and *fling-dust*). Therefore, it is not at all surprising that only several decades later the lexical item *drab* was associated with the morally pregnant conceptual value <COMMERCIALLY UNCHASTE[NEG]> presupposed for the attributive path of **DOMAIN OF MORALITY [...]** when the word started to be used in the morally loaded sense 'prostitute', as evidenced by the following *OED*-quoted historical contexts:

c1530 And than shall the *drabbe*, my daughter, be mured vp in a stone wall.
1605 Birth-strangled Babe, Ditch-deliuer'd by a *Drab*.
↓
1856 And said 'my sister' to the lowest *drab* Of all the assembled castaways.

Additionally, as prompted by the material given in *SS*, to account for the semantics of *drab* one should speak of positing an entrenchment link to the conceptually peripheral **DOMAIN OF SOCIAL STATUS [...]** for which the conceptual value <LOW[NEG]> is activated, which is confirmed by the fact that the *OED* provides *strumpet* in the synonymic definition of the lexical item analysed here.

From the Present-day English perspective, however, the lexical item *drab* seems to have nothing in common with its E.Mod.E. morally loaded senses as the lexicographic works of today, such as *MED*, *LDCE* and *ODO*, define *drab* as bearing either the adjectival sense 'not bright in colour', 'boring' or – as a mass noun – *drabs* is used in the sense 'trousers'. To account for these Pres.E. senses, one needs to take into consideration the homonymic nature of *drab*, which – apart from the female-specific etymological path of development discussed above – is linked to the now obsolete *drap*, borrowed from O.Fr. *drap* 'cloth' (see Ayto 2005).[155] The 16th-century loan-word *drap* was, in the 17th century, applied with reference to natural undyed cloth of dull yellowish-brown colour,

---

155 Interestingly, Schulz (1975) argues that there exists an etymological link between the lexical item *drab* 'untidy woman' and *drap* 'cloth', which, however, seems to be ignored by such etymological sources as the *OED*, Skeat (2005) and Ayto (2005).

and soon for the colour itself. With the passage of time, the dull faded colour became a source domain for the conceptual mapping, through which the current sense 'boring' was born.

In turn, E.Mod.E. Romance *courtesan* became a historical synonym of *prostitute* in the middle of the 16th century although the form itself was first adopted into the English lexico-semantic system from the It. masculine form *cortigiano* via the Fr. masculine form *courtisan* a century earlier. Originally, in the Middle English period, the word *courtesan* was applied in the socially positively loaded sense 'one attached to the court of a prince' and – simultaneously – in the sense 'member of the papal Curia', as seen from the following *OED* historical contexts given below:

> 1426 On Maister Robert Sutton, a *courtezane* of the Court of Rome.
> ↓
> 1563-87 That it should be lawful for a few *Curtisans* and Cardinals... to chuse what Pope they list.

The following century an analogous female-specific adoption took place, namely that of the It. feminine form *cortigiana* via the Fr. feminine form *courtisane*. In this case the newly adopted loan-word *courtesan* was originally used in the female-specific sense 'woman attached to the court' and virtually immediately the word started to be employed in the pejoratively pregnant sense 'court-mistress, prostitute'. Within our theoretical framework, apart from activating the evaluatively neutral conceptual value <FEMALE[NEU]> presupposed for the attributive path of **DOMAIN OF SEX [...]**, the rise of the historically novel sense of *courtesan* is also associated with foregrounding of the negatively loaded conceptual element <COMMERCIALLY UNCHASTE[NEG]> presupposed for the attributive path of **DOMAIN OF MORALITY [...]**. Holder (2008) argues that the immediate rise of the morally pejorative sense 'prostitute' had little, if anything, to do with the lust and lasciviousness so prevalent in Tudor courts. The semantics of *courtesan*, however, owing to its overt association with royalty and court life may be said to involve an entrenchment link to **DOMAIN OF SOCIAL STATUS [...]** for which the conceptual value <HIGH[POS]> is clearly foregrounded. The following *OED*-quoted contexts provide evidence for the 'high-class prostitute' sense of *courtesan*:

> 1549 The rest of the brethren dooe keepe *Courtisanes*.
> 1635 The name *Courtezan* (being the most honest synonymy that is given to a Whore) had his originall from the Court of Rome.
> ↕
> 1868 The ambitious *courtesan* who now ruled the king.

Now, let us draw readers' attention to the fact that the social status of courtesans is reflected in lexicographic definitions. For example, *SS* defines the sense of the lexical item in question as 'high-class prostitute' while Rawson (1981:63) defines the sense of *courtesan* as 'medium-priced whore' with a comment that this particular historical synonym of *prostitute [...] has been working its way down the social ladder for the past four or five centuries.*

Beyond doubt, the position of courtesans on the social status scale tended to lower with time and – towards the end of the 20th century – the Romance borrowing *courtesan* started to be applied with reference to any prostitute that did not walk the streets (*New York Times*, 8/9/71: They call themselves 'working girls,' or, if they are call girls, *courtesans*).[156] Interestingly, the long-gone secondary information pertaining to the high social status once associated with the semantics of *courtesan* seems to have been retained in the present-day lexicographic definitions given in *MED*, *ODO* and *LDCE* all of which include the trait of wealthy and important clientele in their entries. In effect, one may say that in its present-day sense *courtesan* has become closely-related to Pres.E. *call girl*, with some archaic flavour about it. The diachronic story of *courtesan*, especially when contrasted with the historical semantic stability of its masculine counterpart *courtier* used in the sense 'one who attends a royal court', seems to constitute further evidence for the process of democratic levelling, analysed in detail by Schulz (1975) and Kleparski (1990).

The process of lexical borrowing was also a triggering force responsible for the appearance of ***trull*** in the lexico-semantic system of English. According to the *OED*, the word was adopted from G. *Trulle* 'prostitute' at the beginning of the 16th century and corresponds etymologically to Swiss G. *trolle*. Morphologically, the word *trull* constituted a base for the short-lived derivative ***trully*** used relatively infrequently in the same morally contaminated sense 'prostitute' in the first half of the 18th century.[157] Already for the Early Modern English period the historically original sense of *trull* is linked to the morally pejoratively pregnant conceptual value <COMMERCIALLY UNCHASTE$_{[NEG]}$> as well as socially negative <LOW$_{[NEG]}$> presupposed for the attributive paths of, respectively, **DOMAIN OF MORALITY [...]** and **DOMAIN OF SOCIAL STATUS [...]**. In other words, on entering the English word stock the word was used in the sense 'low prostitute, drab, strumpet'. The following *OED* material testifies to this historically original sense of *trull*:

---

156 Following Rawson (1981:63). The quote is taken from a report on the world of big-city prostitutes.
157 Consider the following *OED*-extracted quotation: 1711 Poor Tinker-like, without a *Trully*, Must beat the dusty Road but dully.

1519 I shall apoynt you a *trull* of trust, Not a feyrer in this towne!
1632 Have you as much left... as will Keep you and this old *troul* a fortnight longer?
↓
1871 Coarse orgies with the *trulls* of Wapping.

Skeat (2005) elaborates more deeply on the origins of E.Mod.E. *trulle* and argues that the lexical item may be etymologically related to M.Du. *drol* 'pleasant or a merrie man, or a gester', as well as to Da. *trold* and Sw. *troll* 'merry elf'. In conclusion, Skeat (2005) conjectures that the original sense of *trull* was 'merry or droll companion', which may be treated as an instance of the employment of the device of understatement. However, the *OED* and Green (2003) emphasise that G. *Trulle* was regularly employed in the sense 'prostitute' at the time when the German borrowing was taken into English. This gives us grounds to reject the assumption that the mechanism of understatement played a role in the formation of this synonym of *prostitute*. As for the lexical survival of *trull* in Present-day English, out of the several current lexicographic sources consulted only *ODO* makes a mention of *trull* defined in the sense 'prostitute' with the label *archaic*.

Yet another case of the working of lexical borrowing in the formation of the body of E.Mod.E. synonyms of *prostitute* is **callet**, which – according to the *OED* – has two equally plausible etymological histories. On the one hand, it is suggested that the roots of E.Mod.E. *callet* go back to either Fr. *caillette* 'foole, ninnie, noddie', which is a diminutive form of Fr. *caille* 'quail'[158] or Fr. *calotte* 'small bonnet or cap covering the top of the head'. However, both etymological hypotheses should be discarded as Fr. *caillette* does not correspond phonologically or semantically to English *callet*.[159] In turn, the etymology of Fr. *calotte* fails to provide convincing evidence to link it semantically with E.Mod.E. *callet*.

On the other hand, the data given in the *OED* gives grounds to the feasibility of yet another etymological hypothesis, namely that E.Mod.E. *callet* may have originated from either Gael. or Ir. *caille* 'girl'. One may assume with a fair degree of certainty that the semantics of E.Mod.E. *callet* – from the very start of its existence in the English word stock – was associated with such conceptual values as evaluatively neutral <FEMALE$_{[NEU]}$> as well as morally pejoratively pregnant <COMMERCIALLY UNCHASTE$_{[NEG]}$> presupposed, respectively,

---

158 Note that E.Mod.E. *quail* which was used in the primary sense 'migratory bird allied to a partridge' is evidenced to have undergone semantic extension and started to be used in the sense 'prostitute'. For more details, see section 3.6.1.
159 The *OED* editors conjecture that the French word *caillette* was applied with reference to both men and women.

for the attributive paths of **DOMAIN OF SEX [...]** and **DOMAIN OF MORALITY [...]**, as seen from the following *OED*-extracted quotations:

> c1500 Yf he call her *calat*, she calleth hym knave agayne.
> 1604 Begger in his drinke Could not haue laid such termes vpon his *Callet*.
> ↕
> 1785 I'm as happy with my wallet, my bottle and my *callet*.

As for Present-day English, the lexicographic sources consulted for verification, such as *MED*, *LDCE* and *ODO*, fail to record *callet* in their macrostructure. The conclusion one may justifiably draw is that *callet* became obsolete before the advent of the Present-day English period.

Let us now deal with the etymology of another Romance acquisition. The story of *pucelle*, goes back to the historically primary E.Mod.E. sense of the word, namely 'girl, maid' adopted together with the Fr. form *pucelle* in the first half of the 15th century. The Romance lexical item in question derives ultimately from L.Lat. *pūlicella* 'young girl' mediated through O.Fr. *pucele*, which corresponds to Pr. *piucella* and It. *pulzella*. In terms of the cognitive framework adopted here, the historically primary semantics of the loan-word is accountable for in terms of entrenchment links to two **CDs**, that is **DOMAIN OF SEX [...]** and **DOMAIN OF AGE [...]** for the attributive paths of which such evaluatively neutral conceptual values as <FEMALE$_{[NEU]}$> and <YOUNG$_{[NEU]}$> are clearly activated, as is evident from the following *OED* historical contexts of use:

> c1430 Medecyne to mischeves, *pucelle* withouten pere.
> 1534 This Girle is a metely good *pussel* in a house, neuer idle, but euer occupied and busy.
> ↓
> 1814 My passion can wait, till the *pucelle* is more harmonious.

Another far less plausible etymological hypothesis is – according to the *OED* – to trace the origin of M.E. *pucelle* back to L.Lat. **pullicella*, a diminutive form of M.Lat. *pulla* 'chicken'. If this was the case, E.Mod.E. *pucelle* would constitute a lexical realisation of the zoosemic metaphorical extension that may come under the general label A PROSTITUTE IS A BIRD. It is worth noting at this point that the conceptual metaphor A PROSTITUTE IS A BIRD is realised lexically with the use of the French word *poule* 'hen' > 'girl, young woman' which is employed in Pres.E. *poule-de-luxe* literally 'luxury hen' > 'high-class prostitute'. As could be seen earlier (see section 3.6.1), the E.Mod.E. lexical realisations of the bird metaphor employed in the conceptualisation of the notion PROSTITUTION are frequent and include such words as *Winchester goose*, *quail* and *plover*.

A century later *pucelle* underwent the process of pejoration. It may be said to have associated with the morally negatively loaded conceptual value <COMMERCIALLY UNCHASTE[NEG]> presupposed for the attributive path of **DOMAIN OF MORALITY [...]** when in the first decades of the 16th century the word started to be used in the evaluatively pregnant sense 'drab, slut', as seen from the following *OED* contexts:

> 1520 Here begynneth the maryage of London Stone and the fayre *pusell* the bosse of Byllyngesgate.
> 1617 A *Pusle*, trull, or stinking wench.
> ↕
> a1700 A dirty Quean, a very *Puzzel* or Slut.

The *OED* quotations unambiguously suggest that the short-lived morally pejorative sense of E.Mod.E. *pucelle* must be accounted for in terms of joint involvement of the attributive paths of **DOMAIN OF PHYSICAL CHARACTERISTICS AND APPEARANCE [...]**, as well as **DOMAIN OF SOCIAL STATUS [...]** for which such negatively loaded conceptual values as <FILTHY[NEG]> and <LOW[NEG]> are foregrounded; the low and slovenly nature of anyone referred to as *pucelle* is nothing else but obvious. Again, the directional pattern of pejoration here is for moral pejoration to go hand in hand with social pejoration. The *OED* provides the last quotation from the turn of the 17th and 18th centuries and any attempt to find *pucelle* in major lexicographic works of current English proves futile.

Another short-lived E.Mod.E. *prostitute* synonym is the Romance loan-word *amorosa*, which – according to the *OED* – is a feminine form of *amoroso* 'lover, gallant', both of which were adopted into the English word stock in the first half of the 17th century (see Sp. and It. *amorosa*). As discussed earlier by Schulz (1975), Kleparski (1990, 1997) and Kochman-Haładyj and Kleparski (2011), the semantics of masculine *amoroso* has been invariably associated with the positively loaded conceptual values <COURTEOUS[POS]> and <BRAVE[POS]> presupposed for the attributive path of **DOMAIN OF CHARACTER AND BEHAVIOUR [...]**. On the other hand, *amorosa* must have undergone a virtually immediate downfall on the evaluative scale as the word was used in the morally negatively loaded sense 'female lover, courtesan' from the start of its existence in the lexico-semantic system of English. The account of the E.Mod.E. semantics of *amorosa* requires positing an entrenchment link to the attributive paths of **DOMAIN OF SEX [...]** and **DOMAIN OF MORALITY [...]** for which the evaluatively neutral conceptual value <FEMALE[NEU]> and the morally charged conceptual value <COMMERCIALLY UNCHASTE[NEG]> are clearly activated. The following, and only, *OED* quotation testifies to the negatively loaded sense of *amorosa*:

1634 I took them for *Amorosa*'s, and violators of the bounds of Modesty.

At present, as various current lexicographic sources, such as *MED*, *LDCE* and *ODO* bear witness, *amorosa* is obsolete and there is no trace of this Romance synonym in the Present-day English word stock. On the contrary, its masculine counterpart *amoroso* managed to withstand the diachronic battle for survival, which for many lexical items turns out to be a gallant fight. Note that the story of the semantics of the pair *amorosa/amoroso* provides yet another example of the process of democratic levelling so frequently at work in the development of the human-specific strata of English vocabulary.

The E.Mod.E. synonym **croshabell** constitutes an etymological puzzle as none of the etymological works that have been consulted points to, or even hints at, any plausible hypothesis of the origin of the lexical item in question. The *OED* stresses its incredibly short-lived nature evidenced by a single quotation. Hence, the only way to account for the origin of E.Mod.E. *croshabell* is to resort to speculation, and this leads one to conjecture that the lexical item in question may have been of foreign roots. The reason behind this is that the original phonological layout of *croshabell* fails to meet Anglo-Saxon phonotactic restrictions.

According to the *OED* data, the lexical item *croshabell* appeared in the English word stock towards the end of the 16th century and from the very beginning of its existence the semantics of the word may be said to have been associated with the conceptual values <FEMALE$_{[NEU]}$> and <COMMERCIALLY UN-CHASTE$_{[NEG]}$> presupposed for the attributive paths of **DOMAIN OF SEX** [...] and **DOMAIN OF MORALITY** [...], as seen from the following *OED*-quoted contexts:

a1598 How George gulled a Punk, otherwise called a *croshabell*.

Ibid. In Italian called a curtezan, in Spain a margerite... now the word refined being latest, and the authority brought from... the fruitful county of Kent, they call them *croshabell*, which is a word but lately used.

The *OED* informs us that the lexical item *croshabell* is now obsolete except for its currency in regional dialects. This is confirmed by such various lexicographic sources that have been consulted as *MED*, *LDCE* and *ODO*, which fail to include the entry *croshabell* in their macrostructure.

Last but not least, E.Mod.E. **punk** is yet another synonym which is evidenced to have undergone an intriguing series of semantic shifts. Although several etymological sources, such as the *OED* and Rawson (1989), refrain from determining the origin of *punk*, Partridge (1984) supposes that the lexical item in question may be ultimately linked to Lat. *punctum* 'small hole, usually caused by pricking'. However, diachronically, the original sense with which the word appeared in the E.Mod.E. word stock was 'prostitute, strumpet'. Hence, one may justifiably say that, at the beginning of its existence in the lexico-semantic system of English, the semantics of *punk* was associated with activation of the evaluatively neutral conceptual value <FEMALE[NEU]> presupposed for the attributive path of **DOMAIN OF SEX** [...], as well as with foregrounding of the morally pejorative conceptual value <COMMERCIALLY UNCHASTE[NEG]> presupposed for the attributive path of **DOMAIN OF MORALITY** [...]. The following *OED* quotations testify to the historically original sense of *punk*:

> 1596 He hath a *Punck* (as the pleasant Singer cals her).
> ↓
> 1785 Like a poor pilloried *Punk* he bawled.
> 1928 It amused him to hear the cast-off locutions of duchesses in the mouth of this ageing prostitute... The poor super~annuated *punk* was so gruesome.

Interestingly, at the beginning of the 18th century *punk* developed several senses that are both related and unrelated to the human-specific sense 'prostitute', for example, the unrelated sense 'rotten wood or fungus growing on wood'.[160] This sense of *punk* – as evidenced in the *OED* – underwent the process of meaning generalisation when, in the second half of the 19th century, the word started to be used in the generalised sense 'anything worthless, nonsense, rubbish', as testified by the following *OED*-extracted contexts:

> 1869 Better have the simplest... thoughts, clearly expressed, than what Carlyle calls 'phosphorescent *punk* and nothingness'.
> ↕
> 1973 I don't like the family Stein. There is Gert, there is Ep, there is Ein. Gert's writings are *punk*, Ep's statues are junk, Nor can anyone understand Ein.

In turn, at the beginning of the 20th century, the sense 'anything worthless, rubbish' underwent another process of meaning modification of a metaphorical kind. At that time *punk* developed the derogatory sense 'passive male homosexual, a catamite', especially – as Rawson (1989:313) argues – *in isolated all-male societies*, such as hoboes, sailors and prison inmates. Certainly – as the *OED* suggests – the rise of this novel sense of *punk* may have been conditioned by the historically original sense 'prostitute', as in both cases the attributive value of sexuality comes into conceptual fore.[161] The conceptual schema that may have played a role in the emergence of this male-specific negatively loaded sense may

---

[160] As evidenced by the following *OED* historical context: 1705 Or else they take *Punck*, (which is a sort of a soft Touchwood, cut out of the knots of Oak or Hiccory Trees, but the Hiccory affords the best).

[161] On the contrary, Skeat (2005) advocates the feasibility of the word being imported by sailors from the Low Countries.

be labelled as PROSTITUTION IS DECOMPOSITION/FILTH, through which both passive homosexuality and (male) prostitution are frequently conceptualised as something worthless, dirty or rotten. The male-specific pejoratively pregnant sense of *punk* may be accounted for in terms of activating and foregrounding of such conceptual values as evaluatively neutral <MALE$_{[NEU]}$> and <HOMOSEXUAL$_{[NEU]}$>, as well as negatively loaded <PASSIVE$_{[NEG]}$> and <COMMERCIALLY UNCHASTE$_{[NEG]}$> presupposed for the attributive paths of, respectively, **DOMAIN OF SEX […], DOMAIN OF SEXUALITY […], DOMAIN OF CHARACTER AND BEHAVIOUR […]** and **DOMAIN OF MORALITY […]**. The following *OED* material testifies to the metaphorical sense of *punk*:

> 1904 *Punk*,… a pervert.
> 1926 The '*Punks*', young bums, were sent for 'mickies', bottles of alcohol.
> ↕
> 1977 The involuntary homosexuals tend to be good-looking young men… forced into becoming jailhouse '*punks*' by older men serving long sentences.

Yet another change – apart from that of the female > male kind – is, as Hughes (2006) points out, the shift of the word from the British to the American variety of English with no accompanying shift of semantic value, but merely alteration of register value. As for the survival of the lexical item in question in Present-day English, *punk* is recorded in the informal sense 'worthless fellow, young hooligan, petty criminal' in such modern lexicographic sources as *MED*, *LDCE* and *ODO*, the last of which also includes the sense 'passive male homosexual' with the note that the word belongs to the prison slang.

3.6.5 The role of eponymy in Early Modern English

Evidently, among semantic tools eponymy is a far less productive formative mechanism through which only four lexical items were formed to convey the concept PROSTITUTION in euphemistic or dysphemistic terms, namely *Tib*, *hiren*, *moll* and *hackney*. The last of them was discussed in the section on metaphor.

According to the *OED*, the lexical item ***Tib*** originated as a typical name for a woman of the lower classes as it was frequently employed in the phrase *Tib and Tom*, whereby *Tib* meant 'girl'. This historically original meaning – as the *OED* contexts of use show – became specialised at times and the word was applied in the negatively loaded sense 'strumpet'. Hence, the semantics of *Tib*, apart from the involvement of an entrenchment link to **DOMAIN OF SEX […]** for which the evaluatively neutral conceptual value <FEMALE$_{[NEU]}$> is activated, may also be accounted for in terms of foregrounding the morally negative conceptual value <COMMERCIALLY UNCHASTE$_{[NEG]}$> presupposed for the attributive path of **DOMAIN OF MORALITY** [...]. The following *OED* historical material illustrates both the senses of *Tib*:

> 1533 A Mery Play betwene Johan Johan the husbande, *Tyb* his wyfe, and syr Johan the preest.
> 1681 A *Tib, mulier sordida.*
> ↕
> 1700 *Tib*, a young lass.

The developmental path 'girl' > 'strumpet' may have involved the working of the mechanism of understatement. The feasibility of its application seems to be reinforced by the fact that both female-specific senses co-existed in the Early Modern English period. However, the short-lived nature of *Tib* (the word became obsolete already in the early 18th century) makes it a daunting task to establish with some certainty whether the employment of *Tib* in the sense 'prostitute' was euphemistic in nature. The fact that the *OED* provides the sense 'strumpet', as well as the application of *Tib* with reference to women of lower rank and social standing suggests that the account of the semantics of the lexical item in question necessitates positing an entrenchment link to **DOMAIN OF SOCIAL STATUS** [...] for which the negatively loaded conceptual value <LOW$_{[NEG]}$> is highlighted.

In turn, E.Mod.E. *hiren* may have been – if not a nonce occurrence then at least – a one-off appearance of the word in the English word stock, as its existence failed to exceed the span of half a century. As the *OED* editors conjecture, *hiren* is an adaptation of the female name *Irene*, ultimately from Fr. *Irène*, and was first employed in English as the name of the female character in Peele's play *The Turkish Mahamet and Hyrin the fair Greek* at the close of the 16th century. This particular name must have inspired Shakespeare and several other Elizabethan writers who used the form *hiren* in the sexually pregnant sense 'seductive woman' or 'harlot'. Hence, for the sense 'harlot' one may speak about the involvement of an entrenchment link to the attributive paths of **DOMAIN OF SEX** [...] and **DOMAIN OF MORALITY** [...] for which the evaluatively neutral conceptual value <FEMALE$_{[NEU]}$> and the morally pejorative conceptual element <COMMERCIALLY UNCHASTE$_{[NEG]}$> are clearly activated, as seen from the following *OED*-quoted contexts:

> 1597 Downes: downes Dogges, downe Fates: haue wee not *Hiren* here?
> ↕
> 1615 There be Sirens in the sea of this world. Sirens? *Hirens*, as they are now called... What a number of these Sirens, *Hirens*, Cockatrices, in plaine English, Harlots, swimme amongst vs.

Interestingly, as was the case with such E.Mod.E. synonyms as *amorosa*, *croshabell* or – to a lesser extent – *trull*, the semantics of the lexical item *hiren* seems to be entrenched within only one evaluatively loaded **CD**, that is **DOMAIN OF MORALITY [...]**. One may draw a partial conclusion that the number of axiologically relevant **CDs** in which a word is grounded, in one way or another, seems to influence the length of existence of the word in the lexico-semantic system of a language.

E.Mod.E. ***moll*** – unlike the previously discussed *hiren* – is evidenced to have enjoyed a much longer lifespan in the history of English. Schulz (1975) and Rawson (1989), as well as lexicographic works, such as the *OED*, Partridge (1984) and Green (2003), conjecture that *moll* is a diminutive form derived from the female name *Mary*. According to the *OED* and Green (2003) – in terms of extralinguistic conditions – the pejorative downfall of the semantics of *moll* may be credited to the notorious early-17th-century female character Moll Cut-purse from Middleton and Dekker's play entitled *The Roaring Girl*. Rawson (1989:250), in turn, argues that Daniel Defoe must have been inspired by the morally negative associations of the name *Moll* as the heroine of his early-18th-century novel. *Moll Flanders* is defined in the subtitles as *Twelve Year a Whore, Five Time a Wife (whereof once to her own Brother), Twelve Year a Thief, Eight Year a Transported Felon*.

Originally, that is in the late 16th century, the lexical item *moll* was used in the behaviourally tinted sense 'promiscuous woman', which – soon afterwards – underwent further pejoration when at the beginning of the 17th century the word started to be applied in the heavily morally loaded sense 'prostitute' (see Green 2003). Hence, the shape of its semantics – apart from involving an entrenchment link to the attributive paths of **DOMAIN OF SEX [...]** and **DOMAIN OF CHARACTER AND BEHAVIOUR [...]** for which such conceptual values as evaluatively neutral <FEMALE$_{[NEU]}$> and negatively loaded <PROMISCUOUS$_{[NEG]}$> are activated – is accountable in terms of highlighting of pejoratively pregnant conceptual element <COMMERCIALLY UNCHASTE$_{[NEG]}$> presupposed for the attributive path of **DOMAIN OF MORALITY [...]**. The currency of the sense is documented in the *OED* data from the 17th century:

> 1604 None of these common *Molls* neither, but discontented and unfortunate gentlewomen.
> ↓
> 1753 To nap the Slangs from the Cull or *Moll*; that is,... to take the Things from the Man or Woman.
> 1975 The Psychopath's *Moll*. I'm doing it again, thought Imogen... saving him from the consequences of his follies.

Partridge (1984) and Green (2003) point to the fact that in the early-19th century the semantics of *moll* underwent another modification when the word started to be used in the sense 'girlfriend, female companion of a criminal or a tramp'. From an axiological point of view, the shift in question may be interpreted in two ways, that is either a step towards amelioration because a criminal's female companion need not necessarily be a criminal herself, though close to those who are, or as a rare specimen of reverse order of pejoration where – contrary to the social pejoration to moral pejoration direction, as envisioned in Kleparski (1990) – we are dealing with the moral pejoration to social pejoration pattern. Clearly, the concept of a partner-criminal is by no means positive; the conceptual picture of a female partner of a criminal is far from being axiologically spotless.

It is worth noting at this point that *moll* is also evidenced to have undergone the process of suffixation in the first decades of the 18th century and the derivative ***molly*** started to be applied contemptuously in the sense 'wench' or, less frequently, 'prostitute'. Hence, the original semantics of *molly* – similarly to the 17th-century *moll* – may be rendered in terms of involvement an entrenchment link to the attributive paths of **DOMAIN OF SEX** [...] and **DOMAIN OF MORALITY** [...] for which the evaluatively neutral conceptual elements <FEMALE$_{[NEG]}$> and negatively loaded <COMMERCIALLY UNCHASTE$_{[NEG]}$> are highlighted, as seen from the selected *OED* contexts:

1719 Town follies and Cullies, And *Molleys* and Dolleys, For ever adieu.
↕
1890 The men and girls [at a hiring-fair] are called 'Johnnies and *Mollies*'.

However, already during the course of the 18th century the semantics of *molly* underwent a far-reaching shift. The modification is accountable in terms of novel involvement of the relevant locations within the attributive path of **DOMAIN OF SEX** [...] from <FEMALE$_{[NEU]}$> to <MALE$_{[NEU]}$> when the word started to be applied in the male-specific sense 'male homosexual'. Additionally, to account for the novel sense an entrenchment link to **DOMAIN OF SEXUALITY** [...] must be put to work, for which the conceptual value <HOMOSEXUAL$_{[NEU]}$> is activated. The historically novel mid-18th-century male-specific sense of *molly* is documented by the following *OED*-extracted contexts:

1754 If he goes to school, he will be perpetually teized Miss *Molly*.
1879 Simon is not a *molly*, whatever he may be.
↕
1901 The Langfords are regular *Mollies*.

The historical remains of the discussed senses are variously distributed in the lexicographic sources of today. *Moll* is recorded in the sense 'criminal's girlfriend' in *MED* and *LDCE*, while the sense 'prostitute' is documented within one and the same entry with the sense 'criminal's girlfriend' in the *ODO* macrostructure. As for the status of *molly* in current English, none of the Present-day English lexicographic works includes this entry in their lexicons.

Finally, the compounding productivity of both *moll* and *molly* deserves special attention since it contributes nicely to the whole picture of a panchronic view of both etymologically related words. Green (2003) points out that the L.Mod.E. compound word *moll house* was used in the sense 'brothel' throughout the 18th century while L.Mod.E. *mollyhouse* was employed in the sense 'male homosexual brothel' throughout the 18th and 19th centuries and the senses of the two compounds testified further to the semantics of their heads at that time. In turn, Partridge (1984) proposes a very straightforward explanation of the semantics of the compound *mollyhouse*, when he defines it as 'resort for sodomites, a house where men prostituted themselves to men'. The *OED*, on the other hand, is on the politically correct side in providing a more veiled definition 'private house used as a meeting-place by homosexual men'. The lexicographic works of today confirm that neither *moll house* nor *mollyhouse* survived the test of time.

3.6.6 Early Modern English working of circumlocution

The semantic mechanism of circumlocution is brought about by the coinage of such E.Mod.E. phrases as *lady of pleasure*, *light of love* and *sisters of the bank*, the last of which was discussed in some detail in the section on metaphor. As for **lady of pleasure**, it is essential to scrutinise the semantic evolution of the first element, that is **lady**, in order to be able to draw the whole semantic picture of the phrase in question. According to the *OED*, the Pres.E. form *lady* derives from the O.E. form *hlæfdiʒe*, which is a feminine counterpart of O.E. *hláford* (Pres.E. *lord*), and the word was originally employed in the female-specific sense 'the female head of a household' from the first half of the 9th century. The historically original semantics of *lady*, may be rendered in terms of the involvement of an entrenchment link to **DOMAIN OF SEX** [...] for which the evaluatively neutral conceptual element <FEMALE[NEU]> is clearly highlighted, apart from the involvement of other values such as <ADULT[NEU]> and <HOUSEHOLD HEAD[NEU]> The following *OED* quotations testify to the historically original sense of *lady*:

c825 Swe swe eʒan menenes hondum *hlafdian* hire.
↓
a1100 Materfamilias, hiredes moder oððe *hlæfdiʒe*.
a1745 When you are sent on a Message, deliver it in your own Words... not in the Words of your Master or *Lady*.

Towards the close of the Old English period, the semantics of *lady* is evidenced to have undergone the process of amelioration when – as the *OED* data confirm

– the word started to be applied in the evaluatively positive sense 'woman who rules over subjects', as the sense may be higher up on the ladder of social hierarchy; the element of ruling over others may be perceived as seeing someone higher than the quality of ruling in the household. The historically novel sense – apart from involving an entrenchment link to the attributive path of **DOMAIN OF SEX [...]** for which the evaluatively neutral conceptual value <FEMALE$_{[NEU]}$> is activated – is accountable in terms of foregrounding the positive conceptual value <HIGH$_{[POS]}$> presupposed for the attributive path of **DOMAIN OF SOCIAL STATUS [...]**. Additionally, one is justified to speak about an entrenchment link to the attributive path of **DOMAIN OF KINSHIP AND FAMILIARITY [...]** for which the evaluatively positive or, at least, neutral conceptual value <RULING$_{[POS/NEU]}$> is activated. The socially elevated sense of *lady* is illustrated by the following *OED*-based material:

a1000 Her Æðelflæd forðferde Myrcena *hlæfdiʒe*.
c1205 Bruttes nemnede þa laʒen æfter þar *lafuedi*.
↓
1832 No marvel, sovereign *lady*: in fair field Myself for such a face had boldly died.

From the start of the 13th century onwards the semantics of the lexical item *lady* underwent another slight, yet generalised, sense modification when – according to the *OED* – the word was used in the socially positively loaded sense 'woman of superior position in society, or to whom such a position is conventionally or by courtesy attributed'. One may argue that the novel sense of *lady* may be rendered in terms of activating and foregrounding of the evaluatively neutral conceptual value <FEMALE$_{[NEU]}$> and positively loaded <HIGH$_{[POS]}$> presupposed for the attributive paths of **DOMAIN OF SEX [...]** and **DOMAIN OF SOCIAL STATUS [...]** respectively. However, the activation of the conceptual values <RULING$_{[POS/NEU]}$> and <HIGH$_{[POS]}$> are only contextually not referentially realised for this sense, as evidenced by the following *OED*-based material:

c1205 Alle þa *lafdies* leoneden ʒeond walles to behalden þa duʒoðen.
c1350 Whan þat loveli *ladi* hade listened his wordes... for ioye sche wept.
↕
1888 She was born, in our familiar phrase, a lady, and... throughout a long life she was surrounded with perfect ease of circumstance.

The *OED* editors forward a conjecture that the application of *lady* in the sense 'woman of superior position in society' widened relatively early, and – in this manner – the word became a quasi-synonym of *woman* (cf. Kleparski 1990:77-80). One may thus assume that it was this generalised sense of *lady* that entered the phraseological unit *lady of pleasure* in the first half of the 17th century to be applied euphemistically in the sense 'courtesan, whore'. The semantics of the phrase analysed here is accountable in terms of activation of the morally loaded conceptual value <COMMERCIALLY UNCHASTE_[NEG]> presupposed for the attributive path of **DOMAIN OF MORALITY [...]**, apart from the involvement of attributive values responsible for the notions WOMANHOOD and AGE. The following *OED* contexts testify to the rise of the morally loaded sense of *lady of pleasure*:

> 1637 The *Lady of Pleasure*.
> ↕
> 1708 Kept-Wenches, Kind-hearted-Things, *Ladies of Pleasure*, by what... Names soever dignified.

Evidently, the phrase *lady of pleasure* was the first coinage in the chain of historical euphemisms based on the lexical item *lady*. The second to come was ***ladies of trade***, which – as Ayto (2007:93) argues – surfaced in the English lexico-semantic system towards the close of the 17th century when *trade* became a euphemism used in the sense 'prostitution'. Another one was ***lady of easy virtue*** which came to life towards the close of the 18th century in the sense 'woman whose chastity is easily assailable' (see the *OED*), although Rawson (1981) places the phrase directly among the historical euphemisms for *prostitute*. Last but not least, the first decades of the 20th century brought the rise of yet another euphemistic phrase ***lady of the evening/night***, which – like many of the previously itemised phrases – was also used in the morally loaded sense 'prostitute'. The stylistic value of those phrases varies. Ayto (2007:95) marks the phrase *lady of the evening/night* as *superannuated* while Enright (2005:70) labels *lady of trade* and *lady of easy virtue* as *ironic* in Present-day English.

In Present-day English lexicographic works, such as *LDCE*, *MED* and *ODO*, none of the three *lady*-based euphemistic phrases is recorded. The word *lady* itself is documented both in evaluatively neutral and evaluatively positive senses, for example *ODO* includes the senses 'woman (used as a polite or old-fashioned form of address)' and 'woman of superior social position, especially one of noble birth'. *LDCE* registers, among others, the sense 'woman who is polite and behaves well' and 'woman, especially one with a strong character – used to show approval'. Altogether, somewhat against the mainstream tendency for female-specific words to undergo pejorative downfall, the word *lady* managed to survive as a neutral or positively loaded lexical item, and only in various syntagmas with *trade*, *virtue*, *evening*, *night* did the word yield utterly negative connotations which in a certain way add some, either temporal or other, specific information to the oldest profession.

However, Green (2003) shows that *lady* also appeared in slang register, especially in Am.E. in the course of the 20th century, in much less favourable senses. For example, in the 1930s the word developed male-specific sense 'one's effeminate homosexual partner' in American prison slang. Several decades later, from the 1960s onwards, in Black Eng. *lady* started to be used as a term to convey the sense 'high-class prostitute', and finally – a decade later – the word started to be employed in the modified sense 'prostitute belonging to a pimp' in American slang register, which is confirmed by the *SS*.

The circumlocutory E.Mod.E. expression ***light of love*** constitutes another member of the body of lexical items panchronically related to the concept PROSTITUTION. Interestingly, the phrase may also be treated as an instance of the working of the mechanism of understatement, as *light of love* started its life towards the end of the 16th century with the historically original, both nominal and adjectival, sense 'inconstant/inconstancy in love', as documented by the following *OED*-extracted quotations:

1578 The fickle are blamed: Their *lightiloue* shamed.
↕
1592 And if he should marry her, he will thinke shee will have as good mind to other, as himselfe, when she is so *light of love*.

As is evident from the *OED* material, the existence of the phrase *light of love* used in the abstract sense failed to span more than half a century.

However, at the turn of the 16th and 17th centuries the discussed *of*-phrase started to be applied in the morally loaded female-specific sense 'prostitute'. The semantics of *light of love* is – within the framework adopted – accountable in terms of activation of such a conceptual value as <COMMERCIALLY UNCHASTE$_{[NEG]}$> presupposed for the attributive path of **DOMAIN OF MORALITY [...]**, which together with the prominence of the <FEMALE$_{[NEU]}$> element stands for the construal of the novel sense. The following *OED* quotations testify to the historically novel sense of *light of love*:

1599 Foule strumpet, *Light a loue*, shorte heeles!
↓
1892 'My Kitty a *light-o'-love* – a trollop –' and the wretched father burst into tears.

One may observe a metonymically based relation between the historically primary literal sense of *light of love* and the historically documented female-specific novel sense-thread. It is not far-fetched to say that a major characteristic of sex for sale is high and variable supply, which sounds like a particularised distortion of inconsistency in love. Following this, one may say that the rise of the sense 'prostitute' is based on the metonymic contiguity pattern \\FEATURE FOR PERSON ADORNED WITH THIS FEATURE\\. Although the metonymically conditioned circumlocutory phrase *light of love* is absent from the lexicographic works of today, such as *MED*, *LDCE* and *ODO*, it has contributed to the quantum of lexical items onomasiologically related to the conceptual category **FALLEN WOMAN**.

3.6.7 Early Modern English employment of morphological derivation

Finally, the operation of morphological derivation in the formation of cover terms for the notion PROSTITUTION will be discussed. The lexical items that are attributable to the process of derivation, which have not been discussed in the previous sections, include *occupant* and *doxy*. First of all, according to the *OED* and Partridge (1984), E.Mod.E. ***occupant*** – a derivative of the M.E. verb *occupy* used in the sense 'take possession of, seize' – was employed at the close of the 16th century in the neutral sense 'one who takes possession of something'. The historically original sense of *occupant* is evidenced by the following *OED* quotations:

1596 This land [goeth]… to the party that first entereth; and he is called an *occupant*.
↓
1844-75 The person who had so entered was called a general *occupant*.

The verb *occupy* is documented to have undergone the process of meaning shift at least twice: when the word started to be used in the sense 'employ oneself in, engage in' (c1400 Hit is called Effraym, and there was sciens of Gemetry and masonri fyrst *occupied*) at the beginning of the 15th century, and then when the sense 'trade, deal' developed in the first half of the 16th century (1525 Berthaulte of Malygnes… *occupyeth* to Damas, to Cayre, and to Alexandre). What is of particular interest here is the fact that the next stage in the semantic evolution of *occupy* was sense restriction when – almost simultaneously with the rise of the sense 'trade, deal' – the word started to be applied with reference to a specific kind of dealing, namely offering payable sexual service when it was used in the sense 'deal with sexually, cohabit'. The sexual connotations of the verb *occupy* became so explicit that, as the *OED* authors argue, the word fell into oblivion at the close of the 17th century, as evidenced by the temporal span of the *OED*-based material:

c1520 To make hyme [your husband] lystear to *occupye* with youe.
1597 A captaine? Gods light these villaines will make the word as odious as the word *occupy*, which was an excellent good worde before it was il sorted.
↕
1660 To Lie with, or to *Occupie* a woman.

Presumably, the heavily sexually loaded sense of the verb *occupy* may have influenced the rise of the nominal derivative *occupant* towards the end of the 16th century to convey the sense 'one that deals with sexually', that is 'prostitute'. Both the *OED* and Partridge (1984) conjecture that the commercially loaded sexuality of *occupant* was the outcome of the metaphorical mapping that may have taken place in the semantic evolution of the verb *occupy* 'engage in' < 'deal with sexually'. Interesting as it is, the story of the noun *occupant* used in the sense 'prostitute' did not last for long in the history of English. The *OED* records only one quotation testifying to the sexually loaded sense of *occupant*:

> 1599 He with his *Occupant*, Are cling'd so close, like deaw-warms in the morne That he'le not stir.

Green (2003) informs us of the side effects of the development sketched above; the lexical item *occupant* was employed in the highly specific sense, namely 'brothel prostitute'.[162] As hinted before, brothel prostitutes have always been perceived as better-off than common streetwalkers, and – as such – they come under the general label of *high-class prostitutes*. Hence, for the construal of the sense – apart from involving an entrenchment link to the attributive paths of **DOMAIN OF SEX [...]** and **DOMAIN OF MORALITY [...]** for which such conceptual values as evaluatively neutral <FEMALE$_{[NEU]}$> and morally negatively loaded <COMMERCIALLY UNCHASTE$_{[NEG]}$> are activated – one may propose the process of highlighting of the positively coloured value <HIGH$_{[POS]}$> presupposed for the attributive path of **DOMAIN OF SOCIAL STATUS [...]**.

The present-day semantics of the lexical item *occupant* is entirely devoid of any sexual connotations, much in the same manner as its base verbal form *occupy*. Such current lexicographic works as *MED*, *LDCE* and *ODO* record the historically original senses of both *occupy* and *occupant*, that is 'reside, fill, take up' and 'someone who resides or is present in a house' respectively.

Another instance of the operation of derivation in the formation of *prostitute* synonyms is ***doxy***, which – according to Rawson (1989) – is an English reflex of the Germanic root *dukk-* 'bundle'[163] formed upon either English *dock* used in the sense 'person's buttocks' (16th and 17th centuries) or the Dutch *docke* 'doll'. Whichever etymological path we follow, the ultimate formation of the lexical item in question was based on the root *dock* + *-y* derivational suffix. From the very beginning *doxy* was used in vagabonds' cant in the pejoratively pregnant

---

162 Green (2003) also notes that the verb *occupy* was the base for another 16th-century derivative, that is *occupying house* which was used in the morally pejoratively pregnant sense 'brothel'.

163 Strangely enough, in the history of English there have been several words that started off in the sense 'bundle' and underwent a human-specific pejorative evolution. For example, *faggot* 'bundle of twigs and sticks' > '(male) homosexual'.

sense 'beggar's wench', and soon the word entered English slang with the morally negatively loaded female-specific sense 'mistress, prostitute'. The semantics of *doxy* is accountable in terms of activating and highlighting the conceptual value <FEMALE_{[NEU]}> and <UNCHASTE_{[NEG]}> presupposed for the attributive path of **DOMAIN OF SEX [...]** and **DOMAIN OF MORALITY [...]** respectively. The rise of the sense 'prostitute' necessitates activation of the pejoratively pregnant conceptual element <COMMERCIALLY UNCHASTE_{[NEG]}> presupposed for the attributive path of **DOMAIN OF MORALITY [...]**. The following *OED*-extracted contexts testify to both sexually explicit senses of *doxy*:

> c1530 Of the stews I am made controller... There shall no man play *doccy* there... Without they have leave of me.
> 1611 With, heigh the *Doxy* ouer the dale.
> ↓
> 1857 Spending all my money among *doxies* and strolling players.

Apart from the heavily loaded pejorative sense the word developed a positive sense-thread, too. Interestingly, as Partridge (1984), Rawson (1989) and the *OED* reveal, in regional use *doxy* was used in the sense 'sweetheart', which may be treated as a kind of ameliorative step upwards from the derogatory heavily loaded sense 'prostitute' to a term of endearment. As for the present-day lexicographic works, neither *LDCE* nor *MED* documents the word *doxy* in their macrostructure while *ODO* lists the lexical item in question, yet it is qualified as *archaic*.

Conclusions

The main aim of this work has been to propose a panchronic onomasiological dictionary for the conceptual microcategory **FALLEN WOMAN**, and to investigate the linguistic tools and mechanisms language users employ in order either not to say or to veil the essence of what they mean to say. The data corpus subject to our step-by-step analysis was a body of lexical items onomasiologically linked to the conceptual microcategory **FALLEN WOMAN**, which ultimately may be seen as being hyponymically embedded in the conceptual macrocategory **HUMAN BEING**. Secondly, the focus of the study carried out here was to remain faithful to the cognitive panchronic attitude to the analysis of the lexical material in question with the specific intention of uncovering the relevant linguistic mechanisms operative in the formation of historical synonyms of *prostitute* together with determining the illocutionary force of the lexical items analysed. Furthermore, an attempt has been made to formalise and taxonomise the linguistic mechanisms employed in the historical formation of euphemistic and dysphemistic synonyms of *prostitute*. Thirdly, one of the subsidiary aims set to this work has been to draw a picture – as complete as possible – of the sociolinguistic phenomenon of prostitution, with all its characteristic conceptual traits, and the possible points of departure for metaphorical extensions; also known in the literature of the subject as building-bridges. Last but not least, the analysis proposed was intended to provide a historical and cultural background for the existence of the issue and social attitudes to the phenomenon across time and space. Primary attention was paid to both English and American Anglo-Saxon cultures across different periods of time. While analysing the issue of prostitution in the American West of the 19th century, an intriguing observation was made regarding the occupational stratification, which in some way is comparable to the classification of prostitutes in ancient Greece. According to the *EPSW*, brothel dwellers (and the referents of such lexical items as *wench*, *escort*, *pucelle*, *amorosa* and *call-girl* may be said to fit in this category) occupied the highest position on the socio-economic ladder, followed by saloon/dance hall girls (the concept corresponding to the sense range of such English world lexical items as *harlot*, *tickle-tail* and *wagtail*), then crib women, and streetwalkers closing the list (and this bottom category is in the panchronic dictionary of **FALLEN WOMAN** represented by such historical synonyms of *prostitute* as *beþæcestre*, *fling-dust*, *pavement princess* and *walk-street*). Given the multitude of tasks initially encompassed within this work, it remains to hope that at least some of the aims have been achieved.

Most importantly, it needs to be stressed that, since shaping a somewhat uniform attitude to the phenomenon of prostitution seems beyond any reach, we have – throughout this work – adopted and complied with the view of the relatively tolerant and open-minded oulook and system of values representative of Western Christendom. Obviously, any attempt at analysing axiology-related qualities, actions and attitudes necessitates assuming a certain frame of mind, if not holistically rigid than at least equipped with an axiologically well-defned rigid backbone.

Originally, the ambitious idea underlying the conception of this work was to provide an analytical account of the entire quantum of synonyms of *prostitute* in the history of English, but – as it soon turned out – this enormous task would mean analysing over 70 more lexical items. Yet, the remaining unanalysed Late Modern English and Present-day English material is neither lost, nor shall it be forgotten because it is the implicit intention of the author to continue with the analysis of the microcategory **FALLEN WOMAN** to make the panchronic onomasiological picture, if not complete, then at least as complete as possible. Somewhat prematurely, one may formulate a general hypothesis that the rise and the semantic shifts of the latest synonyms of *prostitute* that have been left out of the analytic account here may have been of an entirely different nature, with varied causes and conditionings. The Enlightenment, the Industrial Revolution, the Victorian Era, the 20th century liberation movements and the post-Second World War Sexual Revolution, coupled with several all-pervading extralinguistic phenomena, such as the drive for political correctness must have had a cumulative impact which, while in no way invisible, remains a loaded question the nature of which may be determined one day, challenging as the task undoubtedly is. The author is fully aware that the analysis of the entire body of historical synonyms would ensure the completion of the work, and to anticipate the richness of the material to be analysed in the future, we have provided a taxonomy of the Late Modern English and Present-day English synonyms into the categories of linguistic mechanisms which were used in their formation; that is structural tools (*market dame, kennel-nymph, prossy, yum-yum girl*), semantic tools (*fille de joie, doll-common, schickster, moonlighter*), and rhetorical tools (*nocturnal, mouse, unfortunate, soiled dove*).

Interestingly enough, the analysis of the phenomenon of prostitution in antiquity has shown that there have always existed two main types of prostitutes, which – in accordance with the ancient taxonomy – were labelled in this work as *porné* and *hetaera*. This division has proved crucial as – a few doubtful cases aside – most lexical items analysed in the foregoing (from Old English to Early

Modern English) come under one of the two subcategories of the conceptual microcategory **FALLEN WOMAN**. Significantly, apart from M.E. *wench* and E.Mod.E. *courtesan, amorosa* and – most probably – *pucelle*, the synonyms of *prostitute* analysed are semantically linked to the conceptual subcategory **PORNÉ**. This immense disproportion reflects the existence of the ever present social stratification into lower classes (the masses) and higher classes (which – as more exclusive – are limited in number). This may be the reason why we speak about an abundance of lexical items linked to the conceptual subcategory **PORNÉ**, but only very few cases of synonyms of *prostitute* which are semantically linked to the conceptual subcategory **HETAERA**.

The phenomenon of prostitution has never been an exclusively female event as even the ancient Romans had a term for male prostitutes, namely *publici cinaedi* although one may hardly speak about the existence of such well-pronounced socially and culturally conditioned dualism as in the case of female **PORNÉ/HETAERA** world. As for the synonyms of *male prostitute* in the history of the English language, the first lexical items with the sense 'catamite' are recorded in the *OED* within the Early Modern English time frames. However, quantitatively speaking, male-specific synonyms of *prostitute* constitute a minority group when compared with the entirety of their female-specific counterparts. Let us stress at this point that the mechanisms that are evidenced in the formation of historical synonyms of *male prostitute* are – by large – the same as those employed in the formation of female-specific synonyms of *prostitute*, which were analysed in detail in the analytical part of this monograph. As shown in Kleparski and Duda (in print) all synonyms of *male prostitute* are associated either with the conceptual value <PASSIVE$_{[NEG]}$> or <LOW$_{[NEG]}$> or both, which places the synonyms of *male prostitute* somewhere at the lowest levels of the (social) perception scale. In conclusion – all facts considered – the body of synonyms of *male prostitute* in no way constitutes a qualitative and quantitative match for the body of female-specific synonyms of *prostitute*.

In discussing etymology, semantics, morphological shape, euphemising/ dysphemising mechanism and illocutionary force of O.E., ME. and E.Mod.E. synonyms of *prostitute*, we have employed a carefully selected body of dictionaries, of which the major lexicographic works are the *OED*, *Historical Thesaurus of English*, *An Anglo-Saxon Dictionary*, *The Slang of Sin*, Weekley (1921), Rawson (1981), Partridge (1984), Mills (1989), Spears (1991), Pearsall (2001), Green (2003), Ayto (2005, 2007), Enright (2005), Skeat (2005), Hughes (2006), Holder (2008), *Macmillan English Dictionary*, *Longman Dictionary of Contemporary English* and *Oxford Dictionaries Online*. Wide as the panorama of lexicographic sources put to use here is, there is always a shadow of doubt whether an inquiry into a wider panorama of dictionaries would provide a more exhaustive range of material for the analysis, and hence lead to formulating more revealing answers to the questions related to the nature of the processes that have been analysed.

Generally speaking, the foundation of the corpus data for the analysis was based on the *Historical Thesaurus of English*, whereby three sections labelled PROSTITUTION and UNCHASTITY provided us with groups of historical synonyms onomasiologically linked to the conceptual microcategory **FALLEN WOMAN**. The author then undertook the necessary task of confronting against other etymological dictionaries the synonymic riches included in the section UNCHASTITY. The result of the search proved fruitful as 40 synonyms included in the section UNCHASTITY are evidenced – both by the *OED* and other lexicographic sources – to be historically linked to the conceptual microcategory **FALLEN WOMAN**. Apart from 93 synonyms included in the *HTE* under the section PROSTITUTION and 40 more included in the section UNCHASTITY, another 21 have been added to the data corpus for the analysis as the outcome of the lexicographic search in such historical sources as Partridge (1984), Rawson (1981, 1989), Spears (1991) and Ayto (2007), to mention but a few, which proved the lexical items to be, beyond doubt, associated with the category determining conceptual value <COMMERCIALLY UNCHASTE$_{[NEG]}$>. Of the entire panchronic body of synonyms of *prostitute* 80 lexical items have been analysed in detail: 12 from Old English, 11 from Middle English and 57 from Early Modern English. A general observation that may be formulated regarding the morphological build-up is that the vast majority of the synonyms take the shape of either single-form or compound lexical items, and only a very limited number of phraseological units have been historically documented for the sense 'prostitute'. The table given below contains the whole body of data that has been the subject of our analysis:

Old English
forligerwif, myltestre, portcwene, hóre, beþæcestre, horcwene, firenhicgend, scand, scrætte, scylcen, synnecge, cwéne
Middle English
strumpet, pute, putain, harlot, common, common woman, tickle-tail, wench < wenchel, bawd < bawdstrot, slut, filth
Early Modern English
cat, drab, strange woman, putanie, stew, hackney, public woman, streetwalker, hackster, punk, croshabell, polecat, walk-street, night-shade, twigger, waistcoateer, hackney-woman, hack, mar-tail, fling-dust, night-trader, lady of pleasure, miss, hackney-wench, occupant, hell-moth, public commoner, moll, Tib, hiren, night-worm, community, Winchester goose, stewed strumpet, laced mutton, meat, wagtail, yaud, mermaid, cockatrice, courtesan, trull, callet, pucelle, succubus, amorosa, doxy, harlotry, loon, limmer, mort, baggage, sisters of the bank, light of love, bat, plover, quail

The analysis of the target material revealed a certain number of general tendencies. To start with, the analysis of Old English synonyms of *prostitute* has shown that – in accordance with the general tendency of that period – Anglo-Saxon language users made use of their own native linguistic resources rather than borrowed from other languages. As a result, one may speak of only one lexical item of either a possible or pseudo-foreign origin, namely *hóre* which may have been adopted from another Germanic language, namely Old Norse. As for exploiting native resources, it is worth noting that the processes of compounding (*forligerwif, portcwene, horcwene*), and derivation (*myltestre, beþæcestre, forligerwif*) were equally productive in the formation of the earliest synonyms of *prostitute*. Interestingly, the lexical items recorded as Old English synonyms of *prostitute* exhibit certain conceptualisation patterns which may turn out to be both historically and culturally universal, rather than language or time specific.

Related to Anglo-Saxon times, the Old English period is characterised by the working of various conceptualisation schemata, such as PROSTITUTION IS PORT CONNECTED (see the evolution of *portcwene*), PROSTITUTION IS WRONGDOING (see the evolution of *firenhicgend*), PROSTITUTION IS A SIN (see the evolution of *synnecge*), PROSTITUTION IS A SHAME (see the evolution of *scand*), and PROSTITUTION IS LYING DOWN (see the evolution of *forligerwif*), the majority of which tend to locate the activity within the limits of either sinful or wrongdoing or, at least, shameful or shamefully perceived frames. Furthermore, two other metaphorical schemata, namely SEX IS CONSUMPTION and SEX IS FIGHT/WAR, this time of much universal application – as recently shown in Kleparski (2013) and Cymbalista and Kleparski (2013) – are represented on a lexical level with the O.E. synonyms *myltestre* and *scylcen*.

It seems that – rather unsurprisingly – the extralinguistic factors related to the phenomenon of prostitution play a crucial role in the development of the lexical items semantically linked to the conceptual microcategory **FALLEN WOMAN**. After all, the most common place of operation for prostitutes in Anglo-Saxon times was a port and the neighbouring area, (stereo)typically a prostitute works in a lying position and, last but not least, sociologically prostitution has always been considered a crime, a sin and/or a shame. Significantly, most synonyms of *prostitute* dating from Old English stage are dysphemistic in nature, as the semantics of the majority of them is associated with negatively loaded conceptual values. However, we need to bear in mind that the lexicographic documentation of the Old English lexical resources is far from being complete and exhaustive, which makes the analysis of O.E. synonyms of *prostitute* a largely speculative task.

As for the Middle English period, the most striking – though historically well-justified – difference is the increased employment of the process of lexical borrowing. To be more specific, the majority of M.E. synonyms of *prostitute* were borrowed from French (*pute, putain, harlot, common, bawd*), and only one is of either Latin or Dutch origin (*strumpet*). Furthermore, during this period new conceptualisation patterns emerge, namely PROSTITUTION IS FILTH, of which four M.E. synonyms *pute, putain, slut* and *filth* have been evidenced to be lexical realisations, PROSTITUTION IS VIOLATING RULES/ WRONGDOING, which is lexically represented by M.E. *strumpet*, as well as *pars pro toto* metonymic extension \\BODY PART FOR A PERSON\\ of which M.E. *tickletail* is a sample. However, the most intriguing conclusion that may be drawn from the analysis of the quantum of M.E. lexical items linked to the conceptual microcategory **FALLEN WOMAN** is that four of the M.E. synonyms, namely *wench, strumpet, harlot* and *slut*, have retained the sense 'prostitute' up to present-day, and – more significantly – till this day these names are almost exceptionlessly employed in the definitional formula of other historical synonyms of *prostitute*, which undoubtedly points to the fact that they are the most central and historically persistent members of the conceptual microcategory **FALLEN WOMAN**.

Moreover, the analysis carried out here clearly points to the dysphemistic nature of the majority of M.E. synonyms of *prostitute*, as they are semantically associated with either the conceptual value <LOW$_{[NEG]}$> (*common woman, common, strumpet*) or <FILTHY$_{[NEG]}$> (*pute, putain, slut, filth*). The only two lexical items dating from Middle English for which the label *euphemism* may be postulated are *wench* and *harlot*.

It has already been acknowledged in the literature of the subject that there is a substantial amount of animal metaphor involved in human conceptualisation of the world, the problem discussed earlier by, among others, Kleparski (1997), Kiełtyka (2008) and Kochman-Haładyj and Kleparski (2011). The analysis of our material clearly shows that the conceptualisation of prostitution is highly metaphorical in nature, and – with the progression of time – the number of metaphorically triggered synonyms of *prostitute* has been constantly on the rise. In Early Modern English alone, twenty synonyms are found which evidently constitute lexical realisations of various metaphorical schemata, animal metaphor including. More specifically, a prostitute is pictured either as a game bird or a nocturnal creature, and – similarly to the picture arising from the analysis of Old English material – a prostitute is viewed as an object of consumption. The metaphorical schemata that have been discerned are labelled in the following way:

- A PROSTITUTE IS A NOCTURNAL CREATURE (see the evolution of *cat, polecat, bat, hell-moth, night-worm*),

- A PROSTITUTE IS A BIRD (see the evolution of *Winchester goose, wagtail, quail*),
- A PROSTITUTE IS A GAME BIRD (see the evolution of *plover*),
- A PROSTITUTE IS A HORSE (see the evolution of *hackney, hackney-woman, hackney-wench, yaud*),
- A PROSTITUTE IS AN ANIMAL (see the evolution of *twigger, mermaid, cockatrice*), THE OBJECT OF SEX IS FOOD (see the evolution of *laced mutton, meat*),
- A PROSTITUTE IS A FAMILY MEMBER (see the evolution of *sisters of the bank*).

Furthermore, the concept PROSTITUTION is evidenced to have been pictured with the aid of several metonymic extensions, namely:

- \\FEATURE FOR PERSON ADORNED WITH THIS FEATURE\\ (*baggage, fling-dust/-stink, light of love*),
- \\LOCATION FOR PROFESSION\\ (*stew, walk-street, streetwalker*),
- \\TIME OF ACTIVITY FOR PROFESSION\\ (*night-shade, night-trader*),
- \\POSSESSED FOR POSSESSOR\\ (*waistcoateer*).

Yet another observation which emerges from the analysis of E.Mod.E. synonyms of *prostitute* is that most of them have been adopted from other languages. The source languages of E.Mod.E. synonyms of *prostitute* seem to reflect the general tendency of the English language in the area of lexical borrowing. Naturally, the obvious priority goes to French and classical languages (e.g. *putanie, courtesan, pucelle, hackney, callet, succubus, punk*). Interestingly, in terms of the illocutionary force evoked by E.Mod.E. synonyms the analysis shows that the vast majority of female-specific synonyms are inauspicious cover terms and should be categorised as dysphemisms.

In more universal tones, the fact that the mechanisms, tendencies and phenomena discussed in this work are not restricted merely to English is clearly demonstrated in the multitude of parallel examples that may be drawn from other natural languages, the phenomenon touched upon in a number of *RSDS* recent publications, such as Kleparski (1997), Kleparski (2010), Kiełtyka (2008) and Kochman-Haładyj and Kleparski (2011). First of all, the ubiquity of zoosemic metaphor is clearly visible since – apart from the cases given above – the general conceptual metaphor A PROSTITUTE IS AN ANIMAL is richly manifested on a lexical level in such languages as Italian (*cagnaccia* < *cagna* 'bitch', *cavallona* < *cavalla* 'mare', *gallinella* < *gallina* 'hen', *vaccaccia* < *vacca* 'cow', *pocella* < *porca* 'sow', *scrofaccia* < *scrofa* 'sow' and *troiaccia* < *troia* 'sow'). In other European languages, as shown in Kiełtyka (2008), the body of metaphorical zoosemic extensions in question includes Mod.Sp. *zorra* 'vixen', Mod.Fr. *poulette* 'small hen', *pouliche* 'young mare', Mod.Pol. *mewka* '(little) sea-gull', Mod.Russ. *бабочка* 'butterfly' and Mod.G. *Mähre* 'old mare'; all being used metaphorically in the sense 'prostitute'.

Another universal conceptualisation pattern related to prostitution is based on the contiguity schema \\LOCATION FOR PROFESSION\\. As early as in ancient Rome a specific term was coined for a prostitute working in the street (Lat. *circulatrix* lit. 'streetwalking'). Similarly, most European languages have corresponding terms in their word stocks, and all may be labelled as counterparts of E.Mod.E. *streetwalker* or *walk-street*, such as Pol. *ulicznica*, Fr. *péripatéticienne*, Sp. *callejera/mujer de la calle*, It. *passeggiatrice*, G. *Straßenmädchen* and Sw. *gatflicka*. Although – in general – availability is largely determined by an act of choice, and the actual physical presence is merely a natural consequence of it, in the case of sex workers public location may only add boost to the trade.

On the methodological side, one of the weaknesses yet to surmount in current semantic research is to determine the ontological status of such conceptual values as <FILTHY$_{[NEG]}$>, <HIGH$_{[POS]}$>, <PORT<CONNECTED$_{[NEU]}$>> and <COMMERCIALLY UNCHASTE$_{[NEG]}$>. To be more specific, their obvious affinity to semantic features as perceived during the epoch of decompositional linguistics has not yet been overcome. Secondly, ideally conceptual values should represent elementary conceptual attributive values; while the former two, that is <FILTHY$_{[NEG]}$> and <HIGH$_{[POS]}$>, seem to meet this criterion to a considerable degree, the latter two, that is <PORT<CONNECTED$_{[NEU]}$>> and <COMMERCIALLY UNCHASTE$_{[NEG]}$>, are nothing short of complex. In addition, regrettably, the analysis offered here to a large extent continues the tradition of answering the question of what has happened, and only on rare occasions do we make an attempt to venture some answer to the question why it has happened and under what conditions. Last but not least, the author is fully aware of the subjective judgement as for the illocutionary force of some – if not many – synonyms analysed here because words may – and often do – evoke varied emotions and reactions when used in specific contexts, though in isolation they frequently appear less marked and harmful even to the naked eye.

Several specific aims that were set to the analysis have been either answered only partially or ignored for the lack of space or lack of sufficient evidence. Regrettably, only few of the subjects raised may be said to have been exhausted and, hence, I feel that there are many questions and issues that must be dealt with more thoroughly in linguistic research to come.

At the same time, we hope to have succeeded in showing that the cognitive apparatus coupled with the traditionally recognised processes and concepts related to euphemisation may be applied to the semantics of other evaluatively specific spheres of the lexico-semantic system of English. Take, for example, such conceptual categories as **DRUNKARD**, **FARMER** and **UGLY HUMAN BEING**. The members of each of the three categories may be treated as representatives of different types of pejoration of meaning content, namely behavioural, social and aesthetic respectively. For example, the body of lexical items historically linked to the pejoratively laden conceptual category **DRUNKARD** includes, to mention but a few, *glow worm, gin hound, drain pipe, staggerer, stewie, juicer, faithful, admiral of the red, true blue*. Even a cursory look at the lexical items suffices to categorise the synonyms of *drunkard* in accordance with the mechanisms which were employed in their formation. For example, the metaphorical extensions may have been at work in the formation of *glow worm, gin hound* and *drain pipe* whereas metonymically-conditioned formations include *true blue, staggerer, stewie* and *juicer*. The lexical item *faithful* may have been the result of the working of the process of understatement and *admiral of the red* may have been formed through the employment of the mechanism of circumlocution. Similarly, the aesthetically loaded lexical items historically linked to the conceptual category **UGLY HUMAN BEING** include, among others, *hag, witch* and *toad*, all of which may be treated as lexical realisations of metaphorical extensions. Yet another conceptual category, namely **FARMER**, is linked to such socially pejorative lexical items as *rustic, peasant, bumpkin, yokel* and *hick*. Interestingly, the historical synonym of *farmer* which may be treated as its euphemistic variant is *man of the country*, may be postulated to have been formed as the result of the employment of the processes of circumlocution. As for the remaining ones, they are all pejoratively coloured with the conceptual value <LOW$_{[NEG]}$> presupposed for the attributive path of **DOMAIN OF SOCIAL STATUS [...]**.

In this work I have consciously been involved in carrying out a well-defined data-oriented study based on the multitude of linguistic facts evidenced for the history of English, and only on rare occasions did I venture to propose theoretical solutions, constructs and generalisations. This is mainly due to the fact that it is my strong belief that although there is a need for new theoretically oriented generalising, systematising and typologising ventures in the field of diachronic semantics, the data-oriented analysis carried out here has shown that the processes of semantic change in general and the mechanisms of euphemisation in particular are not entirely haphazard and unmotivated. In other words, I hope to have forged at least another tiny data-evidenced building block to construct the bridge to understand the realm of historical semantic change.

Index

Early Modern English
- (laced) mutton 160
- amorosa 188
- aunt 164
- baggage 166
- bat 145
- callet 186
- cat 146
- cockatrice 158
- commoner 132
- community 132
- courtesan 184
- croshabell 189
- doxy 200
- drab 183
- fling dust (-stink) 167
- hack 153
- hackney 153
- hackney wench 153
- hackney woman 153
- hackster 153
- hell moth 147
- hiren 192
- lady of pleasure 195
- light of love 198
- limmer 178
- loon 177
- meat 161
- mermaid 159
- miss 175
- moll 193
- mort 179
- night shade 170
- night trader 170
- night worm 148
- occupant 199
- plover 153
- prostitute 181
- public commoner 132
- public woman 173
- pucelle 187
- punk 190
- quail 151
- sisters of the bank 162
- stew 168
- stewed strumpet/whore 169
- strange woman 174
- street walker 169
- succubus 164
- Tib 192
- trull 185
- twigger 157
- wagtail 150
- waistcoateer 171
- walk street 169
- Winchester goose 149
- yaud 155, 157

Late Modern English
- bawd 134
- hackney lady 153
- ladies of trade 197
- lady of easy virtue 197
- molly 194
- mot/mott 179
- strum 137
- trully 185

Middle English
- bawdstrot 134
- common woman 130
- filth 141
- harlot 139
- putain 136
- slut 140
- strumpet 137
- tickle tail 132
- wench 135
- wenchel 135

Old English
- beþæcestre 126
- cwéne 121
- firenhicgend 127
- forligerwif 120
- horcwene 124
- hóre 124
- myltestre 126
- portcwene 123
- scand 128
- scrætte 129

scylcen 128
synnecge 127

Present day English
   hell moth 147
   lady of the evening/night 197

References

Dictionaries and Encyclopedias:

Ayto, J. 2005. *Word Origins. The Secret Histories of English Words from A to Z.* 2nd ed. London: A&C Black Publishers Ltd.
Ayto, J. 2007. *Wobbly Bits and Other Euphemisms.* London: A&C Black Publishers.
Bańkowski, A. 2000. *Etymologiczny słownik języka polskiego.* Warszawa: Wydawnictwo Naukowe PWN.
Bluestein, G. 1998. *Anglish/Yinglish. Yiddish in American Life and Literature.* Lincoln and London: University of Nebraska Press.
Boryś, W. 2005. *Słownik etymologiczny języka polskiego.* Kraków: Wydawnictwo Literackie.
Brückner, A. 1985. *Słownik etymologiczny języka polskiego.* Warszawa: Wiedza Powszechna.
Chaciński, B. 2005. *Wyczesany słownik najmłodszej polszczyzny.* Kraków: Wydawnictwo Znak.
Crystal, D. 1987. *The Cambridge Encyclopedia of Language.* Cambridge: Cambridge University Press.
Crystal, D. 1995. *The Cambridge Encyclopedia of the English Language.* Cambridge: Cambridge University Press.
Cuddon, J.A., C. Preston 1998. *A Dictionary of Literary Terms and Literary Theory.* Oxford: Blackwell Publishers Ltd.
Dalzell, T. 1998. *The Slang of Sin.* Springfield: Merriam-Webster Inc.
Dalzell, T., T. Victor 2008. *Sex Slang.* London/New York: Routledge.
Danesi, M. 2000. *Encyclopedic Dictionary of Semiotics, Media, and Communications.* Toronto: University of Toronto Press.
Dąbrowska, A. 2005. *Słownik eufemizmów polskich – czyli w rzeczy mocno, w sposobie łagodnie.* Warszawa: Wydawnictwo Naukowe PWN.
Ditmore, M.H. (ed.) 2006. *Encyclopedia of Prostitution and Sex Work.* Westport/London: Greenwood Press.
Ember, C.R., M. Ember 2003. *Encyclopedia of Sex and Gender. Men and Women in the World's Cultures.* New York: Kluwer Academic/Plenum Publishers.
Enright, D. 2005. *In Other Words.* London: Michael O'Mara Books Ltd.
Franklyn, J. 1975. *A Dictionary of Rhyming Slang.* London: Routledge and Kegan Paul Books.

Głowiński, M., T. Kostkiewiczowa, A. Okopień-Sławińska, J. Sławiński 2002. *Słownik terminów literackich*. Warszawa, Kraków, Gdańsk, Łódź: Ossolineum.
Gołąb, Z., A. Heinz, K. Polański 1970. *Słownik terminologii językoznawczej*. Warszawa: Państwowe Wydawnictwo Naukowe.
Green, J. 2003. *Cassell's Dictionary of Slang*. London: Cassell.
Holder, B. 2008. *A Dictionary of Euphemisms. How Not To Say What You Mean*. Oxford/New York: Oxford University Press.
Hughes, G.I. 2006. *An Encyclopedia of Swearing: the Social History of Oaths, Profanity, Foul Language, and Ethnic Slurs in the English-speaking World*. New York/London: M.E. Sharpe.
Kunitskaya-Peterson, Ch. 1981. *International Dictionary of Obscenities. A Guide to Dirty Words and Indecent Expressions in Spanish, Italian, French, German, Russian*. Oakland, California: Scythian Books.
Lapidge, M., J. Blair, S. Keynes, D. Scragg (eds.) 2001. *The Blackwell Encyclopaedia of Anglo-Saxon England*. Oxford: Blackwell Publishers.
Macmillan English Dictionary for Advanced Learners. 2002. Oxford: Macmillan Publishers Ltd.
McArthur, T. 1984. *Longman Lexicon of Contemporary English*. Harlow: Longman Group Ltd.
McArthur, T. (ed.) 1992. *The Oxford Companion to the English Language*. Oxford/New York: Oxford University Press.
Mills, J. 1989. *Womanwords. A Dictionary of Words About Women*. New York: The Free Press.
Murray, J., Ch.T. Onions, W. Craige, F.J. Furnivall (eds.) 1971. *The Oxford English Dictionary*. Oxford: Oxford University Press.
Partridge, E. 1984. *A Dictionary of Slang and Unconventional English*. New York: the Macmillan Company.
Pearsall, J. 2001. *The New Oxford Dictionary of English*. Oxford/New York: Oxford University Press.
Pei, M.A., F. Gaynor 1954. *A Dictionary of Linguistics*. New York: Philosophical Library.
Pisarek, W. (ed.) 2006. *Słownik terminologii medialnej*. Kraków: Universitas.
Polański, K. (ed.) 1995. *Encyklopedia językoznawstwa ogólnego*. Wrocław-Warszawa-Kraków: Ossolineum.
Płóciennik, I., D. Podlawska 2005. *Słownik wiedzy o języku*. Bielsko-Biała: Wydawnictwo PARK.
Rawson, H. 1981. *A Dictionary of Euphemisms and Other Double Talk*. New York: Crown Publishers.
Rawson, H. 1989. *Wicked Words*. New York: Crown Publishers.

Roberts, J., C. Kay, L. Grundy 1995. *A Thesaurus of Old English*. Exeter: Short Run Press Ltd.
Sanchez Benedito, F. 1998. *A Semi-bilingual Dictionary of Euphemisms and Dysphemisms in English Erotica*. Granada: Comares.
Skeat, W.W. 2005. *An Etymological Dictionary of the English Language*. Oxford: Claredon Press.
Sobol, E. (ed.) 2002. *Nowy słownik języka polskiego*. Warszawa: Wydawnictwo Naukowe PWN.
Spears, R.A. 1991. *Slang and Euphemism. A Dictionary of Oaths, Curses, Insults, Sexual Slang and Metaphor, Racial Slurs, Drug Talk, Homosexual Lingo, and Related Matters*. Middle Village/New York: David Publishers.
Stomma, L. 2000. *Słownik polskich wyzwisk, inwektyw i określeń pejoratywnych*. Warszawa: Oficyna Wydawnicza Graf-Punkt.
Sussman, E. (ed.) 2008. *Dirty Words. A Literary Encyclopedia of Sex*. New York: Bloomsbury.
Warrack, A. 2006. *The Concise Scots Dialect Dictionary*. New Lanark: Waverley Books Ltd.
Weekley, E. 1921. *Etymological Dictionary of Modern English*. New York: Dutton and Company.

Other Works:

Aitchison, J. 1994. *Words in the Mind: An Introduction to the Mental Lexicon*. 2nd ed. Oxford: Blackwell.
Allan K., K. Burridge 1991. *Euphemism and Dysphemism, Language Used as Shield and Weapon*. Oxford/New York: Oxford University Press.
Allan, K., K. Burridge 2006. *Forbidden Words. Taboo and the Censoring of Language*. Cambridge: Cambridge University Press.
Allyn, D. 2000. *Make Love Not War: The Sexual Revolution an Unfettered History*. Boston: Little, Brown.
Aman, R. (ed.) 1987. *The Best of Maledicta*. Philadelphia: The Running Press.
Aman R. 1996. *Opus Maledictorum. A Book of Bad Words*. New York: Marlowe & Company.
Baugh, A.C., T. Cable 2002. *A History of the English Language*. 5th ed. New York: Routledge.
Bechstein, R. 1863. "Ein pessimistischer Zug in der Entwicklung der Wortbedeutungen", in: *Pfeiffers Germania*, vol.8, pp. 330-354.
Binnie, J. 2004. *The Globalization of Sexuality*. London/Thousand Oaks/New Delhi: SAGE Publications.
Bloomfield, G. 1933. *Language*. New York: Henry Holt and Company.

Boswell, J. 1994. *Same-sex Unions in Pre-Modern Europe*. New York: Villard Books.
Bredin, H. 1984. "Metonymy", in: *Poetics Today* 5, pp. 45-58.
Brown, P. 1990. "Bodies and minds: Sexuality and renunciation in early Christianity", in: D.M. Halperin, J.J. Winkler, F.I Zeitlin (eds.) *Before Sexuality: The Construction of Erotic Experience in the Ancient Greek World*. Princeton: Princeton University Press.
Brundage, J.A. 1987. *Law, Sex, and Christian Society in Medieval Europe*. Chicago/London: The University of Chicago Press.
Bullough, V.L., J. Brundage (eds.) 1982. *Sexual Practices and the Medieval Church*. Buffalo: Prometheus Books.
Burchfield, R. 1986. "An outline history of euphemisms in English", in: D.J. Enright (ed.) *Fair of Speech: The Uses of Euphemisms*, pp. 13-31.
Chamizo Dominguez, P.J. 2005. "Some theses on euphemisms and dysphemisms", in: *Studia Anglica Resoviensia* 3, pp. 9–16.
Chamizo Dominguez, P.J. 2007 "Linguistic interdiction: Forbidden words and the censoring of language", in: *Language Sciences*.
Chamizo Dominguez, P.J., F. Sánchez Benedito 1994. "Euphemism and dysphemism: Ambiguity and supposition", in: *Language and Discourse* 2, pp. 78-92.
Chamizo Dominguez, P.J., F. Sánchez Benedito 2005. CONCEPTUAL NETWORKS OF ENGLISH BAWDY EUPHEMISMS AND DYSPHEMISMS. Unpublished Manuscript.
Cook, H. 2004. *The Long Sexual Revolution: English Women, Sex, and Contraception 1800-1975*. Oxford/New York: Oxford University Press.
Crespo, B. 2013. *Change in Life, Change in Language: A Semantic Approach to the History of English*. Frankfurt a/Main: Peter Lang Verlag.
Crespo Fernández, E. 2008. "Sex-related euphemism and dysphemism: An analysis in terms of conceptual metaphor theory", in: *Atlantis. Journal of Spanish Association of Anglo-American Studies*. 30.2, pp. 95-110.
Cruse, D.A. 1986. *Lexical Semantics*. Cambridge: Cambridge University Press.
Cymbalista, P. 2008. Semantic Development of Selected Items in the Macro-Category of 'HOMO FABER' in the English Language. Ph.D. dissertation, University of Rzeszów.
Cymbalista, P. 2009b. "Do you know what you eat? The phenomenon of food-semy", in: G.A. Kleparski, P. Cymbalista, R. Kiełtyka and K. Pytel. (eds.) *In Medias Res*. Vol.1/2009, pp. 9-29.
Cymbalista, P. and G.A. Kleparski. 2013. *From Michele Bréal to Dirk Geeraerts: Towards the Main Issues in Diachronic Lexical Semantics*. Jarosław: Wydawnictwo PWSTE.

Dąbrowska, A. 1992. „Eufemizmy mowy potocznej", in: J. Anusiewicz (ed.) *Język a kultura*, vol. 5: *Potoczność w języku i kulturze*, pp. 119–163.
Dover, K.J. 1978. *Greek Homosexuality*. London: Duckworth.
Duda, B. 2013. "From *portcwene* to *fille de joie*: On etymology and the word-formation processes behind the historical lexical representations in the category **FALLEN WOMAN** in English", in: J. Fisiak and M. Bator (eds.) *Historical Word-Formation and Semantics*. Frankfurt a/Main: Peter Lang, pp. 259-276.
Enright, D.J. (ed.) 1986. *Fair of Speech: The Uses of Euphemisms*. Oxford/New York: Oxford University Press.
Enright, D.J. 1986. "Mother or maid? An introduction", in: D.J. Enright (ed.) *Fair of Speech: The Uses of Euphemism*, pp. 1-12.
Faraone, C.A., L.K. McClure 2006. *Prostitutes and Courtesans in the Ancient World*. Wisconsin: The University of Wisconsin Press.
Fisiak, J. 2000. *An Outline History of English: External History*. Poznań: Wydawnictwo Poznańskie.
Foucault, M. 1978. *The History of Sexuality: An Introduction*. (trans. Hurley, R.). New York: Random House. Vol.1.
Foucault, M. 1985. *The History of Sexuality: The Use of Pleasure*. (trans. Hurley, R.). New York: Random House. Vol.2.
Freccero, C. 1999. "Acts, identities, and sexuality's (pre) modern regimes", in: *Journal of Women's History* 11.2, pp. 186-192.
Fromkin, V., R. Rodman, N. Hyams 2003. *An Introduction to Language*. 7th ed. Boston: Thomson Wadsworth.
Garton, S. 2004. *Histories of Sexuality*. London: Equinox Publishing Ltd.
Gay, P. 1984. *Education of the Senses: The Bourgeois Experience: Victoria to Fraud*. New York: Oxford University Press. Vol.1.
Gibbs, R.W.Jr. 1999. "Speaking and thinking with metonymy", in: K.-U. Panther and G. Radden (eds.), pp.61-76.
Godbeer, R. 2002. *Sexual Revolution in Early America*. Baltimore: The Johns Hopkins University Press.
Górecka-Smolińska, M. 2012. *Feathered Creatures Speak: The Study of Semantic Evolution and Phraseology of **DOMESTICATED** and **SEMI-DOMESTICATED BIRDS***. Rzeszów: Wydawnictwo Uniwersytetu Rzeszowskiego.
Grygiel, M. and G.A. Kleparski 2007. *Main Trends in Historical Semantics*. Rzeszów: Wydawnictwo Uniwersytetu Rzeszowskiego.
Hoggart, S. 1986. "Politics", in: D.J. Enright (ed.) *Fair of Speech: The Uses of Euphemism*, pp. 174-184.

Jaberg, K. 1901-1905. "Pejorative Bedeutungsentwicklung im Französischen mit Berücksichtigung allgemeiner", in: *Zeitschrift für romanische Philologie*, 25 (pp. 561-601), 27 (pp. 25-71), 29 (pp. 57-71). Halle a. S.: Druck von E. Karras.

Karczmarczyk, J. 2012. "Three terms denoting dragons in Middle English poetry and prose: *Dragon, drake* and *worm*", in: J. Esquibel and A. Wojtyś (eds.) *Explorations in the English Language: Middle Ages and Beyond*. Frankfurt a/Main: Peter Lang Verlag, pp. 257-266.

Kardela, H. and G.A. Kleparski. 1990. *Approaching Diachronic Semantics: The Componential vs. Cognitive Account*. Umea: Printing Office of the Umea University.

Karras, R.M. 1996. *Common Women: Prostitution and Sexuality in Medieval England*. Oxford/New York: Oxford University Press.

Karras, R.M. 1999. "Prostitution and the question of sexual identity in medieval Europe", in: *Journal of Women's History* 11.2, pp. 159-177.

Kiełtyka, R. 2006a. Towards a Historical Account of English Zoosemy: The Case of Middle English and Early Modern English Domesticated Animals. Ph.D. dissertation, University of Rzeszów.

Kiełtyka, R. 2007. "Dark horses, fat cats and lucky dogs: A synthetic view of English zoosemy", in: G.A. Kleparski, R. Kiełtyka, M. Pikor-Niedziałek (eds.) *Aspects of Semantic Transposition of Words*. Chełm: TAWA, pp. 43-55.

Kiełtyka, R. 2008. *On zoosemy: The Study of Middle English and Early Modern English Domesticated Animals*. Rzeszów: Wydawnictwo Uniwersytetu Rzeszowskiego.

Kiełtyka, R. 2011. "Lucky *pigs* and (un)wise *owls*: On the crosslinguistic polarisation of the conceptual dimension **BEHAVIOUR/CHARACTER**", in: G.A. Kleparski and R. Kiełtyka (eds.) *Podkarpackie Forum Filologiczne. Seria Językozawstwo*, pp. 145-158.

Kleparski, G.A. 1990. *Semantic Change in English: A Study of Evaluative Developments in the Domain of HUMANS*. Lublin: Wydawnictwo KUL.

Kleparski, G.A. 1997. *Theory and Practice of Historical Semantics: The Case of Middle English and Early Modern English Synonyms of GIRL/YOUNG WOMAN*. Lublin: Redakcja Wydawnictw KUL.

Kleparski, G.A. 2008. "The joys and sorrows of metaphorical consumption: *Mozarellas, prostisciuttos, muttons* and *yum-yum girls* – Foodsemy with a Romance accent", in: *Studia Anglica Resoviensia* 5, pp. 45-59.

Kleparski, G.A. 2010. "Czy ta **lepsza** jest gorsza niż ten **lepszy** i dlaczego jest **rektor**, a nie ma **rektorki**", in: G.A. Kleparski and R. Kiełtyka (eds.) *Podkarpackie Forum Filologiczne. Seria Językozawstwo*, pp. 127-136.

Kleparski, G.A. 2013. "Historical Semantics: A sketch on new categories and types of semantic change", in: J. Fisiak and M. Bator (eds.) *Historical Word-Formation and Semantics.* Frankfurt a/Main: Peter Lang Verlag, pp. 59-88.
Kleparski, G.A. and M. Martnuska 2002. "Political Correctness and *Bequemlichkeitstrieb*", in: *Studia Anglica Resoviensia* 1, pp. 47-51.
Kleparski, G.A. and M. Grygiel 2003. "Protestants, Puritans, Papists and Logomachy. Some remarks on the role of social factors in the rise of new words and meanings", in: *Gazeta Uniwersytecka* 1/15, p.19.
Kleparski, G.A. and B. Duda (in print) "Cup-bearing in the context of male prostitution: On Early Modern English synonyms of *call-boy*", in: *Inozemna Philologia.* Lviv: Vyd-vo L'vivs'koho universytetu.
Koch, P. 1999. "Frame and contiguity: On the bases of metonymy and certain types of word formation", in: K.-U. Panther and G. Radden (eds.), pp. 139-167.
Kochman-Haładyj, B. 2007a. "Low wenches and slatternly queans: On derogation of WOMEN TERMS", in: G.A. Kleparski (ed.) *Studia Anglica Resoviensia* 4, pp. 206-229.
Kochman-Haładyj, B. 2007b. "The nature of derogation of women terms", in: G.A. Kleparski, R. Kiełtyka, M. Pikor-Niedziałek (eds.) *Aspects of Semantic Transposition of Words.* Chełm: TAWA, pp. 99-115.
Kochman-Haładyj, B. and G.A. Kleparski 2011. *On Pejoration of Women Terms in the History of English.* Rzeszów: Wydawnictwo Uniwersytetu Rzeszowskiego.
Kopecka, B. 2009. The Scope and Nature of Metonymically Conditioned Meaning Transference Related to the Macrocategory **HUMAN BEING**. Ph.D. dissertation, University of Rzeszów.
Kopecka, B. 2011. *Skirts, Jacks, Piece of Flesh Do Make People: Metonymic Developments to the Macrocategory* **HUMAN BEING**. Rzeszów: Wydawnictwo Uniwersytetu Rzeszowskiego.
Körtvélyessy, L. 2010. *Vplyv sociolingvistických faktorov na produktivitu v slovotvorbe.* Prešov: Slovacontact.
Kövecses, Z. 2006. "Metaphor and ideology in slang: The case of WOMAN and MAN", in: *Revue d'Études Françaises* 11, pp. 151-166.
Kröll, H. 1984: *O eufemismo e o disfemismo no português moderno.* Lisbon: Instituto de Cultura e Língua Portuguesa.
Kudła, M. 2010. "Inność od kuchni brytyjskiej", in: G.A. Kleparski and R. Kiełtyka (eds.) *Podkarpackie Forum Filologiczne. Seria Językozawstwo*, pp. 147-156.

Lakoff, G. 1987. *Women, Fire and Dangerous Things*. Chicago/London: The University of Chicago Press.
Lakoff, G. and M. Johnson 1980. *Metaphors We Live By*. Chicago/London: The University of Chicago Press.
Lakoff, G. and M. Turner 1989. *More than Cool Reason. A Field Guide to Poetic Metaphor*. Chicago/London: The University of Chicago Press.
Licht, H. 1932. *Sexual Life in Ancient Greece* (trans. J.H. Freese). London: Routledge.
Łozowski, P. 1994. "The notion of 'prototype' in diachronic semantics", in: E. Gussmann and H. Kardela (eds.) *Focus on Language, Papers from the 2nd Conference of the Polish Association for the Study of English, Kazimierz '93*. Lublin: Maria Curie-Skłodowska University, pp. 153-164.
Łozowski, P. 1999. "Panchrony, or linguistics without synchrony", in: B. Lewandowska-Tomaszczyk (ed.) *Cognitive Perspectives on Language*. Frankfurt a/Main: Peter Lang Verlag, pp. 22-35.
Łozowski, P. 2000. *Vagueness in Language from Truth-Conditional Synonymy to un-Conditional Polysemy*. Lublin: Wydawnictwo Uniwersytetu Marii Curie-Skłodowskiej.
Malinowski, B. 1948. *Magic, Science and Religion, and Other Essays*. Glencoe, 111: Free Press.
Marcus, S. 1966. *The Other Victorians: A Study of Sexuality and Pornography in Mid-Nineteenth Century England*. New York: Basic Books.
Mason, M. 1994. *The Making of Victorian Sexuality*. Oxford: Oxford University Press.
May, D. 1986. "Euphemisms and the media", in: D.J. Enright (ed.) *Fair of Speech: The Uses of Euphemism*, pp. 122-134.
McAnulty, R.D. and M.M. Burnette (eds.) 2006. *Sex and Sexuality*. Westport/London: Praeger Perspectives.
Mitchell, B. and F.C. Robinson 2012. *A Guide of Old English*. Malden/Oxford: Wiley-Blackwell.
Morton, M. 2003. *The Lover's Tongue. A Merry Romp through the Language of Love and Sex*. Toronto: Insomniac Press.
Murphy, M.L. 2010. *Lexical Meaning*. Cambridge: Cambridge University Press.
Nerlich, B. and D.D. Clarke 2001. "Ambiguities we live by: Towards a pragmatics of polysemy", in: *Journal of Pragmatics* 33, pp.1-20.
New American Bible. 1991. St. Joseph Medium Size Edition. New York: Catholic Book Publishing Co.
Outshoorn, J. 2004. *The Politics of Prostitution: Women's Movements, Democratic States and the Globalisation of Sex Commerce*. Cambridge: Cambridge University Press.

Osuchowska, D. 2010. *Talking Dictionaries. An Introductory-Level Course in Lexicography for English-Bound Students*. Rzeszów: Wydawnictwo Uniwersytetu Rzeszowskiego.
Palmer, F.R. 1981. *Semantics*. Cambridge: Cambridge University Press.
Panther, K.-U. and G. Radden (eds.) 1999. *Metonymy in Language and Thought* [Human Cognitive Processing 4]. Amsterdam and Philadelphia: John Benjamins Publishing Company.
Paul, H. 1891. *Principles of the History of Language*. London: Longmans, Green, and Co.
Pearsall, R. 1969. *The Worm in the Bud: The World of Victorian Sexuality*. London: Weidenfeld and Nicholson.
Porterfield, A. 2007. *Modern Christianity to 1900: A People's History of Christianity*. Minneapolis: Fortress Press.
Radtke, E. 1996. "Prostituta in Modern Italian: Suffixation and the semantic field", in: R. Aman (ed.) *Opus Maledictorum. A Book of Bad Words*, pp. 34-42.
Rayewska, N.M. 1979. *English Lexicology*. Kiev: Vyšča Škola Publishers.
Reid, L. 2006. *Talk the Talk. The Slang of 65 American Subcultures*. Cincinnati: Writer's Digest Books, pp. 137-146.
Rodak, M. 2007. "Prostytucja w Lublinie w latach 1918-1939", in: J. Żarnowski (ed.) *Metamorfozy Społeczne*, vol. II. Warszawa: Wydawnictwo Neriton, pp. 189-212.
Rosch, E. 1978. "Principles of categorisation", in: E. Roschand and B. Lloyd (eds.) *Cognition and Categorisation*. Hillsdale, NJ: Lawrence Erlbaum Associates, pp. 27-48.
Sampson, J. 1928. "The Times Literary Supplement".
Saussure, F. de. 1916. *Cours de linguistique générale*. Paris: Payot.
Schreuder, H. 1929. *Pejorative Sense Development in English*. College Park/Maryland: McGrath Publishing Company (reprint 1970).
Schulz, M. 1975. "The semantic derogation of woman", in: B. Thorne and N. Henley (eds.) *Language and Sex: Difference and Dominance*. Rowley: Newbury House Publishers Inc., pp. 64-75.
Self, H.J. 2003. *Prostitution, Women and Misuse of the Law: The Fallen Daughters of Eve*. London/Portland: Frank Cass Publishers.
Seto, K. 1999. "Distinguishing metonymy from synecdoche", in: K.-U. Panther and G. Radden (eds.), pp. 91-120.
Stone, L. 1992. "Libertine sexuality in post-Restoration England: Group sex and flagellation among the middling sort in Norwich in 1706-07", in: *Journal of the History of Sexuality* 2.4, pp. 511-525.
Strugielska, A. 2012. "Conceptual Metaphor Theory as an isolating model: A case for re-conextualization", in: W. Skrzypczak, T. Fojt and S. Wacewicz

(eds.) *Exploring Language through Contrast*. Newcastle upon Tyne: Cambridge Scholars Publishing, pp. 201-218.

Sylwanowicz, M. 2012. "*Clene inwit or fule saule?* A study of evaluative developments in the domain of CLEANLINESS", in: J. Esquibel and A. Wojtyś (eds.) *Explorations in the English Language: Middle Ages and Beyond*. Frankfurt a/Main: Peter Lang Verlag, pp. 339-352.

Taylor, J.R. 1995. *Linguistic Categorisation: Prototypes in Linguistic Theory*. 2nd ed. Oxford: Oxford University Press.

Trumbach, R. 1998. *Sex and the Gender Revolution. I. Heterosexuality and the Third Gender in Enlightenment London*. Chicago: Chicago University Press.

Ullmann, St. 1951. *Words and their Use*. New York: Philosophical Library, Inc.

Ullmann, St. 1957. *The Principles of Semantics*. Glasgow/Oxford: Basil Blackwell.

Warren, B. 1992. "What euphemisms tell us about the interpretation of words", in: *Studia Linguistica*, 46/2, pp. 128-172.

Wełna, J. 1996. *A Brief Outline of the History of English*. Warszawa: Wydawnictwo Uniwersytetu Warszawskiego.

Widlak, S. 1968. "Zjawisko tabu językowego", in: *Lud*, t.52, pp. 7-25.

Więcławska, E. 2011. Semantic Changes and Phraseological Productivity of the English **HEAD**-Related Lexical Items in Diachronic and Contrastive Perspective. Ph.D. dissertation, University of Rzeszów.

Więcławska, E. 2012. *A Contrastive Semantic and Phraseological Analysis of the English **HEAD**-Related Lexical Items in Diachronic Perspective*. Rzeszów: Wydawnictwo Uniwersytetu Rzeszowskiego.

Wilde, O. 2007. *The Importance of Being Earnest*. London/New York: Penguin Books.

Wittgenstein, L. 1953. *Philosophical Investigations*. Oxford: Basil Blackwell.

Internet resources:

Bosworth, J. and T.N. Toller 1898. *An Anglo-Saxon Dictionary.* [available from:] http://lexicon.ff.cuni.cz/search/aa_search.html (date of access: August 2011 – November 2011).
Encyclopaedia Britannica Online. 2010. [available from:] http://www.britannica.com/. (*BRITANNICA*)
Encyclopaedia Romana. Essays on Greek history and culture and the later Byzantine empire. Hetairai. [available from:] http://penelope.uchicago.edu/~grout/encyclopaedia_romana/greece/hetairai/hetairai.html. (*ENROM*)
Harper, D. 2001-2010. *Online Etymology Dictionary.* [available from:] http://www.etymonline.com. (*ETYMONLINE*)
Historical Thesaurus of English. 2009. [available from:] http://libra.englang.arts.gla.ac.uk/historicalthesaurus/menu1.html
Lees, C.A. 1997. "Engendering religious desire: Sex, knowledge, and Christian identity in Anglo-Saxon England", in: *The Journal of Medieval and Early Modern Studies* 27.1. pp.17-46. [available from:] http://muse.jhu.edu/journals/journal_of_medieval_and_early_modern_studies/v027/27.1lees.html
Longman Dictionary of Contemporary English. 2012. [available from:] www.ldoceonline.com
O'Donnell, R.C. 1992. "Freedom and restrictions in language use." University of Georgia: Educational Resources Information Center. [available from:] www.eric.ed.gov/ERICWebPortal/search/
Oxford Dictionaries. 2012. [available from:] www.oxforddictionaries.com
Partridge, E. 2006. *The Routledge Dictionary of Historical Slang.* [available from:] www.eBookstore.tandf.co.uk.
Urban Dictionary. 2012. [available from:] www.urbandictionary.com

Studies in English Medieval Language and Literature

Edited by Jacek Fisiak

Vol. 1 Dieter Kastovsky / Arthur Mettinger (eds.): Language Contact in the History of English. 2nd, revised edition. 2003.

Vol. 2 Studies in English Historical Linguistics and Philology. A Festschrift for Akio Oizumi. Edited by Jacek Fisiak. 2002.

Vol. 3 Liliana Sikorska: *In a Manner of Morall Playe*: Social Ideologies in English Moralities and Interludes (1350-1517). 2002.

Vol. 4 Peter J. Lucas / Angela M. Lucas (eds.): Middle English from Tongue to Text. Selected Papers from the Third International Conference on Middle English: Language and Text, held at Dublin, Ireland, 1-4 July 1999. 2002.

Vol. 5 Chaucer and the Challenges of Medievalism. Studies in Honor of H. A. Kelly. Edited by Donka Minkova and Theresa Tinkle. 2003.

Vol. 6 Hanna Rutkowska: Graphemics and Morphosyntax in the *Cely Letters* (1472-88). 2003.

Vol. 7 The *Ancrene Wisse*. A Four-Manuscript Parallel Text. Preface and Parts 1-4. Edited by Tadao Kubouchi and Keiko Ikegami with John Scahill, Shoko Ono, Harumi Tanabe, Yoshiko Ota, Ayako Kobayashi and Koichi Nakamura. 2003.

Vol. 8 Joanna Bugaj: Middle Scots Inflectional System in the South-west of Scotland. 2004.

Vol. 9 Rafal Boryslawski: The Old English Riddles and the Riddlic Elements of Old English Poetry. 2004.

Vol. 10 Nikolaus Ritt / Herbert Schendl (eds.): Rethinking Middle English. Linguistic and Literary Approaches. 2005.

Vol. 11 The *Ancrene Wisse*. A Four-Manuscript Parallel Text. Parts 5–8 with Wordlists. Edited by Tadao Kubouchi and Keiko Ikegami with John Scahill, Shoko Ono, Harumi Tanabe, Yoshiko Ota, Ayako Kobayashi, Koichi Nakamura. 2005.

Vol. 12 Text and Language in Medieval English Prose. A Festschrift for Tadao Kubouchi. Edited by Akio Oizumi, Jacek Fisiak and John Scahill. 2005.

Vol. 13 Michiko Ogura (ed.): Textual and Contextual Studies in Medieval English. Towards the Reunion of Linguistics and Philology. 2006.

Vol. 14 Keiko Hamaguchi: Non-European Women in Chaucer. A Postcolonial Study. 2006.

Vol. 15 Ursula Schaefer (ed.): The Beginnings of Standardization. Language and Culture in Fourteenth-Century England. 2006.

Vol. 16 Nikolaus Ritt / Herbert Schendl / Christiane Dalton-Puffer / Dieter Kastovsky (eds): Medieval English and its Heritage. Structure, Meaning and Mechanisms of Change. 2006.

Vol. 17 Matylda Włodarczyk: Pragmatic Aspects of Reported Speech. The Case of Early Modern English Courtroom Discourse. 2007.

Vol. 18 Hans Sauer / Renate Bauer (eds.): *Beowulf* and Beyond. 2007.

Vol. 19 Gabriella Mazzon (ed.): Studies in Middle English Forms and Meanings. 2007.

Vol. 20 Alexander Bergs / Janne Skaffari (eds.): The Language of the Peterborough Chronicle. 2007.

Vol. 21 Liliana Sikorska (ed.). With the assistance of Joanna Maciulewicz: Medievalisms. The Poetics of Literary Re-Reading. 2008.

Vol.	22	Masachiyo Amano / Michiko Ogura / Masayuki Ohkado (eds.): Historical Englishes in Varieties of Texts and Contexts. The Global COE Program, International Conference 2007. 2008.
Vol.	23	Ewa Ciszek: Word Derivation in Early Middle English. 2008.
Vol.	24	Andrzej M. Łęcki: Grammaticalisation Paths of *Have* in English. 2010.
Vol.	25	Osamu Imahayashi / Yoshiyuki Nakao / Michiko Ogura (eds.): Aspects of the History of English Language and Literature. Selected Papers Read at SHELL 2009, Hiroshima. 2010.
Vol.	26	Magdalena Bator: Obsolete Scandinavian Loanwords in English. 2010.
Vol.	27	Anna Cichosz: The Influence of Text Type on Word Order of Old Germanic Languages. A Corpus-Based Contrastive Study of Old English and Old High German. 2010.
Vol.	28	Jacek Fisiak / Magdalena Bator (eds.): Foreign Influences on Medieval English. 2011.
Vol.	29	Władysław Witalisz: The Trojan Mirror. Middle English Narratives of Troy as Books of Princely Advice. 2011.
Vol.	30	Luis Iglesias-Rábade: Semantic Erosion of Middle English Prepositions. 2011.
Vol.	31	Barbara Kowalik: Betwixt *engelaunde* and *englene londe*. Dialogic Poetics in Early English Religious Lyric. 2010.
Vol.	32	The Katherine Group. A Three-Manuscript Parallel Text. Seinte Katerine, Seinte Marherete, Seinte Iuliene, and Hali Meiðhad, with Wordlists. Edited by Shoko Ono and John Scahill with Keiko Ikegami, Tadao Kubouchi, Harumi Tanabe, Koichi Nakamura, Satoko Shimazaki and Koichi Kano. 2011.
Vol.	33	Jacob Thaisen / Hanna Rutkowska (eds.): Scribes, Printers, and the Accidentals of their Texts. 2011.
Vol.	34	Isabel Moskowich: Language Contact and Vocabulary Enrichment. Scandinavian Elements in Middle English. 2012.
Vol.	35	Joanna Esquibel / Anna Wojtyś (eds.): Explorations in the English Language: Middle Ages and Beyond. Festschrift for Professor Jerzy Wełna on the Occasion of his 70th Birthday. 2012.
Vol.	36	Yoshiyuki Nakao: The Structure of Chaucer´s Ambiguity. 2013.
Vol.	37	Begoña Crespo: Change in Life, Change in Language. A Semantic Approach to the History of English. 2013.
Vol.	38	Richard Dance / Laura Wright (eds.): The Use and Development of Middle English. Proceedings of the Sixth International Conference on Middle English, Cambridge 2008. 2012.
Vol.	39	Michiko Ogura: Words and Expressions of Emotion in Medieval English. 2013.
Vol.	40	Anna Czarnowus: Fantasies of the Other´s Body in Middle English Oriental Romance. 2013.
Vol.	41	Hans Sauer / Gaby Waxenberger (eds.): Recording English, Researching English, Transforming English. With the Assistance of Veronika Traidl. 2013.
Vol.	42	Michio Hosaka / Michiko Ogura / Hironori Suzuki / Akinobu Tani (eds.): Phases of the History of English. Selection of Papers Read at SHELL 2012. 2013.
Vol.	43	Vlatko Broz: Aspectual Prefixes in Early English. 2014.
Vol.	44	Michael Bilynsky (ed.): Studies in Middle English. Words, Forms, Senses and Texts. 2014.
Vol.	45	Bożena Duda: The Synonyms of *Fallen Woman* in the History of the English Language. 2014.

www.peterlang.com